THE EMBATTLED CONSTITUTION:

—VITAL FRAMEWORK OR CONVENIENT SYMBOL—
by Adolph H. Grundman

ROBERT E. KRIEGER PUBLISHING COMPANY
MALABAR, FLORIDA
1986

Original Edition 1986

Printed and Published by
ROBERT E. KRIEGER PUBLISHING COMPANY, INC.
KRIEGER DRIVE
MALABAR, FLORIDA 32950

Copyright © 1986 by
ROBERT E. KRIEGER PUBLISHING CO., INC.

Library of Congress Cataloging-in-Publication Data

Main entry under title:

The Embattled Constitution.

  1. United States—Constitutional law. 2. United
States—Constitutional history. I. Grundman, Adolph H.

KF4550.E43 1986	342.73′029	85-23079
ISBN 0-89874-904-2	347.30229	
10 9 8 7 6 5 4 3 2		

Contents

Preface

This volume is divided into three sections. The first concentrates on the events which led to the Constitution and how historians have viewed them. The second surveys important constitutional and political issues over two hundred years of American constitutional history. The third section focuses on the contemporary tensions concerning the Constitution.

In general, this volume attempts to analyze institutional and attitudinal changes toward the Constitution and constitutionalism rather than provide an analysis of the wide range of issues that divide Americans. A different kind of book could have focused on abortion, women's rights, affirmative action, the rights of aliens, comparable worth, academic freedom, and the rights of homosexuals—to name only a few of the areas which perplex Americans today. In fact, these issues are on the minds of the contributors to this volume. Their concern in this book, however, is not with the merits of the contending sides in each of these difficult issues. Instead, they attempt to explore how this explosion of issues affects the constitutional process and try to offer suggestions about how to approach these pressing concerns without damaging constitutional government.

In editing this book, I have benefitted from the assistance and encouragement of my colleagues Thomas Altherr, Jett Conner, and Jeremiah Ring. I would also like to thank all the contributors who cooperated with me on this project. Karen Richardson and my wife, Claudia, helped to prepare the final manuscript. Donna Coellen, who organized the Denver Dialogues, and the Board of Directors of the Unitarian Universalist Church of Denver, who sponsored them with a grant from the Colorado Humanities Program, offered much-appreciated support. Finally, I wish to express my thanks to Robert E. Krieger for his advice and patience.

Adolph H. Grundman

Introduction

By the end of this decade numerous Americans of diverse backgrounds will have congregated in a variety of forums to study the significance of two hundred years of constitutional democracy. This volume is the product of such an exercise. In the first half of 1984 scholars, journalists, and citizens gathered together in Denver, Colorado to consider the meaning of the bicentennial of the American Constitution. The program committee organized four dialogues around the following themes: the origin of the Constitution, the nature of constitutional change, the effect of pluralism on constitutional values, and the future of constitutional government. Following the discussions several historians and political scientists were invited to submit papers to further clarify issues raised by the speakers in the course of the dialogues. As a collection, these papers are representative of the numerous concerns of American citizens regarding the nature of contemporary constitutional government. The discussion of philosophical differences is also useful in a historical sense because it offers one way of measuring the evolution of constitutional values over a period of time.

Regarding the Founding Fathers, there is a consensus among the contributors that they were able, realistic, and politically bold in the service of conservative ends. Specifically, the Framers of the Constitution disregarded the instructions of the Confederation Congress and wrote a new constitution rather than satisfying themselves with patching up the Articles of Confederation. The Framers then announced that ratification of the Constitution required the votes of nine states—which was in direct contradiction of the Articles of Confederation, which required unanimity for all amendments. But were the Founding Fathers too realistic, too willing to build a constitution around man as they saw him rather than teaching him how to become a better citizen? Here there is disagreement. Some of the contributors praise the Framers for their ability to compromise on important issues and to create a framework of government flexible and strong enough to solve difficult problems on another day. Other contributors are less enthusiastic about the strategy and results of the men who met in Philadelphia in 1787. Some lament the Framers' rejection of civic education as a method of building politically active citizens who would participate in real communities. They believe that today's constitutional democracy is paying the price for the Founders' decision to build a political society upon the pursuit of private interests. Still others are critical of the Framers for their willingness to compromise on slavery. For these latter critics, the substance of the compromise is made worse by modern perceptions that the Constitution was a neutral document. Finally, some of the contributors see the Framers as victims of historical discontinuity and an incredibly pluralistic society. Without being mean-spirited, the effect of their analysis is to suggest that earlier generations exaggerated the prescience of the Founders.

One other important point of consensus that emerges from this volume is that, for a variety of reasons, the Constitution and constitutional democracy are in deep trouble today. In one sense this concern is not new. By the time of the semicentennial, realistic doubts about a constitutional solution to the slavery question made their appearance. At the time of the centennial celebration of the Constitution, political scientists like Woodrow Wilson doubted whether the institutions of government were a match for an industrial age. Just before Americans celebrated the sesquicentennial of the Constitution, the Great Depression had presented constitutional democracy with its severest threat. Yet there remained substantial confidence that the Constitution contained the flexibility, and the politicians the capacity, to face up to that generation's problems. Americans of the bicentennial era are not new in looking at the future with alarm. But, as evidenced in some of these pages, they seem more unsure of the solutions to modern problems as they have defined them. The tremendous pressure upon government, the complexity of issues, and the seeming inability to educate Americans about their society are some of the themes that run through the chapters.

Three approaches to the dilemmas of contemporary America emerge from these pages. The first, advocated by a strain of conservative thought in America, is to encourage Americans to seek less from their government. In so arguing, conservatives help to clarify the differences between the political values of the eighteenth and twentieth centuries. They stress, in particular, that freedom from government interference is the highest ranking value of the eighteenth century, followed by the right to participate in the political decisions of the society. By the twentieth century Americans turned to the Constitution and government in order to realize equality, security, and special interests. The extent to which Americans achieved these new goals through the judiciary or the bureaucracy was also the standard by which to measure the decline of democratic consent in America and the politicization of the Constitution. However attractive this line of thinking, critics on the other side will charge that a return to eighteenth-century values is simply impossible in a modern society characterized by rapid change, immense differences in private power, and a diverse population.

A second approach to America's contemporary problems is also linked to the eighteenth century. For at least the past decade, some scholars have attempted to revise the foundation of America's political culture. Instead of portraying a society built on individualism and capitalism, some historians characterize eighteenth-century Americans as essentially classical republicans. This idea meant that eighteenth-century Americans recognized that democracy depended on civic virtue or the subordination of the individual to the good of the community. If this view of the American past were correct, could it be revived in twentieth-century America? There are problems with this analysis. The evidence is strong that the Founding Fathers abandoned classical republican theory in devising a constitution. Moreover, scholars have not been very successful in tracing classical republican thought into the nineteenth century.

A third design for meeting the challenge of modern society is to continue on what may be described as a liberal course. In some ways American liberals are less nostalgic than Burkean conservatives or advocates of a return to classical republicanism. When the Founders used words like "liberty" and "equality," they believed these abstractions had a universal meaning that reasonable men could understand and express on paper. The nineteenth and twentieth centuries have eroded faith in natural law, natural rights, and other enlightenment formulas. Ideas such as equality and liberty will ultimately have an empirical and a pragmatic quality. As new groups attempt to give meaning to these abstractions, discord is one obvious result. Another is uncertainty about the direction of society's course. Contemporary liberals seem correct in suggesting that the solution to America's problems will not be found in the remote and poorly understood past. For Americans to ask for less would be to turn back the pages of history. Yet one can appreciate the conservative analysis of a political society which defers to every passion, lacks a sense of direction, and offers little hope of community. American liberals have been slow to acknowledge the merits of this critique, as evidenced by their eagerness to view the Presidential victories of Ronald Reagan as the result of the failed Jimmy Carter Presidency (1980) or a personal victory (1984) rather than as a dissatisfaction with liberal politics. Fifty years ago, when Americans celebrated the sesquicentennial of the Constitution, liberalism was triumphant. As Americans approach the bicentennial of the Constitution they seem to be disillusioned with liberalism but reluctant to commit to a more conservative alternative.

How does the Constitution fit into the dilemma? Politicians and patriots will be prone to find solutions to problems in the Constitution, as they have done in the past. On the day of the sesquicentennial, Idaho Senator William Borah's praise for the Constitution extended to the claim that Americans "cherish and value it [the Constitution], not because of what may be said of it, but because of what it has done for us as a people." Most likely, in September of 1987 the same kind of uncritical eulogy will be repeated. Nonetheless, bicentennial celebrants will try to find a more realistic assessment of the Constitution.

In 1938 Carl Becker wrote that "constitutions are seen to be documents historically conditioned, the imperfect and temporary products of time and place." In words that reflect the modern age Becker observed that "Constitutions, if we do have them, we retain from force of habit; but we do not make new ones if we can help it. Having lost the universal formulas for their construction, the task is too formidable."

The readers of this volume will learn that constitutional democracy is more than the Constitution, but also that the Constitution is much more than a piece of paper.

HISTORICAL
BACKGROUND OF
THE CONSTITUTION

In an introduction to the historical section of this book, Professor George Dennison suggests that the best way to see the Constitution is as part of the revolutionary struggle against Great Britain. In 1763, when the British decided that the colonists should share in the costs of the empire, they precipitated a debate which ultimately led to the American Revolution. Dennison believes that the most ominous part of the new imperial policy to the colonists was the Proclamation of 1763, which closed the western frontier to further settlement. The result, he believes, "was a psychological sense of being penned in." In blocking economic opportunity the British also threatened colonial elites, whose authority rested on their ability to preserve economic mobility in an acquisitive society. Dennison joins other historians in viewing Americans as reluctant revolutionaries who broke with England only when they became convinced that society would not be turned upside down by such an action. The consequences of the American Revolution confirmed their view. One of the threads connecting the Revolution to 1787, according to Dennison, was pressure to keep open the doors of economic opportunity. Consequently, the request for a constitutional convention came from people of authority who believed that political instability under the Articles of Confederation blocked economic advancement and threatened social anarchy. The men who wrote the Constitution wanted a national government strong enough to promote economic growth, but sufficiently restrained to prevent the excesses of democracy. Dennison describes how the Framers attempted to achieve these goals. Their success in drafting a Constitution capable of authorizing or limiting power according to the necessities of the time, Dennison concludes, accounts for the endurance of the Constitution.

GEORGE DENNISON

American Colonial Elites
in the Age of Revolution

To understand the forces that led to the Constitutional Convention
in 1787, it is important to review the background of the late eighteenth
century and the crisis of the British Empire. After defeating France in the
Seven Years' War and concluding the peace of 1763, the English turned
their attention to reforming their imperial system. The goals of the
British were to gain greater control over administration of the empire and
to raise more money by taxing the colonies and exploiting their wealth.
This general program of action was not motivated by evil and deliberate
efforts to subject the colonies to tyranny, but reflected a conclusion that
the colonials should help to pay the costs associated with the benefits
they derived from the empire. However, the colonials perceived a far
different purpose.

The Sugar Act of 1764 and the Stamp Act of 1765 levied taxes that led
to the cry that the colonials could not be taxed without the benefit of
representation. These taxes, along with the Proclamation of 1763 and
other measures that followed, brought a sense of crisis to the American

colonies. Moreover, from the outset the colonials stressed the need for representation before such measures could be instituted even while they denied that effective representation in Parliament could ever be provided to them.

The Proclamation of 1763 was particularly ominous to the colonials since it closed the frontier west of the Alleghenies to their penetration and settlement. The result was that Americans saw economic opportunity blocked to them. Since the American population was crowded along the Atlantic seaboard, there was a psychological sense of being penned in territorially. When absentee landlords in England began to reassert their claims to American land, the tensions between the British and the colonials heightened. These reassertions of ownership resulted from peace in the empire and a burgeoning realization that the lands had value. A good portion of these lands however, had been settled and developed by colonials over the years. Those who had assumed their titles were good reacted sharply to the claims of British absentee owners.

By closing off opportunity in the West and threatening land holdings in the settled East, the British also threatened the place of colonial elites whose positions rested on the ability to sustain an economy characterized by openness and mobility. In other words, if people accustomed to the availability of opportunities see the opportunities closed off for whatever reason, they tend to react with some hostility against all persons in positions of power and authority. Elites typically sustain themselves by preserving within the society some measure of mobility, or at least a perception that such opportunities are available. In addition, elites strive to sustain their own ability to prosper. In a situation of limited opportunity, the conflict between those who have and those who aspire to have gains great intensity. The threat of internal struggle over wealth and place loomed larger in the context of a society losing its openness. Hence, the colonial elites had reason to resist, but they hardly intended to overturn their own societies.

Thus, the British decision to reform the empire not only raised the question of home rule, but it also indirectly focused attention on the question of who would rule at home, as Carl Becker suggested several years ago. It took ten years, however, for the dynamic of political revolution to work itself out in the colonial situation. As scholars have noted, these were very reluctant revolutionaries. People had to be persuaded that they could move from resistance to revolution without destroying the bases for their traditional societies before they would move to separation from the empire. The fact that the colonials waited for two years after the crisis of 1774, initiated by the Boston Tea Party and the British response to it, before they decided to declare independence in July 1776 reveals just how difficult it was for the American colonials to become revolutionaries. By declaring independence, they acknowledged their belief that a decent society did not require the monarchical form of government and that their traditional societies would persist even if the ultimate political authority was destroyed and replaced by a new and novel—for that time—arrangement.

This process of moving from resistance to revolution carried the colonials from an unquestioning belief in the essential soundness and necessity of monarchical government to an acceptance of republicanism. Bernard Bailyn has shown how *Common Sense*, the pamphlet published by Thomas Paine in early 1776, provided to so many Americans an emotional and intellectual foundation for a new and novel approach to government. But a rather strong conservative current characterized these developments. Americans declared their independence and moved to republicanism as the only means they thought available to protect and preserve their traditional societies and culture. There was very little in the way of radical democracy associated with the movement from resistance to revolution. Americans moved to shore up traditional authority vested in their societies and governments, as they defined them, and not to loosen the ties within the society. While the Revolution itself certainly must be seen as an important impetus in the movement toward democratic government in the United States, the point to remember is that Americans overwhelmingly thought of themselves as republicans rather than democrats. The democratic tendencies that surfaced were moderated by a continuing belief in an organic society with a place for all and rule by the better sort, elected because of their position, influence, and ability.

A democratic revolution would, in all likelihood, have involved class conflict of substantial magnitude. This did not happen to any large extent in the American situation. Local elites, by and large, led the movement toward independence that we refer to as the Revolution. This successful effort was republican in character in its substitution of a representative form of government for a monarchical one, but under more or less tightly constrained rules and procedures. Majoritarianism became the rule, but majority rule was of a filtered sort. Direct democracy hardly characterized these events. The source of political authority changed radically, but the authority still retained its hierarchical nature. The better sort would rule because of demonstrated rather than presumed consent, election rather than prescription. Even so, these changes prepared the way for the future of democratic government in the United States in ways that few people appreciated or intended at the time.

Just as the American Revolution essentially represented an effort to preserve authority by preserving opportunity within the society, *because of* rather than *despite* the efforts of the colonial elites, the events leading to the Constitutional Convention involved the same considerations. The men who went to Philadelphia believed that the weaknesses of the Articles of Confederation threatened the opportunities available to Americans in a manner analogous, but opposite, to the British imperial policy prior to the Revolution. That is to say, these men believed that anarchy posed dangers as fearful and substantial as those of tyranny. Therefore, the Framers of the Constitution concentrated upon developing a government structure designed to provide for new opportunities without displacing the people in positions of power and authority. In fact, as Charles Beard, Clinton Rossiter, and Forrest McDonald demonstrated, the Constitution was the work of people in positions of power and authority. In a curious way, these important people found themselves acting as reluctant revolutionaries once again—twice in their political lifetimes—for the actions taken to establish the Constitution violated the provisions of the existing governments of the Confederation and the States. But the process led to the design and implementation of an instrument of government that would allow change to occur as needed in the future.

The concern of those who formulated and successfully offered the Constitution for adoption by the states was to create a society and government in perpetual balance, with change occurring gradually and incrementally in response to the deeply felt needs of the time. The experience of the Revolution taught that the American people wanted a government capable of responding to their needs, and that they were not disposed to destroy their traditional societies if and when governments failed to do so. Rather, they would reconstruct or reconstitute the government toward that end. But if the governmental failure persisted, despite the efforts to correct it, who could predict the outcome? Quite clearly, the American people would act to assure a responsive government, but they could be trusted to act in ways that assured the continuance of authority. This essential faith in the conservative character of Americans goes far to explain the willingness of the elites to act as they did.

What kind of constitution was framed in Philadelphia and adopted in 1787–1788? The Constitution looked toward a government capable of responding to needs but restrained from arbitrary action by internal checks and social balances. Characterized by reliance upon the theory of the separation of powers to assure a balance within government, the Constitution rested firmly upon the premise that social balancing produced governmental balance. There were, of course, some mechanical balances built into the structure of the Constitution itself, but the essential assurance came from the theory of pluralism. The multitude of interest groups and other groups within the society assured that no one could ever dominate the government and thereby the society. This kind of social and governmental balance would guarantee moderation in governmental action.

Because of the belief in the efficacy of social and governmental balancing, and the conviction that the government created by the Constitution could act only if the specific power to act was given in the Constitution itself, the Framers seemingly worried little about the security of rights. One of the most glaring omissions from the product of the Philadelphia Convention was a Bill of Rights, only added in 1789. How did it happen that a society supposedly preoccupied with rights failed to concern itself with a Bill of Rights? But it did. In fact, concern about a Bill of Rights surfaced only in the context of the political fight over ratification, largely because of the struggle for political advantage rather than adherence to principle.

One of the most persuasive answers to the question about the absence of a Bill of Rights was offered by James Madison. He believed that only a fool would presume to list all the rights that mankind would want to secure against the government. To identify a few, he feared, threatened all those that went unstated. Although the Constitution provided no Bill of Rights, Madison argued that it nonetheless protected the rights of Americans against federal encroachment. Since the Constitution granted to Congress and the other branches of the federal government only certain *delegated* powers, Madison reasoned, it followed that Congresss lacked the power to interfere with any other rights of any American. That is to say, the government could only do what it was authorized to do. Creating a government limited to actions sanctioned by specifically *delegated* powers amounted to making the Constitution itself a Bill of Rights.

In the ratification struggle, the Anti-Federalists denounced the omission of a Bill of Rights and made its addition to the Constitution the price of their support. Some historians have taken the view that the Federalists outmaneuvered the Anti-Federalists on this issue, since it represented such a small concession to the opposition. After all, no one denied the need to protect rights. But the consequences of the addition were largely unseen at the time.

The adoption of the Bill of Rights amounted to a reversal of the Madisonian theory of the Constitution. If you begin with the premise that the Constitution authorized the government to do only certain things, it becomes exceedingly awkward to argue that government can do what it is not authorized to do. To insist upon a Bill of Rights in order to guard against governmental intrusion means that government will, in all likelihood, do or seek to do more than it is authorized to to. What is the significance of this construction?

A brief answer is that the addition of the Bill of Rights in the form of a list of restraints placed upon the federal government paved the way for the broad construction of the Constitution developed by Alexander Hamilton and John Marshall. When Hamilton defended the constitutionality of legislation providing for a national bank, he capitalized upon the *form* and *essential character* of the Constitution. He stressed that the object of the bank legislation was constitutional, in this instance to promote the development of a sound national currency. Hamilton then argued that nothing in the Constitution prohibited the establishment of a national bank. In this way, he offered a very neat ends-means test for broadly construing the Constitution. He did not begin the discussion by asking whether the Constitution authorized Congress to create a national bank. Instead, he used the form of argument that insisted that if the ends were constitutional, the means not specifically prohibited, and the means related to the ends, then the means were constitutional. In the Supreme Court case of *McCulloch* v. *Maryland* (1819), Chief Justice John Marshall utilized this logic in an opinion that explained the Supreme Court's decision affirming the constitutionality of the legislation providing for the second Bank of the United States. The circle had been closed.

As a result, what began as an effort to limit government—the Constitution as a limiting instrument with the resultant government having only the powers specifically delegated—ended by virtually destroying all but political limits to power—with the Constitution as an authorizing instrument delegating all powers except those specifically denied. After all, words tend to take on new and desired meanings if subjected to sufficient pressure. Thus, the crisis of the Revolution impelled Americans toward the creation of a responsive government, justified by the concern for rights defined largely as opportunities. But as opportunities became scarce, the concern for rights took on the aura of a demand for action to reopen the opportunities. During the early years, the dynamic tensions within the society gave lasting character to the Constitution as at once the instrument of constraint and power—a limiting *and* an authorizing instrument. That it could be either or both, depending upon conditions, needs, and perceptions, explains its enduring capacity as a basic instrument of government.

In 1774 Thomas Paine traveled from Great Britain to America, where he wrote *Common Sense*, the most famous pamphlet of the American Revolution. Published in January 1776, nine months after hostilities broke out at Lexington and Concord, Paine's tract is credited by historians with hastening the decision by American colonials to declare their independence from Great Britain. Professor Jett Conner argues that Paine's fame as a revolutionary pamphleteer has led scholars to overlook other aspects of Paine's political thought. In this essay Conner shows that Paine devoted considerable attention to outlining a framework of government for the new nation. Between 1776 and 1787, when he returned to Europe, Paine was a consistent advocate of a federal government with the balance of power clearly tipped in the direction of the national government. Paine also anticipated some of the unique features of American constitutionalism: a written constitution, a constitutional convention, and popular sovereignty. In 1802 Paine claimed, "I ought to stand first on the list of Federalists." Although Conner takes this declaration seriously, he is careful not to claim too much for his subject. But he does show how one can usefully study the period between the Revolution and the Constitution by examining the ideas of Thomas Paine.

JETT CONNER

Tom Paine and the Genesis of American Federalism

I.

A generation that commences a
revolution rarely completes it.
—*Thomas Jefferson*

When Tom Paine set out to write *Common Sense*, a pamphlet hailed then and today as truly revolutionary, he had more in mind than just another attack on British rule: he had some notions to offer about what should replace it. Paine's recommendations for our future governance are seldom noticed now, but they did make a few impressions at the time.

11

John Adams, for one, read *Common Sense* with a mixture of admiration and horror. Deciding that Paine was a "keen writer but very ignorant of the science of government," Adams rushed into print his *Thoughts On Government*, partly as an antidote to Paine's "democratical" excesses, partly as a guide to revolution makers on how to form a good government. Adams judged Paine to be much better at tearing down than building up; so have generations of others who have paid the required homage to his revolutionary role and little else. Aside from a few recent works that focus on Paine's political theory, most conclusions about Paine's contributions to the American revolutionary period reflect Adams's initial judgment, as expressed a few years back by Alpheus Thomas Mason when he wrote that *Common Sense* "was a call to arms, not a political treatise."

One of the great difficulties in dealing with famous revolutionists is the relative inattention given to their constructive ideas, for good reason: historically, revolutionary heroes are inextricably tied, in the public mind, at least, to their deeds. The words that live on as vivid as the deeds are words of the battle cry ("Give me liberty, or give me death!"). Less lasting are the ruminations of constitution building, or architectural construction. Moreover, heroes of famous events are people of enormous reputations—reputations that become more enormous over time precisely because history and the retelling of it have conferred upon these individuals a singular place of importance rarely disturbed by the hindsight of cool reflection and reappraisal. Will we ever resolve, for instance, the debate over whether our Founders were benevolent geniuses, or demigods—or just fearful and self-interested human beings blessed with a good deal of foresight? Perhaps not. But their place among other American heroes will remain forever secure.

It is hard to overstate Thomas Paine's place among the heroes of the American Revolution. *Common Sense*, even by today's standards, was a signal publication. Tens of thousands of copies circulated throughout the land and hundreds of thousands of people either read or heard the words. But it is the pamphlet's very success in achieving its goals that may have precluded further scrutiny by many historians and political theorists. Simply put, Paine was the revolutionary hero who had the nerve to stand up and shout what many were muttering: "Tis time to part!" *Common Sense* was the bugle call of the revolution; that is its distinction, and unfortunately, to many its only distinction.

It is not argued here that *Common Sense* is a political treatise. But neither is it only a "bugle call" for the battle to begin. (As everyone knew, the battle had already begun in earnest.) Paine knew his audience, and he understood it very well indeed. It was not for lack of courage that Americans hesitated to declare independence. Instead, it was a fear of the unknown that Paine addressed in *Common Sense*: "If there is any true cause of fear respecting independence," Paine observed, "it is because no plan is yet laid down." It was one thing to argue for independence; the reasons for doing that could be heard everywhere in the streets in late 1775. (Adams figured that Paine had gotten all of his ideas there anyway, since, Adams proposed, no new arguments for independence were offered in *Common Sense*.) It was quite another thing, however, to convince American colonists that they could fill the void left by a separation from British rule. The question was important: What would then serve to promote unity on the continent? Nothing could, Paine argued, but a continental government of our own.

The appeal of *Common Sense* was due to its fiery rhetoric, to be sure, and to its unprecedented, open, and virulent attack on British rule and rulers. If pre-Revolution debate up to the appearance of *Common Sense* had bogged down in ponderous constitutional prose and arguments concerning external and internal taxation, "virtual" representation and the like, Paine single-handedly redirected American attention to that ultimate symbol of English rule—that "hardened, sullen-tempered Pharaoh . . . that Royal Brute of Great Britain," the king of England. It was Paine's ridicule of royalty, aristocracy, and privilege that caught the colonists' attention and caused them to guffaw and later, upon reflection, to snort fire. But while Paine could easily make the Americans laugh or cry at their king, or their own predicament, it was ultimately the strength of *Common Sense* to force Americans to dream of the future. The little pamphlet, it turns out, was not just a compendium of all the excuses one could think of for independence; it offered a sketch of national governance for the immediate future. Within that sketch, I believe, can be found the genesis of the American federated structure of government.

Paine began his "hints," as he called them, for a national government with this proposal: "Let the assemblies be annual, with a president only. The representation more equal, their business wholly domestic, and subject to the authority of a Continental Congress." This remarkably compact passage calls for several things. Unicameral colonial assemblies would be presided over by a president instead of an independent governor appointed by the Crown. The assemblies would be elected annually and, presumably, within the framework of fewer suffrage restrictions than then existed within the colonies. But the most important recommendation for our purposes here was the indication that the colonial assemblies should be defined, limited in scope, and subject to some sort of congressional veto. In essence, Paine was suggesting that the continent should be governed by a dual system of authority clearly weighted at the national level. Thus, a seed was sown for our dual plan of governance.

Suggesting that the assemblies be "subject to the authority of a Continental Congress" is very interesting and deserves some comment before going on to the other proposals in this passage. Almost the same thought as Paine's would be offered by Madison, on the eve of the Philadelphia Convention, in a letter dated April 1787 to Randolph and Washington outlining a constitutional plan: "Let (the national government) have a negative, in all cases whatsoever, on the legislative acts of the states. . . . " It is obvious that Madison, as late as a few months before the Convention, had not conceived of a dual system of powers, each operating independently and directly upon the individual. Instead of restricting state powers by proposing a constitution that carefully divided the powers and functions of the national and state governments so as to limit the latter, Madison initially sought a direct veto by the national government over the state legislatures. In effect, Madison would simply reverse the founding principle of the Articles of Confederation—state sovereignty—and give *all* sovereignty to the national government, so that the national government could decide what role the states would continue to play. While the Convention would not follow this course, to Madison's disappointment, it is nevertheless clear that Paine's "hint" about how to control colonial legislatures was strikingly similar to Madison's thinking and very much in line with early Federalist conceptions.

Paine continues the passage by offering a system of annual rotation for selecting the president of the national Congress (which was, like the assemblies, to be unicameral). Each colony, taking turns, would have a chance to provide a candidate from among its delegates to be selected president. Here again, Paine avoided a fear, that of an independent executive, by making the president directly accountable to the legislature. In order that "nothing may pass into law but what is satisfactorily just," Paine suggested that not less than three-fifths of the Congress be considered a majority when voting. (Such an extraordinary majority was Paine's attempt to provide a check on majority rule, an interesting point for those who have always held that Paine was a straight majority-rule democrat.) Delegates to the Congress should be chosen from colonial districts to be established specifically for that purpose and apportioned by population so that each colony would have a minimum of 30 representatives, giving a total of at least 390 for the whole body. Paine was more concerned with achieving equitable representation of the people than equality among the various colonies. In this, his idea resembles the Virginia Plan much more than the scheme of representation adopted by the Articles of Confederation.

But how was such a continental form of government to be drawn up, and by whom? On these points, Paine's "hints" were full of detail. He knew exactly what he wanted. A "continental conference" should be held to frame a "Continental Charter," or a "Charter of the United Colonies." Furthermore, it was important that this constitutional convention originate from "some intermediate body between the governed and the governors, that is, between the Congress and the people. . . . " Spelling out precisely how the conference should be composed, Paine argued that the group gathered would unite two great principles, knowledge and power, and that since the whole body would be empowered by the people, it would have true legal authority. Paine's teaching was clear enough: Government cannot beget itself. A legitimate government can only arise out of the people or, more specifically, from a representative assembly chosen by members of the governing bodies—local and national—and the people at large.

Getting down to the business of the conference, the group would fix the number and method of choosing Members of Congress and the Members of Assembly "with their date of sitting; and drawing the line of business and jurisdiction between them. . . . " A national constitution, it is clear, would be charged with the authority for establishing the basis of representation and powers of *both* the national and state legislatures. Such a scheme, of course, might well tilt powers in favor of the national legislature, but it is obvious by now that Paine would count among those who came to consider themselves "nationalists." As if to underscore this position, Paine reminded his readers to always remember that "our strength is continental, not provincial."

Paine finished the passage by recommending that the continental charter contain a national bill of rights, of sorts, "securing freedom and property to all men, and above all things, the free exercise of religion, according to the dictates of conscience. . . . " But Paine knew that even all of this might not be enough. Skeptics would surely ask: "Where is the king of America?" In absolute governments, Paine replied, the king is law, in America, the law was to be king. To symbolize this, a crown should be placed on the new charter, and then it should be demolished during a ceremony and "scattered among the people whose right it is." A government of our own was, after all, our natural right. But he concluded the passage with a warning: It would be far safer to compose a constitution "in a cool and deliberate manner" now, while it was in our power, than later, when it might be left up to time and chance. Interesting thought, that, in light of subsequent events. . . .

It is hard to read Paine's prescriptions for a continental government and not be convinced that he was just as interested in what would replace British rule *after* independence as he was in promoting that independence. Should monarchy be overthrown, what would replace it? A continental charter, Paine answered, would take the place of the crown itself in the new country. While it is obvious that these ideas were indeed just what Paine called them, i.e., "hints," they reflected some of the fundamental premises of future constitutionalism in America. As Edward Corwin put it:

> In this singular mixture of sense and fantasy, so characteristic of its author, are adumbrated a national constitutional convention, the dual plan of our federal system, a national bill of rights, and 'worship of the Constitution;' and this was some months before the earliest state constitution and nearly four years before Hamilton's proposal, in his letter to Duane of September 3, 1780, of 'a solid, coercive Union.'

II.

Paine and the Emergence of the Federalist–Anti-Federalist Debate

The years of growing Federalist–Anti-Federalist debate immediately prior to and culminating at the Constitutional Convention of 1787 have been referred to as "the critical period." Something was wrong with the powers of the national government under the Articles of Confederation. On that point there was virtually no disagreement. The Articles would have to be revised in order to strengthen the national government. The short-term questions were how that could be done, and how much power the national government should have. These were indeed difficult questions, which taxed the greatest minds of the period. But the long-term questions were revolutionary, for they focused on those very premises of constitutionalism lying beneath the Articles of Confederation. Upon these grounds the fight would take place.

Crucial to the debate was a difference of vision. On one side stood those whose view was "continentalist;" on the other side were the provincialists. To a great extent, the issues raised by the Federalist–Anti-Federalist debate come back to this single perceptual distinction—a distinction at least as old as the Revolution. The Declaration of Independence had used the phrase "the United States of America" twice, for the first time officially in America. But the language in the Declaration is ambiguous since it echoes the wording of Richard Henry Lee's resolution on July 2, 1776, "to declare the United Colonies free and independent states." John Dickinson, in his first draft of the Articles of Confederation, had spoken of "the United States of America," and John Adams in *Thoughts on Government* had, like Paine, anticipated a "continental constitution" and a "union" of colonies. But the Articles, as ratified in 1781, championed state sovereignty and state supremacy. The first round of the constitutional debate had been lost by those whose vision was decidedly "continentalist."

The Articles had not even been ratified, however, before specific criticism surfaced. As early as 1780, Hamilton wrote to James Duane, a member of the Continental Congress from New York, about the "want of power in Congress." Within a year Hamilton was publishing a series of articles, entitled *The Continentalist*, in which he argued for a strong federal government:

> There is something noble and magnificent in the perspective of a great Federal Republic, closely linked in the pursuit of a common interest, tranquil and prosperous at home, respectable abroad; but there is something proportionably diminutive and contemptible in the prospect of a number of petty States, with the appearance only of union, jarring, jealous, and perverse, without any determined direction, fluctuating and unhappy at home, weak and insignificant by their dissensions in the eyes of other nations.

Hamilton was not the only early critic of the Articles. After the war was over, Washington turned his attention to what the states had achieved by their efforts. His immediate concern, expressed in a letter to several state governors, was the status of the new nation. Like Hamilton, Washington saw the need for a stronger union, and his letter to the governors was written to express his alarm that his men, most of whom had received no pay, might not be able to recover their claims from the states. The army might not even continue to exist. "It is indispensable to the happiness of the individual states that there should be lodged somewhere a Supreme Power to regulate and govern the general concerns of the confederated Republic," he argued. Jefferson, in his letters from Paris, was also beginning to agree that "the want of power in the federal head [was] the flaw in our constitution which might endanger its destruction." Even a sizable number of those who would soon be labeled Anti-Federalists—such men as George Mason, Elbridge Gerry and James Monroe—were in favor of strengthening the national government under the Articles.

Essentially, what had to be done during the "critical" years was to bridge the gap between the theoretical principles of the Revolution (and its Declaration) with those principles which provided the rationale of the Articles. That there was such a gap is obvious. The Articles were firmly rooted in the principles of state sovereignty and supremacy. On the other hand, the Revolution and the Declaration implied, if not national supremacy, the united sovereignty of a people. The Declaration begins with these words: "When in the Course of human events, it becomes necessary for one people. . . . " Clearly, though not quite expressing the will of one nation, the Declaration announces the principle of an aggregate sovereignty whose will is necessary to "institute new government." The act of revolution "to alter or abolish" existing government, the Declaration further declares, "is the Right of the people." But the architects of the Articles refused to legitimize what "one people' had started. Instead, the "United Colonies" became independent, sovereign states. The initial vision of America's early constitutionalists had broken with the vision proclaimed by the Declaration.

Paine's own seminal thoughts on constitutionalism had appeared in *Common Sense*. Without a doubt, that work portrays the vision of a continentalist. The term "continentalist" is chosen carefully here;* it is a grand view of things, a sort of Weltanschauung, that I wish to convey, and not only the ideological meanings associated with "nationalist" or "state rights." In fact, the distinctions often voiced prior to the Philadelphia Convention between such terms as "confederate," "federal," and "national" were not always, if ever, discernible. Even during the convention and after, the meanings were not clear. It was possible, for example, for Paterson of New Jersey to say that "the idea of a national Government as contradistinguished from a federal one, never entered into [the public mind], and to the public mind we must accommodate ourselves." To Paterson, "federal" meant the Confederacy; the idea of a national government as advanced by the Randolph Plan would, to his way of thinking, undermine the "federal" system. The Convention had no authority to establish such a plan, he argued, and even if it did, "*the proposition* could not be maintained whether considered in reference to us as a nation, or as a confederacy." Rufus King admitted at the Convention that "the terms 'States' 'Sovereignty' 'national' 'federal,' had

---

*For an interesting discussion on the continental view, see Stanly M. Elkins and Eric McKitrick, "Youth and the Continental Vision," in Leonard W. Levy, *Essays On The Making of the Constitution* (New York: Oxford University Press, 1976). It is interesting that the article fails to mention Paine.

been often used & applied in the discussion inaccurately & delusively." Finally, the distinction which Madison had labored to make between a national and a federal system in his *Federalist* No. 39, Hamilton dismissed in his *Federalist* No. 9 as "a distinction more subtle than accurate."

Given any chance to express his views, Paine's vision was irrevocably "continentalist," and the translation of that vision always nationalist. This is not to suggest that he harbored any desires, as Hamilton did, to abolish the states. There is no evidence in any of his writings that Paine would have supported a strictly nationalist system. But, like Hamilton, Paine quickly realized that early constitutional thinking in America about national powers left much to be desired. Hence, Hamilton and Paine became America's first critics of the Articles of Confederation, as will be seen shortly.

Paine did not attend the Philadelphia Convention in 1787. But there is ample evidence in his writings to support the contention that if he had been at the Convention he would have cast his lot with the Federalists. At any rate, he thought of himself as the first Federalist. In a letter "To the Citizens of the United States" written after his return to America in 1802, Paine reflected on his role in the Federalist movement of the early 1780s:

> If, then, by *Federalist* is to be understood one who was for cementing the Union by a general government operating equally over all the states, in all matters that embraced the common interest, and to which the authority of the States severally was not adequate, for no one State can make laws to bind another; if, I say, by a *Federalist* is meant a person of this description . . . *I ought to stand first on the list of Federalists.* . . .

Paine goes on in this letter to say that "the proposition for establishing a general government over the Union, came originally from me in 1783." Actually, Paine's own recollection was amiss for, as we have established, the idea emerged in *Common Sense*. In any case, it will be argued here that Paine's most consistent and substantial contribution to American constitutional thought came in the form of germinal ideas on federalism. In order to substantiate this claim, Paine's writings from 1776 to 1787 must be examined carefully.

Prior to the *Crisis Papers*, Paine had several opportunities to amplify his constitutional thinking as initially sketched in *Common Sense*. Shortly after the appearance of that work, several conservative replies were rushed into print. Among these was a series of letters signed "Cato," and written by Dr. William Smith, a clergyman and the Provost of the

College of Philadelphia. Paine's responses to Cato are known as "the Forester's Letters." These letters, written to combat "Cato's Letters" and to continue the arguments for independence laid down in Paine's *Common Sense*, reveal his consistent concern for grounding his revolutionary case upon constitutional premises. Accusing Cato of "loitering in the suburbs of the dispute," Paine goes at once to the heart of the matter by acknowledging and attacking Cato's assumption that reconciliation with Great Britain is compelled by "constitutional premises." Noting that Cato had addressed his letters "To the People of Pennsylvania only," Paine, who had addressed *Common Sense* "To the Inhabitants of America," replies:

> In almost any other writer this might have passed unnoticed, but we know it hath mischief in its meaning. The particular circumstance of a convention in Pennsylvania is undoubtedly Provincial, but the great business of the day is Continental. And he who dares to endeavor to withdraw this province from the glorious union by which all are supported, deserves the reprobation of all men. It is the true interest of the whole to go hand in hand; and dismal in every instance would be the fate of that Colony that should retreat from the protection of the rest.

Throughout the "Forester's Letters," Paine's message is continental, his concern constitutional, in scope. Attacking Cato's reverence for Pennsylvania's chartered constitution, Paine—announcing a theme of popular sovereignty which would recur with great frequency in his writings—charges that the "constitution of Pennsylvania hath been twice changed through the cunning of former proprietors; surely the people . . . may make such alterations in their mode of government as the change of times and things requires." He reminds Cato that the dispute between Great Britain and America cannot be resolved peaceably as long as it is thought of as a family quarrel:

> Whereas were we to make use of that natural right which all other nations have done before us, and erect a government of our own, *independent of all the world*, the quarrel could then be no longer called a family quarrel, but a regular war between the two powers of Britain and America, in the same manner as one carried on between England and France; and in this state of political separation, the neutral powers might kindly render then mediation . . . and bring about the preliminaries of a *peace*. . . .

The perception here is intriguing; only as a nation could America settle her account with Britain. The colonies might win the war and become independent of British constitutional principles and governance, but they would stand no chance of winning and achieving peace unless they exercised their "natural right" to become sovereign and thereby receive recognition by the international community of independent nations. Following Paine's "discussion" with Cato in the "Forester's letters" came sixteen papers known as *The American Crisis* (or *Crisis Papers*). Published between 1776 and 1783, these papers in some cases equaled or exceeded the success and effect of *Common Sense*. Like *Crisis I*, the most famous—as legend has it, written on a drumhead by campfire at a low point during the retreat of Washington's Army across New Jersey ("these are the times that try men's souls")—all of Paine's *Crisis Papers* appeared at critical points in the war and the evolution of the new nation. The pamphlets variously fired up the American patriots and soldiers, denounced and ridiculed Tories and British Army officers, castigated the British for waging a war on the colonies that they would not win, blasted the advocates of reconciliation in America as well as those who wished to negotiate a peace without victory, drew up several schemes of taxation for financing the struggle, and—above all—hammered out a continental message and vision for the American people. Many words of the *Crisis* series are timeless and have been read or broadcast to American troops during more recent times of crisis in this country.

Throughout the war, in his pamphlets written to inspire victory, Paine consistently invoked the imagery of a *nation*, and not mere colonies, at war. His task was to force the readers to believe themselves to be not only united for the purpose of waging a battle, but to be united people with as much potential as any nation on earth. "'The United States of America,'" he proclaimed in *Crisis II*, "will sound as pompously in the world or in history, as 'the Kingdom of Great Britain.'" The man's foresight was sometimes uncanny.

Although it was the war with Britain that had prompted Paine to begin the *Crisis* series, it was the emergence of the Articles of Confederation, and their subsequent adoption, which caused Paine to realize the need for a strong central government. Following the Declaration of Independence, Congress, as mentioned previously, moved to appoint a committee, headed by John Dickinson, to draft some articles for a union. The Congress moved swiftly on this committee's recommendations; it adopted the Articles in November 1777 and submitted them to the state legislatures for ratification. The states were less swift. It took four years for all the states to approve the document because an important hitch had developed in the proceedings. Maryland, acting in behalf of those states with no Western land claims (because of explicit limitations provided in their original charters), refused to ratify the Articles until Virginia and the other states who made such claims agreed to cede those claims to the nation. Paine saw another opportunity to stump for the nationalist cause (some suggested his *own* cause, since Paine was employed with a land company that had a stake in the outcome of the dispute). He published a pamphlet in 1780 entitled *Public Good*, which argued that the Western lands in question belonged to the United States "collectively" rather than to individual states. The tract, more thoroughly argued and researched than many of Paine's other missives, contains some remarkable insights and recommendations for the new nation. After spending some time building a strong case against the historical evidence for Virginia's claims, Paine ended *Public Good* with two unusual recommendations. First, he reminded his readers of his arguments in *Common Sense* that the Western lands constituted "a national fund for the benefit of all." He argued that only the United States, not any particular state, could establish new states and incorporate them into the union. (The argument was not entirely novel: Hamilton had already proposed that Congress be granted "the whole or a part of the unoccupied lands . . . because it is necessary that body should have some property as a fund for the arrangement of finance. . . . ") But it was Paine's second proposal that is most interesting. He called for a convention to be held to remedy the weaknesses of the Articles of Confederation—before the Articles had even been ratified. The entire passage bears quoting:

> I shall in this place take the opportunity of renewing a hint which I formerly threw out in the pamphlet *Common Sense*, and which the several states will, *sooner or later, see the convenience if not the necessity of adopting;* which is, that of electing a Continental convention, for the purpose of forming a Continental constitution, defining and describing the powers and authority of Congress. . . . Those of entering into treaties, and making peace, they naturally possess, in behalf of the states, for their separate as well as their united good, but the internal control and dictatorial powers of Congress are not sufficiently defined, and appear to be too much in some cases and too little in others; and therefore, to have them marked out legally will give additional energy to the whole and a new confidence to the several parts [italics added].

It is now recognized by some that Paine was the first person to call publicly for a national convention to remedy the defects of the Articles. But Hamilton must be given credit for writing the first detailed letter outlining a critique of the Articles and proposing a convention for the purpose of correcting the Article's defects. The letter in question is the now famous letter to James Duane, previously mentioned, in which Hamilton summed up his objections to the Articles with the argument that there was a "want of power in Congress." He went on to suggest what such a convention might accomplish. Once again, a fairly lengthy passage bears quoting:

> The Convention should assemble the first of November next [1781]. The sooner the better. Our disorders are too violent to admit of a common or lingering remedy. The reasons for which I require them to be vested with plenipotentiary authority are that the business may suffer no delay. . . . A Convention may agree upon a Confederation; the States, individually, hardly ever will. We must have one, at all events, and a vigorous one. . . . Congress should have complete sovereignty in all that relates to war, peace, trade, finance, and to the management of foreign affairs . . . of making peace . . . of regulating trade . . . laying prohibitions on all the articles of export or import; imposing duties . . . appropriating funds. . . . The Confederation should provide certain perpetual revenues, productive and easy of collection; a land tax, pool tax, or the like, which, together with the duties on trade, and the unlocated lands, would give Congress a substantial existence, and a stable foundation for their schemes of finance. What more supplies were necessary, should be occasionally demanded of the States, in the present mode of quotas.

Even a cursory comparison of these two passages will reveal which contains more detail and depth. It is obvious that Hamilton was the deeper thinker, but Paine's grasp of the chief problems of the Articles was not far behind. So uncommonly different were these two men that it is highly unlikely their respective ideas will ever be generally associated. All the same, the similarities are often remarkable. Paine's passages certainly illustrate the fact that Hamilton was not alone, in 1780, criticizing the Articles and calling for a convention to strengthen the national government. In fact, while Hamilton went about writing his proposals in private letters to influential friends, Paine—as usual—took up his case directly with the public.

Like Hamilton, Paine thought that the most revealing weakness of the Congress under the Articles was its inability to raise revenues and finance its operations. In a special *Crisis* paper, *The Crisis Extraordinary* of 1780, Paine had issued a plea to the states (and the people generally) to pay their share of the war costs. This *Crisis* paper was ingeniously designed to convince Americans that their portion of the taxes to support the war was actually less than half the taxes which would probably have been levied upon them by the British if the war had been lost. But, once again, Paine argued that a stronger central government was needed. Specifically, he recommended that Congress should have the power to lay and collect a duty on imports (which Congress under the Articles would soon get around to considering), since only Congress, and not the states, would be able to establish equitable rates. Hamilton obviously held similar views, but the comparison has not been noted.

Paine also supported a national bank. Hamilton, whose role in this issue is well known, had begun to argue for such a bank as early as 1779. Hamilton argued that "a national bank . . . will be a powerful cement to our union." He used this phrase later in 1781 in a letter to Robert Morris, with reference to a national debt: "A national debt, if not excessive, will be to us a national blessing. . . . It will be a powerful cement of our union." Paine had expressed the identical thought years earlier in *Common Sense* with the words "a national debt is a national bond." Paine was just as adamant as Hamilton in his promotion of national commerce. He was the earliest writer on the American scene who consistently backed an energetic national government for the purpose of promoting vigorous commerce.

Indeed, the evidence supports the assertion that it was Paine who first published many of the key concerns which would become championed by the Federalists during the so-called Critical Period. Since it is clear that Paine's call for a constitutional convention in *Public Good* was really, as he saw it, no more than a "renewal" of the call made four years earlier in *Common Sense*—and since his later writings remained true to the rudimentary constitutional prescriptions proposed in that work— Paine's boast that he should "stand first on the list of Federalists" has considerable merit. But it remains to be seen whether or not Paine captured and articulated some of the other essential conceptions of American federalism.

A return to the *Crisis Papers* provides some clues. In *Crisis X*, written in March 1782, Paine again addressed the specific issue of united national action and the need for a greater role for centralized government. Arguing that the national government should be supreme, he stated the proposition as follows:

> Each state is to the United States what each individual is to the state he lives in. And it is on this grand point, our happiness as a people, and our safety as individuals, depend.

Paine argued in this *Crisis* that the union was too weak, that it was no longer simply a bond "of common interest and affection" but a "duty of legal obligation:"

> The union of America is the foundation-stone of her independence: the rock on which it is built; and is something so sacred in her constitution, that we ought to watch every word we speak, and every thought we think, that we injure it not, even by mistake. When a multitude, extended, or rather

scattered, over a continent in the manner we were, mutually agree to form one common centre whereon the whole shall move to accomplish a particular purpose, all parts must act together and alike, or act not at all, and a stoppage in any one is a stoppage of the whole. . . .

Once again, the formidable task before Paine was to produce nothing short of a miracle—in the case of this paper, as painlessly as possible to coerce the people in the various states to pay their taxes to the New Congress proposed by the Articles. Without revenue Congress could not finance the war. Paine reasoned in *Crisis X* that the taxes might be more palatable if the expenses of the United States for conducting the war and the expenses of each state for operating domestic matters were kept distinct. The several states should "lay taxes for raising their quotas of money, for the United States, separate from those laid for their own particular use." As long as the finances—taxes, collections and expenditures—were kept separate, the people in the several states would be more inclined to appropriate their share for Congress. But Paine noted—and the similarities to our own time are striking—that there was already a strong movement among the states to lower taxes. Paine's response to this trend would surely give insomnia to the legions of Americans who feel their taxes are too high:

> When we think or talk about taxes, we ought to recollect that we lie down in peace and sleep in safety; that we can follow our farms or stores or other occupations, in prosperous tranquillity; and that these inestimable blessings are procured to us by the taxes that we pay. In this view, our taxes are properly our insurance money; that are what we pay to be made safe, and, in strict policy, are the best money we can lay out.

This passage deserves explanation. The assumption has often been made that the writer of *Common Sense* was a classical liberal on economic matters. The crux of this assumption rests upon principles stated unequivocally in the opening passages of *Common Sense* that the best government is that which governs least and with the least amount of expense. Furthermore, scholars like to remind us that *Common Sense* and *The Wealth of Nations* appeared in the same year, that the two works have much in common, and that their ideas were formed in the same theoretical mold. Precisely because Paine did argue that government ought to secure property rights, among other things, some scholars have attempted to temper his radicalism by suggesting that the adjective "bourgeois" be placed before "radical."

Such ideological meddling only serves to obscure the unique thrust of Paine's thought. Paine was not among those American radicals who had shouted, in so many words, "taxation without representation." To the contrary, *Common Sense*—saying nothing about taxes—does not accuse the British system of being an unjust and overbearing taxing machine. To the extent that Paine did level charges against Parliament, his vehement objections were thrown at hereditary privilege—the underlying source of authority for members of the House of Lords—and not Parliament's taxing powers, the traditional function of the lower house. Throughout *Common Sense* Paine makes it abundantly clear that trade and commerce are to be the primary objectives of the nation. Like Madison, Paine thought that one of the chief objects of government protection is property, although with this important variation: Whereas Madison makes property the chief object of government (*Federalist* No. 10), Paine mentions security, freedom, and property, in that order, and then says that "above all things [is] the free exercise of religion." Yet there is no doubt that by the early 1780s Paine saw the inability of Congress to raise revenue as the number one concern of the new government. Once again Paine and Hamilton thought alike on an issue. In a letter to Robert Morris in 1781, Hamilton wrote that it would be necessary "for keeping up taxation to a degree which, without being oppressive, will be a spur to industry. . . . " For early Federalists, taxation was not an anathema but a necessity for the promotion of industry and commerce.

In 1781 Congress proposed (as Paine had anticipated it would in *Public Good*) a duty on imports, the proceeds to be applied to the war. Unanimous consent of the thirteen states was necessary under the Articles for the 5 percent duty to become law, and by 1782 all states but Rhode Island either had agreed or had promised to approve the measure. Paine was sought out by Robert Morris and Gouverneur Morris (the latter being an old archenemy) to employ his pen in an effort to push Rhode Island into agreement. Paine's "Six Letters to Rhode Island" probably accomplished little more than antagonizing the recalcitrant residents of the state. But some of these letters, all of which appeared in Rhode Island newspapers (with a few being reprinted in several Philadelphia papers), contained an interesting conception of federalism. In "Letter II" Paine wrote:

> Every man in America stands in a two-fold order of citizenship. He is a citizen of the state he lives in, and of the United States; and without justly and truly supporting his citizenship in the latter, he will inevitably sacrifice the former.

Paine had identified the concept of dual citizenship, though he clearly regarded national citizenship as primary. But his thought went even further:

> What would the sovereignty of any one individual state be, if left to itself, to contend with a foreign power? It is on our united sovereignty, that our greatness and safety, and the security of our foreign commerce, rest. This united sovereignty then must be something more than a name, and requires to be as completely organized for the line it is to act in as that of any individual state, and, if anything, more so, because more depends upon it.

There is a prophetic hint in this passage of the concept of "dual sovereignty," as noted by at least one student of Paine's thought. But Paine failed to develop the thought. The passage does indicate, though, his strong advocacy of the federal government's power to regulate commerce. To some, it may seem to be an apparent contradiction, that the "fierce egalitarian," "radical democrat," and famous patron of the "rights of man" should be concerned with such typically conservative matters as fiscal responsiblity. Throughout *Common Sense* and other writings, however, Paine continuously gave equal weight to his arguments for independence and for union and prosperity. To Paine, independence and union were reciprocally bound together:

> It would perhaps be quite as well were [we] to talk less about our independence, and more about our union. For if the union be justly supported, our independence is made secure. The former is the mother, the latter the infant at her breast. The nourishment of the one is drawn through the other, and to impoverish the mother is famishing her offspring.

The union was indispensable to economic prosperity, for only as a sovereign nation could America hope to realize its commercial potential:

> Is there a country in the world that has so many openings to happiness as this? Masters of the land, and proprietors of the government, unchained from the evils of foreign subjection, and respected by sovereign powers, we have only to deserve prosperity, and its attainment is sure. . . . Besides, the European world, or any place we may trade to, knows us only through our national sovereignty, as UNITED STATES. Any infringement on our rights of commerce must be lodged before the United States, and every redress for any such injury must come to us through that line of sovereignty; *consequently the regulation of it must reside in the same power* [italics added].

Over and over in his "Letters to Rhode Island" Paine pounded out the point that "trade is not local property;" that commerce is not just a local affair, "but belongs to all the citizens of America, without distinction of place or state." It was his hope that commerical success and economic prosperity would come to all in America, regardless of the rank within the social and economic order in which people might be found. Paine's belief in union and economic strength is perfectly compatible with his egalitarianism. The promise of greater equality for Paine, was tied to national economic development. The states, because of their narrow interests, were poor repositories of economic policy. The central government had to be made stronger.

The end of the war brought with it Paine's final *Crisis* papers. "'The times that tried men's souls' are over," he declared in *Crisis XIII*, 1783. But the victory was not quite complete. Reminding his readers that it was "the cause of America that made me an author," Paine urged the victors to take immediate steps to strengthen the union. The world would know America not as states but as a sovereign nation, he argued. But in order to become a great nation, the states would have to make some sacrifices:

> It is with the confederated states as with individuals in society; something must be yielded up to make the whole secure. In this view of things we gain by what we give, and draw an annual interest greater than the capital. I ever feel myself hurt when I hear the union, that great palladium of our liberty and safety, the least irreverently spoken of. It is the most sacred thing in the constitution of America, and that which every man should be most proud and tender of. Our citizenship in any particular state is only our local distinction. By the latter we are known at home, by the former to the world. Our great title is Americans—our inferior one varies with the place.

Paine also remarked in this *Crisis* that "sovereignty must have power to protect all the parts that compose and constitute it: and as United States we are equal to the importance of the title, but otherwise we are not." Besides, he continued, "our union, well and wisely regulated and cemented [Hamilton's favorite word], is the cheapest way of being great— the easiest way of being powerful, and the happiest invention in government . . . America can admit of."

Paine's final *Crisis* echoed consistently all his thoughts on union. Given occasion by America's first postwar crisis with Britain, he rushed into print "A Supernumerary Crisis," designed to counter the British decision to close West Indies ports against American vessels. Paine instructed his readers that as long as certain states (obviously meaning Rhode Island) blocked any efforts toward a tighter union, Britain would not fear the new nation but would take advantage of America's disunited status. "United," Paine warned, using perhaps his strongest language yet, America "is formidable, and that with the least possible charge a nation can be so; separated, she is a medley of individual nothings, subject to the sport of foreign nations."

The *Crisis Papers* had all beeen signed "Common Sense," and they left no doubt that "Common Sense" was a staunch nationalist. National unity and national prosperity went hand in hand. America could be one of the great nations among nations, if only it were unified. Paine's final paragraph of the *Crisis Papers* summed up nicely the vision for America that he had begun in *Common Sense*:

> But it is only by acting in union, that the usurpations of foreign nations on the freedom of trade can be counteracted, and security extended to the commerce of America. And when we view a flag, which to the eye is beautiful, and to contemplate its rise and origin inspires a sensation of sublime delight, our national honor must unite with our interest to prevent injury to the one, or insult to the other.

CONCLUSION

Following the *Crisis* series, Thomas Paine continued to write pamphlets on various subjects, including the "bank war" that developed with the establishment of the Bank of North America, paper money, and other issues of the day. His departure for Europe on the eve of the Philadelphia Convention was based on scientific, not political, reasons. There is no doubt that if Paine had attended the Convention he would have voted for the new Constitution. In fact, he later said so. In a letter written to George Washington from Paris in 1796, Paine remarked that he "would have voted for it myself, had I been in America." Like Jefferson, Paine expressed several reservations about specific features of the document: he disliked the single executive and he worried about "the long duration of the Senate." But Paine made it clear that he would have voted for even "a worse" document, as long as the people were given the means to remedy its defects. Moreover, he made it clear that those in Washington's administration who had labeled him an Anti-Federalist were entirely wrong. Paine told Washington in the letter that he, Paine, was the first person to propose "consolidating the States into a Federal Government." (As previously discussed above, Hamilton shares in this honor.) But Paine also reminded Washington that he had called for a "Continental Convention" for forming a "Continental Government" in *Common Sense*. It is clear, at least, that Paine always thought of himself as the first Federalist.

Whether or not Paine really was the first American Federalist does not matter. What matters is that he devoted a considerable amount of attention to constitutional ideas, a fact that is overlooked by many leading scholars of the Constitution today. It is remarkable that Paul Eidelberg could write a book on the philosophy of the American Constitution and not mention Thomas Paine more than once. Alpheus Thomas Mason's classic text on American political thought, *Free Government in the Making,* leaves something to be desired when it comes to the contributions of Paine to American political thinking. It is hard to understand why Paine's political theory has been largely ignored. His writings took a stand on one of the most important constitutional issues—the emerging Federalist–Anti-Federalist debate. Whether there should be a union, a consolidated republic, or a confederation of sovereign, independent states, was the burning question of the period. It was a question which would be only partially resolved in Philadelphia in 1787.

While it is argued, constitutionally speaking, that the debate is over between the nationalists (who have won) and those who regard the Constitution as nothing more than an "intergovernmental treaty among sovereign states," one has to remember that during the last decades two distinct versions of "New Federalism" have appeared to counterattack the steady growth of the national powers. The political debate continues. Indeed, the debate seesaws hotly in the 1980s, just as it did in the 1780s, though it is not likely that the current discussion will fundamentally alter the distribution of powers to the national, state, and local governments. From time to time, the states' rights advocates are given a thin ray of hope, as in the case of *National League of Cities v. Usery* (1976), when the Court—harking back to its pre-1937, "Dual-Federalism" days—used the in-fashion/out-of-fashion Tenth Amendment to strike down federal minimum wage and maximum hours provisions for all state and local employees. On balance, however, the Court has continued its post-1937, nationalist interpretation.*

In spite of President Reagan's recent initiatives, the inexorable growth of national government and powers continues. Toxic waste cleanup (and superfunds), big business (and big city) bailouts and the ever-growing crisis of the American farmer are but three examples of recent issues which easily defy state and local solutions. As if these examples were not enough, national budget deficits alone will continue to establish and dominate the American agenda far into the future. Even Hamilton and Paine might wince at present figures, but it is highly unlikely that either man would have thought much of current initiatives

---

*Less than a week after this was written, it was announced that the Supreme Court had overturned *National League of Cities,* a dramatic affirmation of this conclusion.

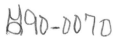

to roll back national powers to solve the problems of modern federal/state relations. (It is equally unlikely, one might speculate, that either man would have supported the current movement among the states to force the national government, through a constitutional amendment, to balance its budget.)

As Tom Paine saw it, the future of American federalism *is* the future of America, as long as federalism is given a strong national flavor. Along with Hamilton, Washington, and Madison, Paine had forcefully and consistently argued for strengthening the union, for expanding the powers of Congress, and for creating a powerful commercial republic during those "critical" years prior to the Constitutional Convention of 1787. He was one of the few democrats of the American Revolution to remain a staunch nationalist in the years following the Convention when an expansive national government began to take shape. Paine went on to other countries and to other revolutions, but he never lost his steadfast belief that his constitutional prescriptions were right for a strong, healthy America. When he left for Europe, on the eve of the Convention of 1787, Paine must have felt somewhat smug, knowing that his call in *Common Sense* for a "Continental Conference" to frame a "Continental Charter" was finally coming to pass. And he must have sensed that his generation was about to accomplish something quite remarkable: it was on the verge of becoming an exception to Jefferson's axiom that only rarely does the generation that produces a revolution manage to complete it.

In Professor William Beaney's succinct description of the Constitutional Convention and the events which led to and followed it, he characterizes the Framers as "children of the eighteenth century" and "earthly realists." He stresses that while the government created by the Articles of Confederation—which preceded the one established by the Constitution—faced immense problems, it satisfied Americans wedded to local control of government and contributed significantly to American constitutionalism. Concerns over national economic problems and fears for an orderly society persuaded men like Alexander Hamilton and James Madison to recommend the convening of a Constitutional Convention. One measure of the difference between the framers' century and our own was that delegates conducted their business in absolute secrecy. They excluded the media, gave no press conferences, and avoided leaking sensitive information. Beaney discusses some of the major issues which divided the Convention and selects the "supremacy clause" in Article VI of the Constitution for special mention. He argues that there would have been little chance for effective government without it. In interpreting the ratification fight, Beaney sees the debate turning on differences of opinion over how far to strengthen the central government rather than diverse economic interests. One consequence of the fear of a dangerously consolidated government was the addition of a Bill of Rights as the price of ratification. Beaney concludes that the Framers did not solve all the problems facing the new nation, but he credits them with writing a document flexible enough to adapt to a much different kind of society.

WILLIAM M. BEANEY

The Constitution of 1787

BACKGROUND

The constitution which emerged from the Convention of 1787 is deservedly regarded as an outstanding achievement in the agelong search for effective, representative, and free government. The great English statesman and prime minister William Gladstone proclaimed it "the most wonderful work ever struck off at one time by the brain and purpose of man."

Frequently lost in the understandable veneration of the great document is a proper recognition of the blending of intellectual inheritance, practical experience, and political skills that made possible the writing and adoption of this relatively short document, which, though modified in a number of ways, still retains its basic original form. Except for the post–Civil War amendments, the great changes in the structure and operation of the American political system have resulted from the actions over time of political forces, changes in the social scene, and confirmatory decisions of the United States Supreme Court. Wars, both internal and external, cyclical economic depressions, and the persistent drive toward equality have driven the national government into roles not fully anticipated by any of the participants in the Constitutional Convention. Yet, the Framers of the Constitution must receive full credit for creating a constitution which, in the oft-quoted words of Chief Justice Marshall, was "designed to endure for ages to come. . . ."

The fifty-five men who served as representatives of their respective states were familiar with the classical political writers, such as the Englishmen John Locke and James Harrington, and the Frenchman Charles de Montesquieu (1689–1775). The former two stressed the critical social role of property, broadly conceived, for which government was the necessary protector, while the latter's contribution was the central structural concept of separation of powers as a way of protecting the people's liberties. But there were other strains of thought of purely American derivation that influenced the Framers. Roger Williams (1603–1683), an early dissenter against the Puritan theocracy, stressed that government was the creature and servant of a sovereign people. Another nonconformist, Thomas Hooker (1586–1647) of Connecticut, believed in the ecclesiastical equality of all men—whose free consent was as necessary to the formation and conduct of government as it was to the creation and operation of a church. A latter democratic philosopher, John Wise (1652–1725), based his compact theory of government on the necessity for protecting natural rights, one of which was the equality of rights shared by all. Even more important in the world of political thought in which the Constitution emerged was the long period of debate leading up to the separation from England, characterized by detailed arguments on the vital subjects of the location of sovereignty, the doctrine of representation, higher law theories, and discussion of federalism. Such worthies as James Otis, Benjamin Franklin, John Dickinson, James Wilson, Alexander Hamilton, and John Adams not only addressed trenchant criticisms against the rulers of Great Britain and their policies, but in the process provided a fund of materials from which a popular-based successor government could be fashioned.

The governments created after the gauntlet had been laid down to the British took the form initially of new state governments welded together by a very loose central mechanism, the Continental Congress. Then, in 1777, because of the widely acknowledged inadequacies of the Congress in carrying out military and foreign activities, the Articles of Confederation were proposed by Congress. By March 1, 1781, they were ratified by the last state, Maryland.

STATE CONSTITUTIONS

Of the state constitutions and the governments they established, little will be said except that, while all possessed some form of separation of powers and guaranties of certain liberties, the dominant institution in the states was the legislature—reflecting the bitterness resulting from the quarrels between colonial governors and colonial legislatures. Several state constitutions provided for legislative amendment of the Constitution; many gave the legislature the power of appointing most state officers. In only three states (South Carolina, Massachusetts, and New York) did the Governor have even a partial veto power. The judicial branch, like the Governor, was made clearly subordinate to the legislature, being fully dependent on that body for its organization, functions, and the salaries of judges. The Articles of Confederation simply gave fuller expression to the idea that the separate, sovereign states should continue to act through a legislature in which each state had a single vote. None of the more important powers granted in the Articles could be exercised "unless nine states assent to the same," and the injunction that "every state shall abide by the determinations of the United States in Congress assembled" was purely hortatory, since no mechanism existed for compelling states to accept a congressional decision.

In the absence of an effective central government, the policies of the individual states dominated the political scene—not only in the domestic sphere, but in the international arena as well.

THE ARTICLES OF CONFEDERATION

The most serious complaints by critics of the Articles government centered on commercial and financial matters, but many took a friendly view of its development. As historians have made clear, the conditions then existing benefited some groups, who, quite naturally, viewed predominant state power and a weak central government as a blessing. Wholly apart from economic arguments, these people who became Anti-Federalists insisted strongly that liberty is safer at the hands of a government close to the people. The debtor class was obviously pleased with stay laws, paper money, and other measures protective of their interests. The most alarming of these incidents took place in Massachusetts, where armed farmers led by Daniel Shays closed inland canals and threatened to march on Boston on behalf of inflationary legislation demanded by the debtor class.

There were other economic developments that, while pleasing to some interests, were perceived as threatening to others. One was the tendency of certain states to use their strategic geographical location to impose excise taxes and other tax burdens on commerce passing through their borders.

The triumph of "cheap money" parties in seven states resulted in various statutes suspending legal actions to collect debts, or allowing payment in kind or in land. Those who had property interests feared that the revolutionary period stress on "liberty" was being exploited, resulting in a system where the accepted rules and laws counted for little. They feared that the misuse of the power of the ballot box could destroy the society as effectively as the tyranny of George III and his ministers.

The Articles of Confederation did little or nothing to improve the strength of the central government or eliminate the weaknesses and dangers exhibited by the states. As a result, many American leaders believed that their country faced perilous economic and political problems. These men, later described as Federalists in the debate over the ratification of the Constitution, concluded that some of the fundamental problems facing America arose from serious deficiencies in the Articles of Confederation as well as dangerous tendencies in the states. As they viewed America's place in the world, they recognized that the confederation government was incapable of conducting an effective foreign policy. England, France, and other countries treated our ministers with disdain, since they failed to represent a sovereign nation but rather a collection of virtually independent warring states. The inclination of the American states to consider themselves independent sovereign states also made it difficult to promote commerce and economic development among the colonies.

It is true that the men who traveled to Philadelphia were men of property. This fact led Charles Beard, in his *Economic Interpretation of the Constitution of the United States* (1913) to suggest that they went to

Philadelphia to secure their investments, particularly in securities used to finance the war. In the eighteenth century, however, property meant something quite different from Beard's more familiar twentieth-century definition. For instance, it meant responsibility, status, and the deference which came with this status. The debtor legislation of the 1780s symbolized an assault on an orderly society which the Federalists led, defended, and believed necessary to self-government. Because of the revolutionary arguments, the Federalists already had a well-developed sense that governments were easily corrupted. If revolutionary propaganda led Americans to falsely blame all their problems on the king, debtor legislation reminded Federalists of the need to limit the most popular branches of government.

Because of the success of the Federalists, school books often fail to reflect the fact that there were many people who did not share the view of a people in peril. Some revolutionaries, such as like Patrick Henry, "smelled a rat" and refused to go to Philadelphia. Some historians, like Merrill Jensen, have considered the so-called Anti-Federalists men who wished to carry on the democratic experiment begun but not completed by the American Revolution. Although historians have hotly debated the revisionist positions of Beard and Jensen, they have agreed that the Articles of Confederation made a significant contribution to American government. Extradition, the full faith and credit clause, and the privileges and immunities clause serve as examples of Confederation provisions that passed directly into the United States Constitution. Finally, some of the problems faced by revolutionary America were not susceptible to easy solutions regardless of the structure of the government. It required a decade of experience following 1776 to suggest some of the more appropriate remedies to cure the new nation's ills.

MAKING THE CONSTITUTION

Between May 25, when enough delegates were present to proceed, and September 17, when thirty-nine delegates signed the document, a distinguished body of American political leaders drafted a new framework of government. Fifty-five men appeared in Philadelphia, but the real work was done by about a dozen. In a symbolic sense, George Washington was among the most important. Viewing him as a living legend, the advocates of a new constitution believed his presence crucial to success. For substantive contributions to the Constitution, the most important delegate was another Virginian, James Madison. Believed to be the author of the Convention's working document, the Vriginia Plan, Madison was also a careful recorder of the proceedings as well as a major contributor to the *Federalist Papers*, a collection of famous articles designed to win support for the newly proposed document. Other noteworthy contributors were James Wilson, Gouverneur Morris, Oliver Ellsworth, Rufus King, and William Samuel Johnson.

Very early in the Convention, the nationalists demonstrated their influence when they passed a resolution which concluded "that a national government ought to be established consisting of a supreme Legislative, Executive and Judiciary." By so resolving, the Convention made it clear that its goal was not to patch up the Articles but to create a new national government. Despite this consensus, there were plenty of differences concerning the structure of this new government. One of the Convention's major disputes centered on how to elect and apportion representatives to the new Congress. The Virginia Plan provided for the popular election of the House of Representatives, whose members, in turn, would elect members to the Senate. While the small states offered no resistance to the method of electing representatives, they vigorously opposed the method of electing senators. After a brief debate, the delegates rather easily decided to leave the election of the Senate to state legislatures. Not until the Seventeenth Amendment, ratified in 1913, would the people of the United States have an opportunity to elect their senators. The stickier question before the Convention was that of apportionment. Small states simply feared the proposal made by the large states that representation in Congress should be apportioned according to population. The solution was to elect one representative to the House of Representatives for every 40,000 people and to give each state an equal vote in the senate. This "Great Compromise" was hardly a step in the direction of greater democracy. But there was no thought of populism among these men. They were children of the eighteenth century, who were fascinated by checks and balances. As political scientists, they wished to refine and control government. There was no discussion of one man–one vote. Requirements for voting were left to the states. After all, the Framers saw value in qualifying suffrage by requiring the ownership of property. They also excluded women and blacks from the privilege of voting. Blacks were property, and any thought of protecting them withered in the face of the South's demand that its property remain protected. The United States Constitution provided for a democracy, but, from the twentieth-century perspective, it was of a very qualified kind.

Another important debate revolved around the related issues of federalism and the judiciary. The Virginia Plan permitted the national government to define its authority, gave Congress the authority to disallow state laws, and allowed the national government to coerce errant states. This was an extremely nationalistic solution to the problem of federalism and was strongly opposed by moderates and defenders of states' rights. The Convention's response was to delegate specific powers to Congress and then to declare, in Article VI of the Constitution, that the new national government was supreme in its sphere. To later generations, the supremacy clause (Art. VI, par. 2) was the most important clause in the Constitution. There was absolutely no chance that the Constitution could have provided an effective government without it. If this seems doubtful, study the history of the Civil War. Even with the benefit of the Civil War experience, there were southern jurists and commentators in the 1950s who still claimed that individual states were sovereign, as they protested Supreme Court decisions which destroyed barriers to civil rights and civil liberties of blacks.

While the powers of the Congress and judiciary were fairly well defined, the Constitution provided enough flexibility to allow statesmen to shape this document to the demands of subsequent generations. Although the Constitution delegated specific powers to Congress, the last clause of Article I, Section 8, clause 18 gave Congress the authority "to make all laws which shall be necessary and proper for carrying into execution" the delegated powers. Shortly after the ratification of the Constitution, Alexander Hamilton seized upon this clause to justify legislation establishing the creation of a national bank. The powers of the Supreme Court also seemed pretty well defined. Yet, when John Marshall argued that the Supreme Court was the final interpreter of the Constitution, his opponents protested vehemently, and several generations of scholars have spilled a great deal of ink arguing the merits of this assertion. The Constitution's provisions in Article II for the powers of the President were not specific. This reflected a division in the Convention over how powerful the delegates wished to make the office. Revolutionary ideology stressed that a republican form of government required a weak executive. The difficulties of the 1780s prompted a revision of the view in the minds of some American political leaders. The Presidency they created was clearly stronger than the state governorships and reflected the need to balance strong legislatures.

The men who drafted the Constitution were earthy realists with a good idea of their priorities, which included protection of their interests and a good understanding of how to conduct public affairs. They did not solve all of their (and future generations') problems, but they created a system that proved adaptable to an ever-changing world.

RATIFICATION

The Congress was hardly enthusiastic about the proposed Constitution, but submitted it, according to its terms, to the individual states—whose legislatures in turn set convention dates and called for election of delegates. Merchants, large landowners, land speculators, and Confederation bond holders—most of them living along the tidewater (fifty miles inland from the coast)—generally supported the new Constitution. Called Federalists, they opposed the populist legislation of the states, wanted protection of commerce, and favored sound national credit. They feared the growth of popular demands that would convert a free society into one dominated by the demands of a vociferous legislative majority.

As has already beeen discussed, the Federalists—led by Hamilton, Madison, Jay, Washington, and other prominent Convention figures—had the task of convincing a majority of delegates in at least nine states that the objections raised by their opponents had no basis either in fact or in logic.

Few of the items over which Federalists and Anti-Federalists quarreled had an obvious economic basis. Instead, the Anti-Federalists stressed the tendency of the new Constitution to diminish state authority through the taxing and spending power, the "necessary and proper clause," and the supremacy clause (Article VI, par. 2). The very size of the proposed government which had the power of acting directly on the citizenry was also a source of concern, as was the two-year term allowance in the popularly elected House of Representatives. Worst of all, the proposed Constitution failed to include a Bill of Rights.

These criticisms were answered by various writers and spokesmen, none more effectively than Madison and Hamilton (Jay playing a minor role) in a series of eighty-five articles appearing between October 1787 and July 1788. Later commentators have noted the "split personality" of these articles, meaning that Madison and Hamilton differed on many points. Still, their joint endeavors produced a picture of a new central government which, while competent to achieve a successful foreign policy and national defense posture—as well as to eliminate the commercial interference by the states—was hardly a threat to the people's liberties. They stressed the divided powers of the branches of the federal government, the impact of localism through the legislative branches, and the power of the Supreme Court to retain the national government within its enumerated powers.

The writers minimized the role that the national government would play in the lives of Americans and stressed the prominent part that state governments would continue to play. As to the absence of a Bill of Rights, they agreed that the whole organization and national operation of the new government had the effect of a Bill of Rights, since the intricate set of checks and balances was the most desirable way to ensure that liberties were effectively safeguarded. They also played up the dangers of an attempted enumeration, since it could be argued that any liberty claim that was not included in a Bill of Rights would, as a result, be unprotected and would invite governmental intrusion.

At the state conventions, many delegates were won over to the ratification side by the promise of amendments guaranteeing rights. The narrow victories in the important states of Massachusetts, Virginia, and New York were attributable in large part to the promise of "rights amendments." (The respective votes were 187–168, 89–79 and 30–27.) The last state to ratify was Rhode Island, on May 29, 1790, by a vote of 34–32.

THE BILL OF RIGHTS

Madison, Hamilton, and many other Federalists originally resisted the plea that a Bill of Rights—delineating those rights which every citizen could claim from the proposed national government—was essential if the liberties of the people were to be fully protected. To Madison and Hamilton the limited powers of the new government, the separation and blending of the powers of each of the branches, and the check of federalism were sufficient guaranties of the people's liberties. They agreed that a bill of rights was needed in state constitutions because of the many ways that citizens could be directly affected by state and local government, but this was not likely at the national level. An additional argument which Madison and the other Federalists gave up reluctantly was that the enumeration of certain rights in a written constitution gave rise to an inference that these were the only rights worthy of protection— and thus might encourage government action interfering with those unmentioned rights. A modern example of the realization of their fears was the position taken by Justice Black, dissenting, in *Griswold* v. *Connecticut* (381 U.S. 479: 1965), where the United States Supreme Court held that a state statute punishing the user (or adviser as to the use) of contraceptive devices violated the constitutional right to privacy, at least in the case of married persons. Since "privacy" was not mentioned in the Constitution, Black would not give it constitutional protection.

Madison assumed the chore of culling from numerous proposals those guaranties which he thought most desirable, though some of the drafting reflected his personal choices as to the most important rights. At the first session of Congress in 1789 he began implementation of his plan. Madison's original intention was to add amendments at appropriate places in the body of the Constitution, and, at first, this was agreed to by the House. The sheer number of proposals offered by the Anti-Federalists and a recognition that a separate Bill of Rights would give greater prominence to the amendments, led Madison to abandon his original plan.

Some of the proposed amendments—such as one stating that government was intended for the benefit of the people and derived from their authority—were dropped as redundant. An attempt of the Anti-Federalists to add the word "expressly" to the eventual Tenth Amendment was defeated. Finally, in September 1789, Congress submitted twelve amendments to the states. Since there were now fourteen states, approval by eleven was necessary. Ten of the amendments were approved by the eleventh state in November 1791. The two proposed amendments that failed ratification would have required at least one representative for each 50,000 persons and postponed any effort to alter the salaries of members of Congress until an election had intervened.

The amendments that compose the Bill of Rights are not of equal importance. Madison himself stressed the religious clauses of the First Amendment and, secondarily, the remaining provisions of the Amendment protecting free speech, press, and assembly. Amendments Four through Eight deal with procedural guaranties sought by those who, with great foresight, were persuaded that the national government would become involved in criminal prosecutions.

The Ninth and Tenth Amendments represent soothing balm to the Anti-Federalists, who feared the dominance of the national government. The Second and Third Amendments dealt respectively with the right to bear arms and the quartering of troops.

During the discussion of the proposed amendments, there was an attempt to make one or more apply to the states as well as the national government. That effort failed and was confirmed by the Supreme Court's 1833 opinion in *Barron* v. *Baltimore*. The first ten amendments, by their own terms, pose limits only on the national government.

In this essay Richard D. Miles explores the meaning of the Constitutional Convention as an event in American history rather than as law. He begins by speculating upon the reasons why the Constitution was so widely embraced by all Americans almost immediately after the bitter struggle to ratify it. There was no anti-Constitutional party, in the 1790s. Moreover, politicians defended their positions by arguing that, unlike their opponents, their proposals had the virtue of constitutionality. Later extreme abolitionists and state sovereignty theorists challenged the accepted view of what occurred in Philadelphia, but the Civil War, by force of arms, confirmed the view of the Constitution enunciated by Alexander Hamilton, John Marshall, and Abraham Lincoln. By 1887, the centennial of the Constitution, comfortable Americans congratulated the Framers for providing them with the basis for the "American way of life." Added to natural boosterism came praise for the Framers from foreign observers like Alexis de Tocqueville, William Gladstone, and James Bryce. As a result, Americans worshipped the Constitution and made the Framers into demigods. As the nineteenth century came to a close, professional historians began to dominate the study of the Convention and ratification. Of these, Charles Beard's *Economic Interpretation of the Constitution* (1913) swept the field. Despite the widespread influence of Beard's book, Miles emphasizes that it was no match for the Constitution and Supreme Court as secular religious symbols during the "court packing" controversy of the late 1930s. After World World II, Beard's work took a severe beating at the hands of some scholars as the Framers' political sagacity won applause from other historians. Recently, historians have tried to get outside the Beardian framework, but, after two hundred years, Miles concludes that there has been a surprising lack of diversity in how we think about the events surrounding the summer of 1787 in Philadelphia.

RICHARD D. MILES

The Philadelphia Convention: Two Hundred Years of Thinking About It

American independence—the "Glorious Cause," as it was known—did not immediately bring the glorious life which people had expected. The blessings of liberty were many, of course, but the daily struggle to make a living was not much easier for most people than before the Revolution. Nearly everyone heard rumors about worrisome things happening in other places. Prospects seemed uncertain or bad for solving the really big problems, such as the payment of public debt, the maintenance of reliable currencies, the availability of foreign markets, and above all the continuing menace of a hostile Britain.

Soon there was a general understanding that the resolution of these and other problems would require once again a united effort of the sort which had generated such enthusiasm in 1776. Congress, which had somehow managed to wage the war and arrange the peace, seemed poorly equipped for dealing with postwar problems. Another *kind* of Congress was needed, it seemed. To that end, Congress itself, somewhat belatedly and reluctantly, finally agreed that the states should send delegates to a convention at Philadelphia "for the sole and express purpose of revising the Articles of Confederation."

This led to a most astonishing turn of affairs. The delegates who assembled in Philadelphia in May 1787 proceeded to do something quite different. Rather than revising the Articles, they set about drawing up an entirely new plan of government, to be known as the United States Constitution.

Most people, of course, did not know about this until the Convention ended its work in September, for the delegates had deliberated behind closed doors under a pledge of secrecy. Naturally, during the four months of its sessions, rumors abounded. At one point there was a persistent report that they were considering a king for the United States. For once, the Convention responded promptly to rumor: "We never once thought of a king." Another report had it that they were concentrating on the public debt. Finding how difficult it was to pay foreign debts, one nameless correspondent said the Convention had resolved to recommend to Congress "to set up the whole state of Rhode Island [they had no delegates at the Convention] for sale to the highest bidder . . . in a view to applying the net proceeds of such sale to the liquidation of the . . . debt."

The Convention concluded its work on September 17. The next morning the official secretary, William Jackson, set out for New York, where Congress was meeting, to present its work to them. Within a few days, newspapers printed the text of the U.S. Constitution. The debate as to its acceptability was now joined. Congress sent the document, without comment, to the state governments—which would find in the document's final article that it was not really their approval that was sought, but rather the approval of ratifying conventions gathered solely for that purpose. By early November, we are told, "it was a lonely or uncaring American . . . who had not read the proposed Constitution." Many found it a deeply troubling issue.

Some people voiced immediate disapproval; for a while they were known simply as "anti's." Much of that disapproval, especially at first, arose from their thinking about the Convention itself, which is our concern here: we must make some effort to separate disapproval of the Convention from disapproving views of the Constitution itself, a much larger subject altogether. The most serious observation which the "anti's" made about the Convention was that it had exceeded its authority. All along, many persons, including some members of Congress, had had deep suspicions that a centralized tyranny was in the making. An excess of centralized power was their greatest apprehension.

As long as the Convention was limited to proposals for reform of the existing system, it had been supposed, things might not go too far. But now the suspicions of the "anti's" were confirmed: the men at Philadelphia had indeed gone way beyond their instructions. One said that they had forged "gilded chains . . . in the secret conclave." In fact, a few of the delegates had even left the Convention when they realized how "consolidated" the proposed new government would certainly be, asserting that such strong action violated their instructions.

Beyond this, there was the extreme irregularity of the Constitution's final article, whereby the Convention plainly proposed to circumvent current constitutional arrangements for changing the Articles of Confederation. According to the Articles, which was the prevailing "constitution," changes were to be ratified by the *legislatures* of *all* the states. The Philadelphia Convention asserted that the Constitution would be in effect when ratified by *conventions* in *nine* states. This is central to the later characterization of the Philadelphia Convention as "counter-revolutionary."

There were many at the time who were eager to see the worst of motives in this maneuver. Thus, Samuel Bryan of Pennsylvania spoke darkly of "the masqued aristocracy . . . the aristocratic juntos of the *well-born few*," anticipating a theme of early twentieth-century descriptions of the Convention. The charge was heard often, but never more tellingly than in Amos Singletary's melancholy remarks in Massachusetts:

> These lawyers and men of learning and moneyed men . . . expect to get into Congress themselves . . . and get all the power and all the money in their own hands, and then they will swallow all us little folks . . . just as the whale swallowed up Jonah!

Supporters of the Constitution were troubled by such characterizations of the Convention's motives. Alexander Hamilton vigorously denounced Governor George Clinton of New York and other Anti-Federalists (as the Constitution's opponents soon came to be called) as men "who gain influence by cajoling the unthinking mass . . . " Such a description of the American people, of course, might well seem to have proved his opponent's point. Edmund Pendleton in Virginia responded somewhat more temperately. "Why bring into the debate," he asked, "the whims of writers—introducing the distinction of *well-born* from others?" Everybody, he thought, was "*well-born* who comes into the world with an intelligent mind and all his parts perfect." There was some shock at seeing a distinguished group of men led by The Great Man himself being maligned—surely that could only be the work of irresponsible riffraff. "The *Federalists* should be distinguished hereafter by the name of WASHINGTONIANS," declared one writer, and he deftly turned the point against the Convention's detractors by continuing, "and the *Antifoederalists* by the same of SHAYITES, in every part of the United States"—a reference, of course to the notorious defiance of government in western Massachusetts in 1786, led, presumably, by one Daniel Shays.

If early critics of the Philadelphia Convention had had their way, we would have had *two* constitutional conventions to think about (at least) for the last two hundred years, for they frequently suggested that the work of the 1787 Convention could be regularized, or made proper, by having it submitted to yet another convention which would be arranged for just this purpose. This idea had been discussed briefly during the Philadelphia Convention and overwhelmingly rejected. Now, in the heat of the ratification battle, such a notion horrified Washington, Hamilton, Madison, and the others who had invested a whole summer of arduous thought and negotiation in a heroic effort to get the best and the fairest constitution humanly possible. There was, however, substantial appreciation of their work at the time, for the ratifications by the states went forward without being derailed by suggestions of a second convention.

Before the end of June 1788 the ratification of the Constitution was assured. By all accounts then and in most accounts written in the last two hundred years, the ratification of the U.S. Constitution was achieved by some of the most severely contested battles of American political history. Those who had drafted the Constitution, no less than those who did battle for it (in some cases they were the same people), withstood a great deal of criticism and even vituperation. Once the procedure for establishing the new government got under way, however, the aspersions no longer flowed so freely. In fact, "all serious controversy over the Constitution ceased abruptly once it had been adopted," according to one authority. Within a year or two after Washington took office as President, little was heard about the deficiencies of the Convention and its work. Those who opposed some of the administration's policies did so, not because the Constitution was flawed as a product of a suspect convention but, they insisted, because the Constitution forbade those policies.

Historians have found a number of reasons for the sudden embracing of the Constitution and the praising of the Convention. For one thing, economic conditions in many parts of the country were already improving in 1787, and that happy trend continued. Furthermore, the public trust in Washington, so potent a force in the ratification controversy, also continued; people just could not believe that tyranny was imminent if he were the President. Fears of potential oppression were further assuaged by the early proposals for amendments to the Constitution launched by a Congress dominated by Federalists, for those amendments had the character, as we have said ever since, of a Bill of Rights. Such leadership as the Constitution's opponents once had almost withered away. Some leaders abandoned public affairs, while Virginia's George Mason and Richard Henry Lee died between 1792 and 1794. Some became converts to federalism, conspicuously Patrick Henry and Samuel Chase. Finally, entirely new issues came before the country, rendering further antagonism to the Constitution simply quaint. In an astonishingly short time, it had become both useless and unpopular to complain any longer about the Philadelphia Convention.

*   *   *

So it remained for more than a generation. During the young nation's trials and tribulations, it was the true meaning of the Constitution rather than the Convention itself that was the center of controversy. One exception to this occurred near the end of the War of 1812 at the Hartford Convention, where, many believed, disunion was contemplated. But this rapidly came to seem an aberration—a terrible abandonment of the central purpose of the Philadelphia Convention. A burst of new nationalist feeling followed the war. One powerful manifestation of it was the emergence of a vigorous U.S. Supreme Court, led by the formidable John Marshall. He had personally witnessed part of the process of founding the national government as a member of the Virginia ratifying convention. By now he was into his long career of expounding the meaning of the work produced by the Philadelphia Convention. Along with Marshall, other important national leaders of the time—Henry Clay, the young John C. Calhoun, John Quincy Adams, Daniel Webster, and others—paid unquestioned tribute to the work of the Constitution's Framers. Even Andrew Jackson, whose ideas of the Constitution seemed erratic to some, is remembered for his resolute "The Union will be preserved," uttered during the South Carolina nullification crisis.

A major storm in American life had already been brewing during these early years. Its beginnings may very well have been at Philadelphia in 1787 or even before, but it had long been believed that the presence of slavery need not seriously harm the nation. The intense argument occasioned by Missouri's admission as a state in 1821 portended a problem of major proportions. Presumably an argument about the extension of slavery, it launched a newly bitter argument over the very institution of slavery. As to the stand of the Constitution and its Framers on the matter, it now became much clearer that they had accepted compromises on the subject in the interest of achieving their first goal, a strong national government. The Missouri Compromises may have seemed to be a resumption of the original style of conflict resolution— i.e., compromise—but the spirit of the procedure was now quite different. They left a residue of anger and sullen resentment.

The escalation of the quarrels over slavery which followed the Missouri Compromises is a story which is all too familiar, with its conclusion in the Civil War. But there is a remarkable feature of it which is germane here: for the most part, *both* sides insisted that if the U.S. Constitution were properly observed, their cause would be served. And so both sides long made mighty efforts to find solutions which were derived from the language and style of the Philadelphia Convention. To this there were two exceptions—one on each side. First, John C. Calhoun's particular development of constitutional theory, evident as early as 1831, asserted a view of the nature of the union which was palpably at odds with the thinking of the Philadelphia Convention. He saw the formation of the union as the action of sovereign states whose domestic institutions (e.g., slavery) remained under their exclusive control. Therefore, he felt that the federal government had an obligation to help maintain such domestic institutions because the acceptance of the Constitution had created a kind of compact among the states "to protect and defend each other." Plainly this "compact" made room for nullification and even secession if the terms of the "compact" were violated.

Meanwhile, on the other side, some militant antislave people, who were demanding the immediate and total emancipation of the slaves, knew full well that the U.S. Constitution prevented action of that sort by the national government. Their response was to denounce the Constitution as "an agreement with hell!" Along with this came the belief, once eloquently voiced by William H. Seward, that there was a "higher law" than the Constitution. These departures from the spirit of the Philadelphia Convention commanded only limited support for some time. Inflammatory events, especially in the 1850s, influenced more and more people on both sides to accept these views.

Southern anxiety about the future of slavery after the election of 1860 led to secession, which precipitated the Civil War. During all the excitement of that terrible winter (1860–1861), the air was filled with talk of the Constitution and what its Framers had intended in 1787. Secessionists asserted, as Calhoun had over twenty years before, that the Constitution was a compact among sovereign states, whose sovereignty could never be entirely relinquished. Hence, the aggrieved states had every power and right to leave the union if ever they thought that the compact had been violated. Secessionists asserted that this was precisely what had happened. The principal charge of such a document as the Mississippi Resolutions on Secession, for example, is that the states of the North were guilty of violating the Constitution.

Lincoln's view of the nature of the union created at Philadelphia was, of course, a far different one. It was his responsibility as President to "preserve, protect and defend the Constitution of the United States," as his oath of office stipulated. After denying that any state "upon its own mere motion can lawfully get out of the Union," he noted, "All profess to be content in the Union if all constitutional rights can be maintained." Since none had been violated, and he did not foresee that any would, secession was "the essence of anarchy," a lawlessness which he was duty bound to suppress.

In the secessionists' view, then, the Philadelphia Convention became a far less "counter-revolutionary" body than the Anti-Federalists had originally claimed. For the secessionists, the Framers of the Constitution had apparently not abandoned the quintessential nature of the Articles of Confederation—which had plainly prescribed a union of states whose sovereignty was clearly guaranteed, along with every power "not . . . expressly delegated to the United States." The Philadelphia Framers, in this view, had merely delegated *additional* power to the United States government. Lincoln, on the other hand, saw the Convention as creating coercive power which might be applied to individuals (not states) who were in violation of "the supreme law of the land." Furthermore, Lincoln, particularly in his First Inaugural Address, repeatedly attempted to invoke the spirit of compromise which had been so conspicuous in the Philadelphia Convention as a way of resolving sharp differences of opinion. Looked at this way, one could say that the rejection of the Philadelphia formula by the secessionists left only war as a way of resolving such a crisis.

*   *   *

The victory of the North apparently settled the question of the nature of the union. But the fundamental question which precipitated the great constitutional crisis could be resolved only by adding amendments to the Constitution. Those which were forthcoming (the Thirteenth, Fourteenth, and Fifteenth) represented the first truly important departures from the original intent of the Philadelphia Convention. The compromises regarding slavery which the Framers had made were undone. "Citizenship" was now given a constitutional definition. On the other hand, the central purpose of the Philadelphia Convention—the creation of a strong central government—had been well served by the victory of the Union. Never before had the national government seemed so strong.

The age which followed was one of unprecedented economic development and demographic change marked by the further settlement of many remaining parts of the vast expanse of land within the United States, the astounding increase in population, the emergence of a superb national transportation system, the exploitation of abundant natural resources, and, above all, by the policies of a business-minded national government. These and other elements combined to produce a domestic market without parallel in the world, serviced by a business community whose most striking feature became the giant corporation. For some, it was in many ways truly a Gilded Age. The few who belonged to the established order—along with the many who thought they belonged, or hoped to belong—regarded the American constitutional system as a principal beneficence of the land. This was a time, then, when the praise for those who had created the Constitution became the loudest yet.

By this time, too, there were far more extensive efforts to disseminate that praise. Public schools were becoming an important part of American life, and there was much concern that they should inculcate proper civic attitudes. Earlier, there had been bits and pieces in school books which were directed to this matter. They had come from the pen of such men as Jedidiah Morse, Noah Webster, Samuel Goodrich (a.k.a. Peter Parley), and, latterly, William McGuffey. Their books, usually known as "readers," were intended to enhance literacy but, as one writer has observed, "taught mostly manners and morals."

Six states had attempted to require the study of American history in the public school before the Civil War, but the effectiveness of such action was very limited. After the Civil War there was a greatly heightened concern about this. "A gradual extension of the requirements grew out of the spirit of the times," one writer has said, "and to American history was added the study of the constitution. . . . " By the end of the century, twenty-three states (about half) required such study. Before 1900, though, great numbers of American children did not attend school or did so very irregularly.

Apart from what may have been learned in school, Americans learned American history from oral accounts, from occasional pieces in magazines and newspapers, and, of course, from historians who wrote for an educated, influential adult readership. But most of those who succeeded in attracting substantial numbers of readers—men like Prescott,

Motley, and Parkman—did not turn their attention to the framing of the Constitution. A striking exception is seen in the remarkable achievements of George Bancroft.

Born in 1800, Bancroft was "at thirty-four . . . the leading historian of the United States." A Jacksonian in politics, democratic in philosophy, nationalist in purpose, he saw the divine hand of Providence in the affairs of the United States. From 1834, when his first volume of American history appeared and was roundly applauded, to the end of his long life, he labored with unprecedented success in telling the nation's story. By 1874 his tenth volume of *A History of the United States* brought the narrative to the close of the American Revolution. Surely, it would appear, he was telling people more than they wanted to know, but such was not the case. Public acclaim continued, and, thus encouraged, he added a two-volume work, *History of the Formation of the Constitution of the United States of America*. It was published in 1882.

With the elaborate preparation of ten volumes, the advent of the Constitution in another two was, of course, an episode of high climax. Bancroft took an entire chapter to praise the genius and the glory of the work of the Philadelphia Convention. He included William E. Gladstone's remarks, widely known at the time, that the Constitution was "the most wonderful work ever struck off at a given time by the brain and purpose of man." The account of the last moments of the Convention was especially moving. Bancroft reported that "the members were awe-struck at the result of their councils; the constitution was a nobler work than any one of them had believed it possible to devise." "Washington," he added as if whispering reverently, "then retired to meditate." He omitted to mention that when the Convention adjourned for the last time the delegates—including Washington—retired to the City Tavern.

Bancroft somehow managed to make his celebration of the Constitution a part of his lifelong celebration of democracy. This was no small feat, for he had to reconcile the fact that the Philadelphia Convention's members were unquestionably the ultra-distinguished elite of society with his assertion that their work represented a triumph of democracy. This was done by asserting that everything was done for the people by men who were the authentic agents of the people—hence, the great work was done by the people. And a remarkable people they were: "a new people" who had "risen up without king, or princes or nobles," and who "were more sincerely religious, better educated, of serener minds, and of purer morals than the men of any former republic." His final lines rhapsodized:

By calm meditation and friendly councils they had prepared a constitution which, in the union of freedom with strength and order, excelled every one known before. . . . In the happy morning of their existence . . . they had chosen justice for their guide . . . and while they proceeded on their way with well-founded confidence and joy, all the friends of mankind invoked success on the unexampled endeavor. . . .

Such sentiments were much in demand in the nineteenth century, particularly during the turbulent final decades. John Bach McMaster's eight-volume work, entitled *A History of the People of the United States*, began to appear at about the same time as Bancroft's *History of the Formation of the Constitution*. Despite the title, McMaster's work was less an attribution of all great deeds to "the people" than was Bancroft's; what McMaster had in mind was something like what today is styled "social history." But he was equally awed by the Philadelphia Convention, which he referred to as "a most remarkable assemblage of men, to whom, under God, we owe our liberty, our prosperity, our high place among the nations." At about the same time, John Fiske was giving a course of lectures in Boston, St. Louis, and New York, which became the basis of a book, *The Critical Period of American History, 1783–1789*, "probably the most influential work on the adoption of the Constitution before Beard's." For generations, this was the most familiar description of the 1780s, which Fiske saw as a time of crisis graver than that of the Revolution or that of the Civil War. Those crises were resolved at Yorktown and Paris, and at Appomattox; the crisis of the Confederation period was resolved by the Philadelphia Convention and its "wonderful work—this Iliad, or Parthenon, or Fifth Symphony of statesmanship."

This was also centennial time for the Philadelphia Convention. Americans seem especially prone to commemorate great occasions every fifty years: by now we have had many a semicentennial, centennial, and sesquicentennial celebration. Philadelphia experienced one great centennial in 1876. The first international exposition held in the United States, it was visited by nearly ten million people—close to a world record at the time. Nonetheless, ten years later plans were under way to observe the Constitution's centennial in Philadelphia. It materialized as a "three-day festival of parades, banquets, receptions, and orations extending from the 15th through the 17th of September" of 1887. The rhetoric, of course, echoed in style and theme the leading histories of the time which we have sampled.

The celebrations of 1887 apparently achieved one further thing. Frank Wesley Craven has found these to be occasions which stressed national unity of the sort associated with the Revolution, and thereby "encouraged a new emphasis in the interpretation of our national origins upon the years which had given birth to the Republic." He saw this as the time when those who conducted the Revolution, and especially those who formed the Constitution, were beginning to be referred to as the "Founding Fathers," a term which previously had been used for those who founded the colonies. "I think it may be suggested also," he continued, "that this was the time at which their chief claim to glory first tended to become the drafting of the constitution rather than the signing of the Declaration." Within another generation, most Americans would agree that the "Founding Fathers" were the men of the Philadelphia Convention.

The American experiment in government naturally engaged the attention of foreign commentators. The most distinguished one of the early nineteenth century, Alexis de Tocqueville, expounded at length on the specific features of constitutional government in the United States. As to the Philadelphia Convention, it included, he said, "the men of greatest intelligence and noblest character ever to have appeared in the New World. George Washington presided over it." This accounted for the excellence of the result: "The great cause of the superiority of the federal Constitution lies in the actual character of the lawgivers."

Late in the nineteenth century another foreign observer found a vast reading audience. He was James Bryce, a distinguished English scholar and diplomat. His *American Commonwealth* first appeared in 1888, to be followed by many subsequent editions well into the twentieth century. It has recently been described as a great treatise, "a classic that is still read and used." For Bryce, the men who assembled at Philadelphia were "delegates unlike those usually sent to Congress," for they were "the leading men of the country" and they were men of "admirable boldness, boldness doubly admirable in Englishmen and lawyers." He was impressed with both "the magnitude of the task and the splendour of the result." The Constitution, he was certain, "deserves the veneration with which Americans have been accustomed to regard it." Both Tocqueville and Bryce told Americans what they wanted to hear about the Framers of the Constitution; both, along with their multitudes of readers, were quite sincere in their praise.

*   *   *

Toward the end of the nineteenth century, the study of American history was becoming systematic ("scientific" was the favored term) and *professional.* No longer the exclusive preserve of leisured gentlemen and literary craftsmen, the American past was now rigorously investigated by learned scholars in academic institutions striving to be among the best in the world. These trained historians undertook careful, thoroughly documented research into what really had happened in the past. For some time the results of this newly rigorous scholarship confirmed the prevailing reverential attitude toward the Constitution and its Framers, but within the ranks of professional scholarship another view could occasionally be found.

As early as 1849 Richard Hildreth provided a model for revisionists when he published the first three volumes of his *History of the United States* (three more appeared in 1852), which he considered superior to Bancroft's work. For, he insisted, he had avoided "meretricious rhetoric" and the portrayal of the Founders as having a "mythic and heroic character." He meant, he said, "to present for once on the historic stage, the founders of our American nation unbedaubed with patriotic rouge, wrapped up in no fine-spun cloaks of excuses and apology." Well! That was a slap at Bancroft, perhaps, but neither did it endear him to potential readers, who had not thought there was anything to excuse or to apologize for regarding the Founders.

The members of the Philadelphia Convention, Hildreth said, belonged "almost exclusively to what is called the conservative class" and they "had seemed to look upon property not so much as one right, to be secured like the rest, but as the great and chief right, of more importance than all the others." "The democracy," he continued, "had no representatives, except so far as the universal American sentiment was imbued, to a certain degree, with the democratic spirit." He had words of praise for the Convention, but not Bancroft's notion of "the people" nor Bancroft's discovery of democratic values in 1787—yet admitted that democracy was not entirely absent. His account of the ratification of the Constitution, a subsequent historian said, was done "in terms that Charles Beard would later find congenial." Hildreth's work gained the respect of other historians, but it did not find the popular audience which Bancroft's did— which suggests, as has been said, that his books "were a good index of what the American reader did not want."

Another jarring note had been sounded at the end of the Reconstruction period by a German immigrant who ultimately came to be regarded as a distinguished authority on American constitutional history, Hermann von Holst. Rigorous in his methods and outspoken almost to the point of unpleasant bluntness, von Holst had little use for the prevailing veneration of the Constitution and its Framers. In the first volume of his eight-volume work *Constitutional and Political History of the United States*, the second chapter was entitled "The Worship of the

Constitution and Its Real Character." The Philadelphia Convention had done well, he thought, but their struggle to draft a constitution and get it adopted was a rough-and-tough political battle. "The current view places the labors of the Philadelphia convention in a totally false light," he complained; "the difficulties that convention had to surmount were so great that they can scarcely be exaggerated." In a characteristically tactless passage, von Holst castigated the Americans:

> The masses of the American people in their vanity and too-great self-appreciation are fond of forgetting the dreadful struggle of 1787 and 1788, or of employing it only as a name for the "divine inspiration" which guided and enlightened the "fathers" at Philadelphia. . . . In America this is an inexhaustible theme for Fourth of July orations. . . . With history, however, it has nothing to do.

So much for the American tendency to regard the Constitution as "the political Bible of the people."

One of the new, professionally trained young scholars, Woodrow Wilson, published his best known book in the 1880s. As its title, *Congressional Government*, suggests, it is more an analysis of the system than an account of its origins. Yet he did touch on the Philadelphia Convention; he was rather cool toward their work so far as democratic values were concerned—and indeed he seemed not to think much of the prevailing veneration of the Constitution. "The Constitution," he said, "is not honored by blind worship." Eight years later, in a book which was more history than political science, Wilson was again making a realistic search for democratic values in American national origins. He didn't find much. "The federal government," he wrote, "was not by intention a democratic government. In plan and structure it had been meant to check the sweep and power of popular majorities." Then came the real challenge to the still popular beliefs of Bancroft: "The government had in fact, been originated and organized upon the initiative *and primarily in the interest of the mercantile and wealthy classes* (emphasis added)." It was, furthermore, ratified by a minority, he said.

By the end of the century, a good number of scholars and writers had repeated Wilson's first theme: that there was little regard for democracy at the Philadelphia Convention. This had been in some of the historical writing all along. Bancroft, the most widely read historian, had been a special case—few writers of American history had been Jacksonian Democrats—and one might almost say that he had smuggled democracy into the story of the Constitution by impressive literary legerdemain. Many people in the nineteenth century surely understood, however, that the Framers themselves were mainly aristocrats, worried about an excess of popular whim in public affairs, the influence of the "licentious," and, above all, the "spirit of Shays." The prestige of the Constitution had always been high, but before the Civil War there had clearly arisen a profound difference of opinion as to what was so prestigious about it. Constitutionally speaking, democracy had not really been at issue; what had been crucial was the arrangement of power in the federal union and, therefore, the nature of the union. During the years of Civil War and Reconstruction, amendments were added to the Constitution which were expressive of democratic values, but once that was accomplished it was as if—now that duty had been done—the country could turn to other matters. If the Framers of the Constitution had been elitist, aristocratic, and even doubtful of democracy—well, they had labored so brilliantly that one could only be grateful for such able leaders, and, meanwhile, states and communities at least were free to indulge in as much democracy as their people might wish. Deference to the wisdom of the Constitution meant deference to its creators.

As to Wilson's second point, that the government had been organized in the first place to serve the interests of the wealthy—that, of course, was a central theme of populism in the 1890s and progressivism just after 1900. Here is where a new boldness became evident in the growing spirit of skepticism about the Philadelphia Convention. Among those who are still well remembered for their audacity is J. Allen Smith. His influential book *The Spirit of American Government* (1907) made it very plain not only that democracy had been no part of the Philadelphia Convention's intent, but that, in truth, it was the very thing they struggled to avoid. The crucial chapter in this book was entitled "The Constitution: A Reactionary Document." Early in the book he said, "It is strange that the American people know so little of the fundamental nature of their system of government." Near the end, he asserted that the members of the Convention must have been entirely aware "that their economic advantages could be retained only by maintaining their class ascendancy in the government."

The moment was just right for such a book as Charles A. Beard's *Economic Interpretation of the Constitution* when it appeared in 1913. His book was very readable, it had the appearance of impressive scholarship, and it had a ready, vast audience among the would-be reformers eager to believe that the work of the Convention was not beyond reproach. It was also greeted with uproar and vituperation. One distinguished historian's review simply called it "little short of indecent." Nicholas Murray Butler, president of Columbia University, where Beard was a member of the faculty, believed that Beard's ideas were reminiscent of the "crude, immoral, and unhistorical teachings of Karl Marx." Despite such criticism, the book set the terms for a new look at the Philadelphia Convention, it dominated the discussion of it for over forty years, and its influence is in some ways still visible today.

Beard described those who attended the Philadelphia Convention as men who were concerned about the security of "personalty," a kind of property which consisted of public securities, money loaned at interest, merchandising and shipping facilities, lands held for speculation, and slaves. The Convention's members, Beard said, were mainly concerned with devising a national government which might protect such property; in turn, they had to work hard to get their plan ratified somehow, despite the opposition of the majority of the people—farmers and planters whose property was mostly "realty." There were plenty of inflammatory ideas here. Instead of the traditional heroic, inspired, and patriotic labors, he saw a kind of economic self-interest, rampant elitism, and calculated manipulation of public opinion.

Within the scholarly community there was much less outrage at Beard's suggestions than among the general public. Presumably, scholars were already familiar with the writings of Hildreth, von Holst, J. Allen Smith, and others who had been saying something like this in one way or another. Beard's account was not an especially novel one for them. But prominent public figures in the world of government and business, along with eminent persons in the academic establishment, were able for a time to perpetuate the longstanding idea of the Philadelphia Convention as an assemblage of inspired patriots whose motives had been wickedly impugned. Events reinforced this. Beard resigned from the Columbia faculty a few years later over issues which, though different, were not entirely unrelated. American entry into World War I brought with it the inevitable tide of conformist patriotic sentiment, followed by the Great Red Scare which spilled over into the 1920s, a time of conservative civic attitudes for the most part.

Meanwhile, Beard's approach to the Convention and its work was gradually gaining a place in the school books of the country. A new edition of his book was published in 1935. By that time, Beard's approach was nearly standard in American history textbooks. Of course, it was a time when some sort of economic interpretation of history, broadly speaking, was at least understandable to people suffering the hardships of the Great Depression. The apparent rejection of many New Deal measures by the Supreme Court on the ground that they violated the Constitution seemed to many further evidence that the Constitution was

in the service of a privileged elite—quite possibly the intent of its
Framers. For all that, it should be noted that there were limits. When
Franklin Roosevelt undertook his court reform plan (court packing, many
said) in 1937, the effort was widely taken to be an attack on constitutional government and even on the Constitution itself. The project
became an embarrassing failure. The deep-seated traditional reverence for
the Founding Fathers was still strong.

*   *   *

There had been some thoughtful rebuttal of Beard's work from the
start. A number of able scholars pointed out flaws in reasoning and
evidence, but for some considerable time these criticisms had little
general influence, even in the academic world. After World War II, a new
generation of scholars began a substantial reassessment of *An Economic
Interpretation*, subjecting it to a rigorous examination of its method,
reasoning, and evidence. The results were devastating—so devastating
that within a dozen years or so of such attacks, it was authoritatively
said, "Today Beard's reputation stands like an imposing ruin in the
landscape of American historiography."

Of the half-dozen or so major assaults, two became especially well
known—those of Robert E. Brown and Forrest McDonald. Brown presented his work in 1956, calling it a "critical analysis." It was a very
tightly reasoned, point-by-point refutation, stressing the defects in
Beard's historical methods. To Brown, the members of the Philadelphia
Convention seemed to be the kind of men who were expected, by the
people of the time, to direct public affairs. The notion that most of the
men of the Philadelphia Convention held a special kind of property which
their Constitution enhanced was severely flawed. The Convention's
work, furthermore, was promulgated by a procedure (ratifying conventions) more democratic than any prior American political movement,
including the Revolution itself. "The men who wrote the Constitution,"
Brown declared, "believed they were writing it for a democratic society."
Continuing in language suggestive of Bancroft, he added that they did not
act "without regard to the views and interests of 'the people.' More than
anything else, they were aware that 'the people' would have to ratify what
they proposed."

Two years after Brown's work appeared, Forrest McDonald published
his *We The People; The Economic Origins of the Constitution*. Based on
impressive research—far more than Beard had believed possible—he
found the economic interests of the men at the Philadelphia Convention
and their supporters to be far more complex than Beard's crude two

categories could possibly accommodate. McDonald's minute inspection of the delegates' material possessions revealed that a fourth of the delegates "had important economic interests that were adversely affected, directly and immediately, by the Constitution they helped write." He continued, "The most common and by far the most important property holdings of the delegates were not, as Beard has asserted, mercantile, manufacturing and public security investments, but agricultural property." Furthermore, the proceedings of the Convention do not, he insisted, reveal anything like the behavior of a "consolidated economic group." The Constitution could not be understood in Beard's way. On the other hand, during the ratification contest, McDonald found, there were many appeals to economic self-interest on both sides—so much, indeed, as to lead to the conclusion that the outcome seemed "to have turned largely upon the anticipated effects of the Constitution on economic interest." This may have brought the reader back, not to Beard—who had stressed that his was *an* economic interpretation—but to the expectation of an alternate, *another* economic interpretation. An attentive reader might have anticipated this by careful notice of the wording of McDonald's title.

We The People was a learned critique of Beard. McDonald's own idea of the Philadelphia Convention appeared a few years later in his narrative account, *E Pluribus Unum* (1965). Here was unfolded an alternate economic interpretation, leading many to style the work "neo-Beardian." But the tone of the work was not at all Beard's. Where Beard artfully led the reader to think of the Philadelphia Convention as something of a conspiracy—whose members' self-serving labors were to be deplored— McDonald found in the Convention a crucial cadre of men who made great things happen. They were, he said, "men possessed of an idea of a great nation, and possessed of the ruthlessness and the daring and the skill that make ideas into reality. . . . " He has also praised them as "men of almost unbelievable ability; and taken as a whole, the convention comprised possibly the most able group of statesmen gathered under one roof." *E Pluribus Unum* concludes in language reminiscent of the nineteenth century: "But there were giants in the earth in those days, and they spoke in the name of the nation, and the people followed them. As a result, the Americans were despite themselves doomed forever to be free."

Other writers found new reasons for admiring the Framers of the Constitution during these years. John P. Roche (1961) saw them as skilled practical politicians who pulled off a peaceful coup d'etat by doing everything just right—from designing a plan which would please the right people in good numbers to conducting a brilliant campaign for its ratification. There is no need, in Roche's view, for an excursus in heavy thinking, for the Constitution "was not an apotheosis of 'constitutionalism,' a triumph of architectonic genius; it was a patch-work sewn together under the pressure of both time and events by a group of extremely talented democratic [!] politicians." The men at the Philadelphia Convention, he insisted, were not a "College of Cardinals or a council of Platonic guardians. . . . " They were *political men*—not metaphysicians. . . . " They deserved admiration for their "magnificent demonstration of the art of democratic politics."

Stanley Elkins and Eric McKitrick, also writing in 1961, found much to admire as well in the astute *political* management of affairs in 1787 and 1788. Noting that "a legend of a transcendant effort of statesmanship, issuing forth in a miraculously perfect instrument of government" had been extraordinarily durable, they undertook an explanation of its persistence. The conditions and circumstances of the Convention were very special indeed. In addition to the unusual array of talent present, "there had also been at work a remarkably effective process of self-selection, as to both men and states. Rhode Island ignored the convention, and as a result its position was not even considered there." How fortunate it was, too, that Patrick Henry and R. H. Lee refused to attend. A strong nationalist consensus at Philadelphia allowed the delegates to proceed on their own terms. They ignored their instructions to limit their work to amendments for the Articles; they planned a government whose coercive power would apply to individuals rather than states; and they stipulated that the ratification would be done by special conventions (not existing state governments), with nine states' acceptance enough to launch the new government. They had to overcome the most severe obstacle of all— inertia. They did it by long, hard political work. "The revolutionary verve and ardor of the Federalists, their resources of will and energy, their willingness to scheme tirelessly, campaign everywhere, and sweat and agonize over every vote meant in effect that . . . the Anti-Federalists would lose every crucial test." The momentum thus generated carried the cause to victory with impressive speed, "and the ease with which the Constitution so soon became an object of universal veneration, still stands as one of the minor marvels of American history."

There were some historians after World War II who seemed to be retreating from Beard's ideas only slowly—on some points, perhaps not at all. Merrill Jensen's important book *The Articles of Confederation* (1940) had provided something of a rescue operation for that document. The longstanding idea of dreadful conditions in the 1780s had included a severely negative view of what Jensen now wanted to think of as the first constitution of the United States. The glaring flaws of the Articles were central in the traditional tale of woe, from which predicament the Philadelphia Convention delivered the country. Now Jensen said, "The Articles of Confederation was a constitutional expression of the philosophy of the Declaration of Independence," and it served the cause of democracy. Conservatives of the time, unhappy about this from the start, became nationalists, with a view to restoring the domination of American government by the elite. In language reminiscent of Beard, Jensen said that "in the name of the people they engineered a conservative counter-revolution and erected a nationalistic government whose purpose in part was to thwart the will of 'the people' in whose name they acted." There was, furthermore, an important connection between centralization on the one hand and speculation in land, speculation in currencies, and the interests of the business community on the other—again close to Beard's picture of things. These views and many more were the leitmotif of two subsequent books and a number of articles, including one written in 1973.

There were a few other historians who did not always applaud the Philadelphia Convention during the postwar decades. E. James Ferguson, one of Jensen's students, explored much of the economic dimension of the period in his *Power of the Purse: A History of American Public Finance, 1776–1790* (1961). There he spelled out in authoritative detail the maneuvers of Robert Morris and his many associates who sought political and constitutional change through the support of public creditors, merchants, and other elements of the business community. The importance of economic self-interest was taken for granted in the eighteenth century, he argued, and the nationalists intended to make the most of it. As Ferguson put it in a subsequent article directly on our subject, by the end of the war "what one might call a mercantile capitalist reorganization of the country's economic institutions had become integrated with constitutional revision." While this was extremely important in the movement toward the Philadelphia Convention, there were many other elements in the circumstances of the time which led Ferguson explicitly to deny the validity of Beard's interpretation. "The Constitution," Ferguson said, "does have an economic interpretation," but it did not "have to be elucidated by doubtful attempts to construct the inner motives of the Founders or depend upon a Beardian or anti-Beardian assessment of the role of security holders."

Another student of Jensen's, Jackson T. Main, undertook at least a partial defense of Beard in a lengthy 1960 review of McDonald's *We The*

People. Many readers may have been intimidated by the mass of material in that book; not so Main, who had been through much of it while writing *The Antifederalists, Critics of the Constitution* (1961). It became evident in that book and in his next, *The Social Structure of Revolutionary America* (1965), that the nature and composition of classes in early American society were a central concern of his, as a foremost explanation of political behavior. Main's assessment of McDonald's work was specific, detailed, and largely negative. A number of times he remarked that "Beard's analysis is the more nearly correct one." "It can be maintained," he wrote, "that the Constitution was written by large property owners and that the division over its acceptance followed, to some extent, class lines." "The full story of the Constitution and its ratification remains to be written," he concluded. "Until this is done, the historian seeking an interim interpretation will be better advised to follow Beard than McDonald."

One area of agreement emerged from this stage of thinking about the Philadelphia Convention: most scholars now seemed to agree that there was a consensus among American political leaders in the 1780s that, under the Articles of Confederation, the plan of government was inadequate—and that changes had to be made. The older style had been to describe advocates of change as "intelligent statesmen" or "thinking men"; those opposed to change were "the ignorant or the narrowminded." For Beard, of course, it had been "large and important groups of economic interests" who had made unsuccessful attempts to amend the Articles, and who had then "set to work to secure by a circuitous route . . . the adoption of a revolutionary programme." Now the Anti-Federalists had become the subject of thoughtful, serious study, and it was clear that they deserved it. For, rather than being complacent, narrowminded, or simply self-serving local politicians, they were now seen as men who knew very well that changes had to be made and that those changes consisted of additions to the power of the central government. Jensen, for example, declared that both the nationalists who attended the Philadelphia Convention—along with their supporters—*and* their opponents "agreed that the central government should be strengthened." The Anti-Federalists, though, supported only proposals for "grants of specific powers to Congress for limited periods of time, not amendments to the Articles of Confederation."

*   *   *

Recent thinking about the Philadelphia Convention, and about early American history generally, is based on a greatly expanded range of information. The Convention is still regarded as a major turning point in American history, but it is seen as far more than just the resolution of the woes of the Confederation. The picture has been extended to reach back well into the colonial period for the economic, social, religious, and political tendencies evident by the eve of the American Revolution; to recover the original understanding as to the nature and meaning of the Revolution; and to bring this to bear on the experiences of the 1780s, which led people to accept the idea that a stronger central government of some kind was needed. Much of the work which has been done to provide this giant canvas has had a sophistication and an array of detailed information which has made it all but inaccessible to many readers.

Some features of the scene, as now depicted, do seem clear. First, the political landscape in America, from colonial times to the day of the Constitution, seems far more varied and diverse in every respect than earlier generations had acknowledged. The very different nature of the separate states—derived from the very different circumstances of their origin and development as colonies—was still an outstanding deterrent to nationhood in the 1780s, despite all the cooperation which had been summoned up in the common cause of independence from Britain. It had seemed amazing, even to those who labored so hard for it, that in 1776 "thirteen clocks could be made to strike as one," as John Adams had phrased it. At that time, though, there had been an army and a navy present in America to subjugate them. Now, in the 1780s, they might very well be facing the common menace of disunion (as well as other perils)—but many did not believe it, and some did not seem to care. Their first concerns were those of their own neighborhood. Although this is scarcely a new idea, or a departed one, the pervasiveness, intensity, and persistence of it is more appreciated than before.

Second, many detailed studies of the social history of eighteenth-century America have probed into the experience of the "lower orders" of American society, people hitherto given little serious attention. Class conflict has been found—a matter often considered so un-American as to warrant automatic rejection. For example, urban strife has been described by Pauline Maier in her influential article "Popular Uprisings and Civil Authority in Eighteenth Century America" and in her book on the Sons of Liberty. The theme is present in Dirk Hoerder's book *Crowd Action In Revolutionary Massachusetts, 1756–1780* and in Gary Nash's *Urban Crucible*—as well as in many other books and articles. Taken together, they provide a picture of a turbulent, volatile social order unknown to the readers of Bancroft, or even to the readers of most twentieth-century historians, down to 1960 or so. Alfred F. Young, the editor of a substantial volume of essays in this vein, observes shrewdly that this social tension in turn produced a "sophisticated kind of American conservatism," which mastered the tactic of "swimming with a stream which it is impossible to stem," a process "brought to a climax when the Founding Fathers—the men who shaped the federal Constitution in 1787—created a government which attempted to take into account 'the people out of doors'"—the phrase used by the framers for the numerous humble folk who were not in any direct way movers and shakers of public affairs.

Finally, impressive studies of the development of eighteenth-century American political ideas have stressed several new themes. The best known, perhaps, is the notion that American ideas of liberty took shape under the influence of the writings of radical English Whigs, whose writings were abundantly reprinted in colonial America. Bernard Bailyn's *Ideological Origins of the American Revolution* (1967) set the terms of the discussion. In addition to identifying influences on colonial American thought, Bailyn also described the subsequent development of American political ideas as "a transformed as well as a transforming force." This included a new conception of constitutionalism—one far different from earlier notions—which was centrally "the concept of a fixed, written constitution limiting the ordinary actions of government." This, he asserted, had "new meaning and propulsive power." The American idea of the nature and function of fundamental law by 1787, whether as new as Bailyn contends or not, is crucial to an understanding of the constitutional problems of the 1780s and of the Philadelphia Convention.

The story was carried forward by one of Bailyn's students, Gordon S. Wood, in his *Creation of the American Republic, 1776–1787* (1969). He described the thinking which dominated the Philadelphia Convention as the product of another transformation. Since 1776, he said, "in newspapers, pamphlets, town meetings, and legislative debates, the political assumptions of 1776 had been extended, molded, and perverted in ways that no one had clearly anticipated." The old "scattered strands of Whig thought" were now "picked up and brought together by the Federalists and woven into a new intellectual fabric. . . . " As for those who feared the proposed new order, they were either bemused or outmaneuvered, much as the Loyalists of an earlier day had been. Now, in 1787, as before in 1776, new ideas had a dynamic energy which generated enthusiasm and spirit, and they carried the day.

Wood therefore labeled the Philadelphia Convention and subsequent events "the Federalist Revolution." "All had expected some change to be effected by the Convention," he wrote, "but they had hardly expected what they got—a virtual revolution in American politics." The idea that this was at least irregular and extraconstitutional, and perhaps revolutionary, is an old one; it even bothered Washington somewhat at the time—to say nothing of the Anti-Federalists. Wood, however, was thinking well beyond revolutionary *procedure*, for he asserted that it was "a virtual revolution in American *politics*, promising a serious weakening, if not a destruction, of the power of the states (emphasis added)." Fortunately, Wood did not seriously try to pursue the notion of "destruction" of state powers as William W. Crosskey had, without much success, in the 1950s.

Much of the recent writing about early American political ideas has stressed the theme of republicanism, wherein the notion of "virtue" was apparently a fundamental one. It meant, Robert Shalhope said in his second survey of the literature on republican thought, "maintaining public and private virtue, internal unity, social solidarity, and vigilance against the corruptions of power." To be sure, it has been pretty well accepted for nearly twenty years that the Revolution of 1776 had been based on the assumption of the perfectibility of human nature, whereby virtue would become the hallmark of a new kind of American polity. Now, Wood maintained, considerable disillusionment had set in. Making good use of a familiar Washington sentiment, *"We have, probably, had too good an opinion of human nature in forming our confederation,"* Wood went on to find "the profoundest disillusionment" in Madison, too. The object of the Philadelphia Convention was to create something new and original: "a republic which did not require a virtuous people for its sustenance." "If they could not," he continued, "as they thought, really reform the character of American society, then they would somehow have to influence the operation of the society and moderate its viciousness." The nobility of the cause was expressed by its advocates as a struggle of "the worthy against the licentious."

For the most part, the great interest of recent years in republican ideology has not been applied in depth to the Philadelphia Convention, apart from Wood's deft handling of the matter. It would also appear to be useful for understanding the subsequent battle over the ratification of the Constitution—applicable both to the Constitution's opponents and to those who opposed Federalist policies in the 1790s.

*   *   *

It is a common notion that every generation has its own questions to ask of the past and that written history changes to reflect the current interests of the living generation. Two hundred years of thinking about the Philadelphia Convention reveals a measure of this, though less than might have been expected—far less than the variations in our ideas of the Constitution itself, insofar as they can be disentangled from the Convention as such. To those living at the time, criticisms of the Convention must have seemed short lived. Something of a consensus about the greatness of the Convention emerged rather quickly, despite the persistent disputes about the actual meaning of their work. It was a hundred years or more before serious doubt about the Convention gained much attention, even among scholars who took great care and much time to understand that body.

Twentieth-century Americans, who pride themselves on their more detailed and more precise knowledge of the past, have wobbled the most in their thinking about the Convention. Some of the ideas of the very earliest critics, which a few historians had tried to take seriously along the way, became congenial to the reformers of the Progressive period. The influence of some of these ideas, rather unflattering to the Convention, grew steadily until the 1950s. Then the Anti-Federalists became the object of serious, sophisticated study. While their ideas may seem far more respectable and interesting now than ever before, an approving view of the Philadelphia Convention nonetheless persists.

There is much in American thinking about the Philadelphia Convention which has endured throughout two hundred years. First, it has always seemed that it was an assemblage which included unusually gifted, farsighted men, possessed of an extraordinary combination of audacity and political common sense. Our praise is more discriminating now, for we know that not all were "giants on the earth," but this is only to acknowledge that it was a gathering of human beings, not gods or even demigods.

Second, there has always been a clear understanding that the Convention's boldness in bypassing its instructions was indispensable to the success of its work. Congress had authorized them to meet

> for the sole and express purpose of revising the Articles of Confederation and reporting to Congress and the several legislatures of such alterations and provisions therein as shall when agreed to in Congress and confirmed by the states render the federal constitution adequate to the exigencies of government and the preservation of the Union.

But how many "alterations and provisions" would ever be approved by Congress *and* be accepted by *all* the states? Clearly, they understood that they faced problems which were both constitutional and political, requiring tremendous exertions of both intellect and organizing zeal. This led the Framers to defy existing notions of regular procedure—at the start by quickly abandoning the "authorized" discussion, and at the end of their labors by a unilateral declaration in Article VII of the new manner in which their work was to assume authority. Considered in the abstract, this was so highly irregular as to be revolutionary.

This irregularity bothered Washington. "The legality of this convention," he wrote more than three months before it convened, "I do not mean to discuss." Nonetheless, he thought the most "direct" way of acting will, "under present circumstances, be found best; otherwise, like a house on fire, whilst the most regular mode of extinguishing the flames is contended for, the building is reduced to ashes." Americans have usually thought of the matter in the same way.

Third, there has commonly been an appreciation of the importance of compromise in the work of the Convention. The members had to show a great deal of patient forbearance and willingness to listen as well as to speak. Many of them must have left Philadelphia with much disappointment at having yielded some portion of their profound convictions for the sake of getting the Constitution written. As to posterity's approval, there is one important exception. Antislavery writers of the nineteenth century (as well as some recent writers) saw the compromises regarding slavery as a serious flaw. There can be little doubt, though, that an American nation could not have been realized in the eighteenth century without compromise on the matter. It was left to later generations to make such efforts anew, only to find that this had become one subject on which compromise, apparently, was impossible. A start at resolving the matter was made possible, however, by the existence of a strong national government.

Finally, there has nearly always been wide agreement that the Convention had the right priorities in mind in making nationhood the first concern. Their sense of urgency about this fueled their audacity and drove them to strike out into new constitutional ground; yet, it also induced them to restraint and accommodation when that seemed necessary to the main chance. The importance of Washington's influence in this matter can scarcely be exaggerated. Long before the end of the war he had been an advocate of expanded Congressional power. In his famous letter of 1783 to the governors of the states, circulated when the army disbanded, the first item in his list of things indispensable to the continued existence of the United States was "an indissoluble union of the States under one federal head." A few years later, he complained, "Thirteen sovereignties pulling against each other, and all tugging at the federal head, will soon bring ruin on the whole."

The Convention's achievement is often described as a solution to the central problem of federalism: how to have a federal union which is also a nation—more exactly, how to accommodate a plurality of sovereignties in the construction of a harmonious whole which is itself possessed of sovereignty. It is well to remember that on the sole occasion when the Convention's success in creating an enduring nation was seriously in doubt, during the Civil War, the disaffected party did not repudiate the Convention or the U.S. Constitution—it charged the other side with doing so. Washington's vision of an indissoluble union, which later became Jefferson's and Jackson's, inspired Lincoln to make ultimate sacrifices in its behalf. Since then, nearly everyone has found it unthinkable that there should not be an American nation. This was the foremost achievement of the Philadelphia Convention.

SOCIETAL CHANGE
AND THE
CONSTITUTION

Some scholarly commentators are critical of the quality of American citizenship, and they usually blame the schools, media, or public apathy. Dennis Hale traces the problem of citizenship right back to 1787 and the ideas of James Madison and Alexander Hamilton. He argues that the Federalists, in order to avoid the problem of faction, helped to undermine citizenship by encouraging Americans to prefer their personal interests as opposed to those of the community. The separation of powers, Hale believes, compounded the problem by leaving the people without a clear authority in government. Forty years later, Alexis de Tocqueville believed that America's dilemma was not faction but indifference to public life. If America continued to encourage a political system based on an apathetic citizenry, Tocqueville feared, America would slide from democracy to some form of authoritarian rule. In the nineteenth century, under the pressure of industrial and demographic revolutions, citizenship became social rather than political. By the opening of the twentieth century, as Hale shows, citizenship and "Americanism" had merged—to the disadvantage of the former. Fifty years later, some political scientists—influenced by voter studies which revealed the political deficiencies of the American citizen—considered political apathy a blessing. Consequently, Hale finds it no surprise that James Madison's reputation as a political theorist also blossomed in the 1950s. If Americans are to recover their lost citizenship and revive their weakened communities, Hale concludes, they should turn to Alexis de Tocqueville, rather than James Madison, as their guide.

DENNIS HALE

Citizenship and the Federalist Tradition

The *Federalist Papers*, the Constitution, and the apologia which have grown up around them—these are among the most powerful themes and symbols American political thought has to offer. The Framers of the Constitution—and in particular its most famous defenders, Madison and Hamilton—brought American politics firmly within the liberal tradition, and anchored it there with a set of institutions that has survived longer than perhaps even they could have hoped. The work they accomplished has been preserved and enlarged by generations of scholars, jurists, and politicians, who made of the Constitution a powerful symbol of solidarity and continuity—so much so that the thirteen years of America's existence as an independent nation prior to the adoption of the Constitution have nearly passed from our historical memory.

Political science, almost from its inception as a separate academic discipline, followed the approved custom of venerating the Constitution, the Framers, and particularly the *Federalist Papers*. James Bryce praised the "pessimism" of the *Federalist Papers*, finding it a more useful quality than the excessive "abstraction" which he found in the second volume of Tocqueville's *Democracy in America*. Charles Beard, who was by no means a blind enthusiast for the Framers, nevertheless felt that the *Federalist Papers* was the only American political book bound for immortality. More recently, Clinton Rossiter bluntly stated that

> *The Federalist* is the most important work in political science that has ever been written, or is likely ever to be written, in the United States. . . . [It] stands third only to the Declaration of Independence and the Constitution itself among all the sacred writings of American political history. . . . an exposition of certain timeless truths about constitutional government.

The significance of the Framers, Norman Jacobson has pointed out, is that they "provided more than a theory, they set the conditions for its verification." The Constitution they helped to write would train citizens to behave in ways expected of them by the theory, launching what Jacobson termed a "gigantic self-fulfilling prophecy." In this paper I want to show that the Framers gave us a theory of politics and a set of institutions—which both grow from that theory and fulfill it—that have made American citizenship difficult to comprehend and to preserve.

1.

In *Federalist* No. 9, Alexander Hamilton announces what will be the basic theme of his defense of the Constitution. The history of republics, he argues, shows that they are inherently unstable, constantly subject to "tempestuous waves of sedition and party rage." Republican citizenship would be impractical in America were it not for the happy fact that "the science of politics . . . has received great improvements." The most important improvement concerns the new understanding of the relation between the size of a nation and the performance of republican institutions. Hamilton's audience was familiar with the standard argument that the small state is the most appropriate setting for republican government. Of more significance, his audience had inherited a strong tradition of local self-government, and they were now being asked to alter that inheritance in important but unpredictable ways. The small state, long the object of philosophy's praise and the citizen's affection, was now listed among the "wretched nurseries of unceasing discord and the miserable objects of universal pity. . . . " Small republics, Hamilton declared, were the breeding ground of all those faults which "the advocates of despotism" had used to discredit free governments: factional strife, inefficiency, fiscal disorder, divided counsel, stagnant commerce, and war. These faults the Constitution proposed to remedy by the ingenious discovery Hamilton now recommended: the "enlargement of the orbit" of democratic institutions, the chief advantage of such a union being its tendency to "repress domestic faction and insurrection."

It was left to Madison, however, in *Federalist* No. 10, to refine this argument and lay to rest some of the apprehensions it must have aroused. Much has been written about this famous essay, but what concerns us here is what its argument reveals about an emerging Federalist conception of citizenship.*

Despite John Jay's optimistic appraisal, in *Federalist* No. 2, that Americans had become a "band of brethren, united to each other by the strongest ties," Madison paints a grim picture of America's fate under the Articles of Confederation: "instability, injustice, and confusion introduced into the public councils," and "interested and overbearing majority" ruling by force rather than by the "rules of justice." His response to this problem is more interesting for what it omits than for what it says. Factional strife can only be dealt with by: 1) eliminating the liberty that fires it; 2) eliminating the differences of opinion and interest that nurture it; or 3) controlling its effects.

What is omitted here is the classic remedy for a diseased polity: civic education. In the seventeenth century, Madison's view would have seemed more novel than it apparently did in the eighteenth. In some places it would have seemed heretical. The Puritans held to an image of

---

*The term "Federalist" has been used in two ways, historically: it refers to a set of principles associated with the Constitution and with the *Federalist Papers*, and it refers to the less formal doctrines of the Federalist Party. The two sets of ideas did not always run along parallel tracks. In this essay, the term is used in the first sense unless otherwise indicated.

human nature "grimmer" than Madison's but they deduced from that image the necessity of a strict system of moral education. John Winthrop had equated "civil liberty" with moral education, defining liberty as the "liberty to that only which is good, just and honest." The Puritan commonwealth was based upon a covenanted patriotism, in which, John Schaar observes, "individuals became members of the community only upon acceptance of certain articles of religious faith and morals. . . . Social institutions were designed to encourage performance of the covenant." An elaborate teaching was the centerpiece of this convenanted community, and moral education was as strict as anything in *The Republic* or *The Laws*.

Controlling the effects of a corrupted liberty would have seemed, to a man of Winthrop's training, as sinful as setting aside a reservation for the worship of the devil. Since men *are* corrupt, civil government must help them to be virtuous. The city exists in order to help men make the right choices with their liberty. That task did not recommend itself to the Framers, for several reasons.

First, the tendency to combine in factions grew from the depths of human nature. Fallible men, seeing and reasoning differently, would ultimately be led to that form of behavior which typified faction for Madison: actions that were "adverse to the rights of other citizens, or to the permanent and aggregate interests of the community."

Second, factions were nurtured by an immutable feature of the human personality: differences in faculties and talents, which gave rise to the different classes in society, to the division of labor, and thus to human progress itself. And while it might be possible to abolish classes, or at least to regulate the pursuit of economic gain, such a course would be the very antithesis of liberty and an intolerable interference with private rights.

But there was another reason for departing from the stern moralism of the Puritans, or the equally severe civic education of antiquity. The nation the Framers were contemplating was a large one, and had every prospect of growing larger. The Union was in fact an empire, as ancient political science would have understood the term: a confederation of small states banded together for the purposes of self-defense and commerical expansion, with some provision for guidance from the center. (Hamilton called the proposed union a "most interesting empire," and did not see any need to explain what he meant.) Such an empire was simply too large for civic education to be practical: it was too large, that is, for the direct participation and the "moral unity" that would have been major elements of such an education. States small enough to be managed directly by their citizens—and they would have to be *very* small, Madison thought, since even a moderately large body of citizens tends to degenerate into a mob—would not be large enough to engage in any but the pettiest of projects, and would in any case be the constant prey of larger states. A republic large enough to defend itself and to pursue "great national projects" would be a danger of another kind, unless its power were hedged about by complex checks and balances. Such a state would certainly not be able to tolerate frequent direct intervention by the people in its government, since this would invite instability and injustice of the worst sort.

But Madison is apparently conscious of his audience's fear that a large federal union would be unmanageable except by autocratic means, and he engages in an ingenious and somewhat devious argument to the contrary. First, he must accustom his readers to thinking of the new Union as a republic instead of a direct democracy, and then he must show why the former is not only preferable to the latter but the only viable alternative to the drift and decay of the Articles. The first reason is the republic's ability to manage factions. A large republic with a representative system of government would "refine and enlarge the public views by passing them through the medium of a chosen body of citizens, whose wisdom may best discern the true interest of their country. . . . " This argument raises a question which Madison moves quickly to answer. Why should we assume that this "medium of chosen citizens" will be any more immune to the vagaries of human nature than the common run of citizens? Madison's answer is somewhat disingenuous:

First, he argues, let us agree that, regardless of the size of the country, the number of representatives must be at least large enough to "guard against the cabals of a few. . . . " But the number must not be *so* large that it becomes a "confused multitude." He appears to believe that this point is not controversial, but it is not clear (even before the discovery of the "iron law of oligarchy") why a small body is more likely than a large one to be run by a "cabal." Nor is it clear why a large group must always be a "confused multitude." Madison merely assumes these propositions and proceeds to the next point.

Since the proportion of representatives to voters is greatest in a small republic (that is, each representative represents a smaller number of voters than in the larger state), it follows that if the proportion of fit citizens is the same in a large as in a small state, then the larger state offers the greater number of good citizens from among whom representatives can be chosen. Second, since more voters must choose the representatives in the larger state, it will be harder for a bad representative to pass himself off as a good one (because he will have to fool a larger number of voters).

But what if the large *state* were to share the characteristic Madison attributes to large *assemblies*? What if, that is, it were to become a confused multitude? If that were the case, then Madison's conclusion would be exactly wrong, and the larger state would contain a *greater* proportion of corrupted (or at least confused) citizens. And in the general confusion, it would be easier for a dishonest or incompetent politician to convince a crowd of utter strangers of his fitness for a seat in Congress or for election to the Presidency.

It was just this possibility that haunted the advocates of the small state, who were convinced that in a large union with a complex government, public officials would grow distant from the people— resulting in a situation in which the officials not only failed to *represent* their constituents adequately but were no longer in a position to be *judged* by them, either. Dazzled by the trappings of federal power, they would come to constitute a separate class, and "soon feel themselves independent of heaven itself." Not only would direct participation be impossible in the large state; so would the atmosphere of trust upon which citizenship depends.

Having proceeded this far, Madison was prepared for the part of the argument that has become the classic defense of the Constitution:

> Extend the sphere and you take in a greater variety of parties and interests; you make it less probable that a majority of the whole will have a common motive to invade the rights of other citizens; or, if such a common motive exists, it will be more difficult for all who feel it to discover their own strength and to act in unison with each other.

Of course, Madison is talking only of those combinations motivated by sinister designs against private rights or the public interest, but the difficulties that restrict factions also restrict majorities of *any* sort, as Hamilton was candid enough to admit in *Federalist* No. 73:

> It may perhaps be said that the power of preventing bad laws includes that of preventing good ones; and may be used to the one purpose as well as to the other. But this objection will have little weight with those who can properly estimate the mischiefs of that inconstancy and mutability in the laws, which form the greatest blemish in the character and genius of our governments. . . . The injury which may possibly be done by defeating a few good laws will be amply compensated by the advantage of preventing a number of bad ones.

But since American government is to be ultimately responsible to society—the same society that is to be "broken into so many parts"—it follows that authority itself will be shattered. This, too, is part of the plan. In order to insure this result, the government will be broken also into parts, each part given a material interest in seeing that no one part usurps the rights of others. The division and separation of powers will complement the division and separation of citizens, "by so contriving the interior structure of the government as that its several constituent parts may, by their mutual relations, be the means of keeping each other in their proper place."

A divided citizenry and a shattered authority—it is hard not to see in such a prescription evidence of a novel citizenship. Sheldon Wolin has written of the eighteenth-century constitutionalists that they "longed to transcend the political," forgetting that doing so "meant denying the central referent of the political, abandoning a whole range of notions and the practices to which they pointed—citizenship, obligation, general authority. . . . " The regenerative potential of politics, the "moral mission of the polis," is absent from Federalist constitutional theory. In its place is a world view which Martin Landau has termed a "monument to the image of the machine," a clockwork mechanism designed to work as nearly as possible without human attention, a "government of laws, not men." It is Harrington's dream of "sinful citizens in a perfect commonwealth" all over again.

There is a well-known sentence in Madison's *Federalist* No. 51 that reveals a great deal about the premises of this view of politics. The sentence is particularly striking when we remember the experience of revolution against arbitrary government through which the American people had recently passed.

> In framing a government which is to be administered by men over men, the great difficulty lies in this: you must first enable the government to control the governed; and in the next place *oblige it to control itself.*

A government that could control itself was surely a novelty in the world of political speculation. That such a utopian vision could have such appeal is the result of a particular set of circumstances that have their own implications for American citizenship.

2.

When Alexis de Tocqueville visited the United States, the Constitution was scarcely a generation old, and the eastern seaboard had been settled by "Americans" for just over two hundred years. So it was a relatively new country that Tocqueville observed, with an even newer regime to govern it. Yet patterns had already emerged and habits of mind had developed, so that Tocqueville was able to gather enough evidence and impressions to justify a general theory about American politics. That theory has much to teach us about what citizenship had become in the American context, and what effect constitutionalism was having on its continued development.

Briefly, Tocqueville argued that republican institutions, citizenship especially, were liable to be eroded by American culture, specifically, by individualism and social equality. "Democracy," he observed, "loosens social ties, but tightens natural ones; it brings kindred more closely together, while it throws citizens more apart." Democratic individualism—the "atomistic social freedom" that Louis Hartz has identified as the "master assumption of American political thought"—interfered with the creation of a lasting republic because it hampered the growth of a vivid public consciousness.

Certain aspects of American culture were especially troubling to Tocqueville. The love of material gratification, a uniquely American belief in self-reliance, the absence of a hereditary aristocracy, the wide expanse of territory, the availability of cheap land as an inducement to mobility—all these led Americans to a love affair with privacy and a withdrawal from public affairs. In America, John Schaar has observed, "liberty was defined as private liberty, namely, as the liberty to enhance one's private estate and possibilities to the limits of his power." The corollary, Tocqueville concluded, was an indifference to the common life and to public business. "Private life in democratic times is so busy, so excited, so full of wishes and of work, that hardly any energy or leisure remains to each individual for public life." But even when Americans found time to pursue the public's business, certain difficulties intruded— or, rather, the culture's individualistic bias lent to political awareness a certain distortion of its own.

Specifically, individualism and equality eroded the supports that citizens needed in order to participate effectively in political life. The sense of connection to others, of sharing a common life, which is crucial to any cooperative endeavor, grew only fitfully in America. American culture broke the chain that aristocracy and immobility had forged between all classes in society; it encouraged men to believe that their "whole destiny is in their own hands," and made any other view of the citizen's destiny difficult to conceive or, once conceived, to communicate.

In place of a sense of connection to his fellows, the American citizen nurtured a much wider, but vaguer, sense of belonging, one that encompassed the entire nation: "the bond of human affection is extended, but it is relaxed." The sense of solidarity, stretched so far and so thin, could not provide the emotional support that citizens needed in political life.

> Thus not only does democracy make every man forget his ancestors, but it hides his descendants and separates his contemporaries from him; it throws him back forever upon himself alone and threatens in the end to confine him entirely within the solitude of his own heart.

From this solitude, the American looked out upon a vast and often frightening world. Compared to this vastness, the citizen felt himself to be only a small part of something immeasurably large, a "very puny object. . . . Nowhere do citizens appear so insignificant as in a democratic nation; nowhere does the nation itself appear greater or does the mind more easily take in a wide survey of it." Between the isolated individual and the "great and imposing image of the people at large" lay a void. But it was in that empty space—the space between the one and the many— that politics took place. American politics was consequently weakened from within because the arena in which it took place appeared to most citizens to be "extremely general and vague," a shadow world of indistinct shapes and unknown quantities. Tocqueville feared that few Americans would be bold enough to venture into that void alone and that the time would come when corrupt or foolish leaders might encourage that fear, preparing the way for despotism.

To combat this possibility, Tocqueville looked to political organization.

> As soon as a man begins to treat of public affairs in public he begins to perceive that he is not so independent of his fellow men as he had at first imagined, and that in order to obtain their support he must often lend them his co-operation.

This effect could be produced by associations of various kinds. First of all, Tocqueville looked to the legislatures of the several states to focus the citizen's attention on public objects. Second, he looked to the general political associations formed for promoting public safety, commerce, industry, religion, education, and so on. It is important to note here that Tocqueville had in mind something different from the "interest groups" of twentieth-century American politics. Whereas the modern interest group is an office supported by the dues of thousands of strangers who will never meet, and whose officials are paid merely to effect certain changes in legislation, Tocqueville was thinking about an association whose major characteristic is its effect on the lives of those who belong to it and who directly shape its policies. A political association in this sense is defined by "the public assent which a number of individuals give to certain doctrines . . . and the engagements which they contract to promote . . . those doctrines." The example he provided was the Anti-Tariff Convention which met in Philadelphia in 1831: a public meeting called to debate a matter of public policy, whose conclusions were framed in terms of public law.

Associations of this type often grew into political parties; these, especially at the local level, also brought citizens out of their isolation into closer contact with one another, even though they did so at some expense to public harmony and tranquility.

> The desire of being elected may lead some men for a time to violent hostility; but this same desire leads all men in the long run to support each other; and if it happens that an election accidentally severs two friends, the electoral system brings a multitude of citizens permanently together who would otherwise always have remained unknown to one another. Freedom produces private animosities, but despotism gives birth to general indifference.

Finally, there were the nonpolitical associations which Tocqueville saw blossoming everywhere for a thousand purposes: sponsoring entertainments, founding seminaries, building inns, fixing roads, distributing books. These were the social projects which in England would normally have been sponsored by members of the landed gentry, but which in the United States were taken up by small groups of neighbors united by at least a temporary sense of solidarity and common concern.

Tocqueville understood that Americans were not, in fact, a "band of brethren" and that their normal relations would be characterized by distance rather than intimacy. Under these circumstances, factions were not to be feared as much as the general indifference to public life that American conditions encouraged. Bertrand de Jouvenel has pointed out that in modern states "amity" is not and cannot be the general rule in citizen relations. Nations are too large for that, and factions are often no more than an attempt to create a partial city-state within the larger community. Tocqueville was making a similar argument, understanding that the education of citizens through political life was a better medicine for a diseased polity than all the mechanical devices embedded in the Constitution.

In the second volume of *Democracy in America* there is a paragraph on this subject that seems a direct response to Madison's *Federalist* No. 10, and which might serve to sum up the paradox of Federalist teaching on the subject of citizenship:

> When social conditions are equal, every man is apt to live apart, centered in himself and forgetful of the public. If the rulers of democratic nations were either to neglect to correct this fatal tendency or to encourage it from a notion that it weans men from political passions and thus wards off revolutions, they might eventually produce the evil they seek to avoid, and a time might come when the inordinate passions of a few men, aided by the unintelligent selfishness or the pusillanimity of the greater number, would ultimately compel society to pass through strange vicissitudes.

"Strange vicissitudes" is a fair description of what American citizenship would suffer during the nineteenth century, partly because Federalist teaching and Federalist institutions only deepened the cultural problem Tocqueville identified. Federalist hostility to "petty republics" weakened local government. Madison's attempt to make "the private interest of every individual" stand "sentinel over the public rights" called forth the very tendency Tocqueville most distrusted in Americans: the constant quest for private enrichment. Federalist hostility to the "little arts of little politicians" and the Constitution's system of divided authority inhibited the growth of just those forms of organization which Tocqueville hoped would penetrate the citizen's isolation and educate him to his larger role in a democratic community.

Two attitudes competed during the Revolutionary period, Norman Jacobson has argued. One was "notable for its expression of friendship and brotherhood, for its insistence upon individual spontaneity and uniqueness. . . . The other displayed a preoccupation with social order, procedural rationality, and the material bases of political association and division. . . . " This latter view prevailed with the Constitution and became the seed of a form of political education that was passed on from generation to generation, training citizens to "prefer certain goods and conduct over others." The Federalist tradition taught citizens to prefer social mobility to community, privacy and the pursuit of private gain to political commitment and participation, equal opportunity to equality itself, and change to tradition. The teaching did not succeed entirely, of course: trends counter to these could always be found. But these other elements did not benefit from the sanctity of the Constitution, nor did they benefit from the assistance of Federalist ideology and Federalist law.

The Federalist ascendancy, ironically, survived the Federalists themselves. As the nation began to grow, the Constitution carried to the newer territories the Federalist conception of citizenship, which over time came to seem not a Federalist but an American conception.

3.

Scarcely fifteen years after Madison tried to persuade his countrymen that America was not too large for a centralized government, President Jefferson doubled the size of the nation in one masterful stroke. The Louisiana Purchase opened a vast domain in the West, and shortly thereafter American society began to undergo tremendous expansion and change. Between 1810 and 1830, two million people moved West. Indiana's population increased by 100 percent; Illinois tripled its population. By 1840 one of every three Americans lived west of the Appalachian range. The ratio of rural to urban residents declined between 1800 and 1830 from fifteen to one down to ten to one; by 1850 it was near five to one. Cities over 8,000 in population quadrupled in number between 1820 and 1850. Banks proliferated; from the founding of the first bank in 1782 until 1828, 329 banks were created—and "unofficial" banks, little more than storefront operations, were innumerable, especially along the frontier. In each decade, thousands of new businesses were formed, and the corporation, rare and controversial in 1800, was the established form of doing business by 1850. On top of all this, between 1828 and 1844, one-half million immigrants arrived in the United States.

Society was shaken, rearranged, and then shaken again. Between one decade and the next scarcely any American community was able to retain its distinctive character. Everything changed. One of James Fenimore Cooper's characters describes the times: "The whole country is in such a constant state of mutation, that I can only liken it to the game of children, in which as one quits his corner another runs into it, and he that finds no corner to get into, is the laughing-stock of the others." Soon the costs of such uncertainty became visible. Tocqueville noted the burgeoning manufacturing sector and asked a pertinent question about the future of modern commerical societies: "What can be expected of a man who has spent twenty years of his life in making heads for pins?"

While the workman became attached to his machines and the manufacturer grew more powerful, the American community became a spectacle, alternately hopeful and terrifying, of boom and bust. Individuals, Chancellor Harper noted, were "tantalized, baffled, and tortured" by the pursuit of wealth they could not attain. In the midst of a fantastic abundance, economic anxiety became a perennial feature of the American character, as Americans found themselves squeezed between the fear of losing what they had achieved and their desire to gain more. This atmosphere and these paradoxes had their inevitable political results. Myers has suggested that the Jacksonian movement might best be understood as an expression of this anxiety. The Jacksonians, hating the Second Bank of the United States as a symbol of the industrial and commercial oligarchy, at the same time yearned to see the country's wealth thrown open to all who could exploit it. Rejecting the "Eastern oligarchs," they dreamed of the day they would be oligarchs themselves. Jackson, Myers concludes, tried to "recall agrarian republican innocence to a society drawn fatally to the main chance. . . . to reconcile again the simple yeoman values with the free pursuit of economic interest, just as the two were splitting hopelessly apart."

Citizenship did not escape these pressures. That was only to be expected. But the problem was complicated by the fact that the Constitution did not provide a clear definition of "citizen" or "citizenship" to begin with, leaving the concept and the experience doubly vulnerable to the forces of social and economic change.

The Constitution confused matters in two ways.

First, it did not define precisely who was a citizen of "the United States," or how new citizens were to be created. It is unclear in the Constitution, for example, whether state citizenship *precedes* federal citizenship, or whether there is any certain relation between the two at all. Under the Articles of Confederation, Congress had no power to naturalize citizens, and each state was free to make its own provisions in this regard. Inevitably, provisions differed, some liberal and some severe. Article I, Section 8 of the Constitution, accordingly, gives Congress the power "to establish an uniform Rule of Naturalization," but the Constitution is silent on the question of state citizenship. Nor is it clear to what entity new citizens would belong: to a state first, and then to the "united States," or the reverse? The problem was raised on a practical level when the federal government naturalized immigrants living in the territories, thus creating an anomoly: the citizen who was a citizen *only* of an empire, with no connection of any kind to a local government.

The records of the Constitutional Convention show, according to John Roche, that citizenship "referred to national citizenship as secondary to, and derived from, citizenship in a state." This would be a natural inference, given both theories current in 1789: that states were joining together to form a confederated republic (one version) or that citizens of the several states were creating some *additional* form of community (the other version). In both versions Americans were *already* citizens of communities that, however altered their powers, were to continue under the new regime. It seemed to be the Convention's belief that naturalization would be accomplished by the individual states, "with the national government merely exercising supervision in the interests of conformity."

But it soon became apparent that the naturalization of "American" citizens involved issues more complex and controversial than length of residence, and conformity proved difficult to achieve without a basic definition to work from. Americans were united by the "self-evident" truths contained in the Declaration of Independence and the Preamble to the Constitution, and the possibility that some new immigrants might not recognize these truths provoked the first great crisis of American national politics.

In 1790 Congress passed a Naturalization Act, providing for the "progressive naturalization" of immigrants. One year's residence earned all of the "rights of citizenship" save the right to hold office, which was granted after two years. States-rights advocates objected that this bill went beyond the authority of the Congress to guarantee "uniform" rules. Others thought that the two-year requirement for office holding should be dropped, since it created a body of citizens with fewer rights than others. Congress ducked the issue by giving the courts the responsibility for supervising the entire naturalization process.

Five years later, a fresh wave of immigration, sparked by war and revolution in Europe, sent to the United States a large number of immigrants suspected of harboring "royalist" sympathies. Federalist politicians wanted to raise the residency requirement to five years, and they succeeded. "Republicans" wanted immigrants to submit to an inspection of their political views. The final amendments, after raising the residency requirement, compromised on the political questions. New citizens would be required to give a declaration of intent to become a citizen three years before being naturalized, renounce foreign allegiances, and swear an oath in support of the Constitution; they would then have to satisfy a court that all of these requirements had been met and, in addition, that they were of "sound character."

These fears were intensified in 1798. In that year, the Alien and Sedition Acts were passed, reflecting the Federalist Party's fear that "republican" and "jacobin" immigrants were bringing to America an unstable new element which would only add to the mounting chorus of invective directed at the Federalists. A new Naturalization Act was passed that year, requiring fourteen years of residence before becoming a citizen; the bill was repealed in 1802.

In 1824 Chief Justice Marshall settled once and for all the vexing question of whether Congress could make distinctions between native and naturalized citizens not made by the Constitution. In *Osborn* v. *Bank of the United States*, Marshall held that since the Constitution makes certain distinctions between the two kinds of citizenship, Congress may not add any more. The naturalized citizen is "distinguishable in nothing from a native citizen, except in so far as the Constitution makes the distinction." Other court decisions firmly established the principle that Congress has the authority to set naturalization requirements of whatever kind it wishes, so long as naturalized citizens are not left with any disabilities not mentioned in the Constitution.

Nevertheless, the old controversy about what makes American citizenship "American" has been with us ever since the Founding, and is still very much alive. The operative naturalization law, dating from 1943, denies naturalization to anyone who advocates or belongs to a group that advocates "the overthrow by force or violence of the Government of the United States or of all forms of law"—i.e., Communists and anarchists. Some philosophical element, then, remains a part of the legal conception of citizenship in the United States—but whether American citizenship requires any further doctrinal commitments is unclear.

Another source of confusion has not received nearly as much attention from the courts and from political institutions as naturalization has received. Stated simply, the question is this: What are the rights and duties of American citizens? Article IV, Section 2 states that "the Citizens of each State shall be entitled to all Privileges and Immunities of Citizens in the several states." These "privileges and immunities" are not listed, however; it has remained to the courts to infer them from other sections of the Constitution (particularly from the Bill of Rights and, lately, from the Fourteenth Amendment) and to decide what, specifically, this particular clause requires the federal and state governments to do. The settled doctrine of the Supreme Court is that this clause only means that a state may not discriminate against the citizens of other states residing within its borders in favor of its own citizens, although the Court has permitted exceptions even to this general rule.

This is not the place to record the Supreme Court's gradual assumption of responsibility for the protection of various rights against interference by state or federal officials. Suffice it to say that this has been a vast and confusing terrain, over which a complicated battle has raged. There has never been a settled consensus about what rights American citizens enjoy, and there is still less agreement about their duties. In the confusion, a bewildering variety of rights has been asserted or denied—

from the right to be born to the right to die—and a similarly confusing body of court doctrine has emerged to deal with these questions.

The important point here is that since "American citizenship" has been ambiguous from the start, it came to be many things to many people. The social institutions that had helped to give it definition in the early republic vanished or declined. Town government, for example, which Tocqueville had praised so fervently, became impossible as the "close New England town gave way to the isolated homestead or to the city of recent immigrants." Furthermore, "our teachers began to teach, and we to value, private life and liberty above all." Industrial and commercial expansion quickened the pace of erosion, altering familiar landscapes and shifting populations to distant places.

> Outward changes of such magnitude were not without devastating effects on the quality of inner experience. Venerable institutions, especially family and church, were twisted into strange shapes. Respected habits of thought, notably the doctrines of the moral individual and the higher law as the sources of ethical canons, were attenuated and weakened. . . . [A] new material environment tore great chunks from the moral codes which had held liberty in check and kept men united in a sense of community.

In the second half of the nineteenth century, however, citizenship began to assume a more precise meaning, one impressed on it by social and economic changes. By the turn of the century, the transformation was nearly complete. The new meaning of citizenship was compounded of many different materials: immigration, industrial growth, urban expansion, new economic ideologies, the decline of traditional institutions, the weakening of political organization, and the sentiments of "reform." It differed almost entirely from ancient notions of citizenship and substantially even from the eighteenth-century liberal concepts which were its forebears.

4.

One characteristic of the new understanding was its emphasis on the "social" dimension of citizenship, at the expense of the political. In 1918 R. L. Ashley's *The New Civics* expressed this new conception more bluntly than most: "The citizen . . . is a regular member of the large society which we call the United States of America. Citizenship is therefore *social* rather than *political*. It is a *natural right*, not a conferred privilege." A decade later John Dewey said that the citizen is no more than "a thoroughly efficient and serviceable member of society."

Arguments such as these took several forms, but all called attention away from politics to the private groups and circles within which the "real" or "fundamental" life of men and women took place. Economics rediscovered "interest," and Charles Beard used that discovery to reassess the Framers—without, however, losing his respect for the "greatness" of their work, or identifying in it a particular political theory. Sociology dwelled on the small groups in which men worked and played and worshipped. Psychology discovered the unconscious. As new analytic categories were added, however, each was accompanied by a rejection of political categories and political life (this was especially clear in Dewey's work), partly because politics was so clearly in need of "reform," but mostly because the discovery of "society" seemed to offer a richer method for understanding man's world. The new social science disciplines—economics, sociology, psychology, and political science—urged thinkers to look below or beyond the formal institutions of the community and the formal behavior of men and women to find the hidden springs which made the whole thing work. As Tocqueville had predicted, the vividness of the private sphere had grown; the public sphere had become a void.

This approach made a contribution to the new understanding of citizenship that can best be described by comparing it to the classic conception. The city had lost its center, which was the forum. Men no longer went out from their private spaces to the space they shared in common; the life of society was now to be sought closer to home: in the routines of daily existence such as marriage, vocations, dreams, and commerce. Here men led the only lives that had any concrete meaning—visible, analyzable, measurable. And just as the city had lost its center, the citizen had lost his relation to the city. No longer a citizen of a particular place, he became a member of a particular group, and that membership became his most important possession.

The mass immigrations of the late nineteenth and early twentieth centuries made their own contribution to the conception of "group" or "social" citizenship. It was during this period that *citizenship* became hopelessly entangled with *nationalism*. The most visible sign of this new equation was the formation of nationalist organizations such as the Daughters of the American Revolution (1890), the Sons of the Revolution (1883), the Colonial Dames (1890), the Aryan Order of St. George (1892), the Daughters of the Cincinnati (1894), and the Society of Mayflower Descendants (1894). Purely defensive in character, these organizations made "Americanism" a part of the definition of citizenship and then defined "Americanism" in terms of what it was not—revealing better than anything else₁ the insecurities among "native" Americans about their own citizenship. Where the fears prompted by immigration did not lead directly to the demand that immigration be halted (as the American Protective Association demanded), they did lead to various attempts to "Americanize" immigrants as they arrived, the chief vehicle for this transformation being the public schools.

While it had many facets and many motives, the "citizen education" movement—which was only fitfully an attempt to educate *all* citizens and nearly always an attempt to educate *immigrant* citizens—was hampered by its inability to disentangle the idea of citizenship from the simpler idea of nationality. Well-meaning groups such as the Young Men's Christian Association and benevolent projects such as the School of Citizenship founded by the American International College gravitated very quickly to the most easily grasped idea, namely, that a citizen of the United States was first of all an *American*. How do Americans talk? How do they dress? What symbols do they hold sacred? What opinions do they profess? These were to be sought out and passed on to those of doubtful loyalty and foreign nationality. Jacob Riis, no hysterical nativist, was deeply moved by one public school experiment designed to turn immigrant pupils into "Americans":

> Very lately a unique exercise has been added to these schools that lays hold of the very marrow of the problem with which they deal. It is called 'saluting the flag' and originated with George T. Balch of the Board of Education [of New York City], who conceived the idea of instilling patriotism into the little future citizens of the Republic in doses to suit their childish minds. . . . In the flag it was all found embodied in a central idea which they could grasp. . . . The thing took on at once and was a tremendous success. . . . Every morning sees the flag carried to the principal's desk and all the little ones, rising at the stroke of the bell, say with one voice, 'We turn to our flag as the sunflower turns to the sun!' . . . Then with a shout that can be heard around the corner: 'To our country! One country, one language, one flag!'

Unfortunately, once the children grew up there was no one to instruct them in the deeper subtleties of citizenship (with the exception of Tammany Hall, an organization much older than the DAR and, for all of its unsavory reputation, steeped in the republican imagery of the early nineteenth century), and the simplistic notion of a nation of immigrants held together by nationalist symbols carried the day by default. Under the circumstances it is not surprising that efforts to Americanize the immigrants were often taken over by conservative business interests whose major concern was the suppression of "Bolshevism" and the creation of a placid work force.

Parallel to the Americanization movement was the social work movement, examples of which are Jane Addams's Hull House in Chicago and the Boys' Club organizations in New York and other big cities. This movement, like the Americanization movement, hoped to nurture a "higher" citizenship in the nation's slums, but was not as susceptible to the confusion of citizenship with nationalism. The social work profession, however, with its natural concentration on the more urgent needs of its desperate clients, did not have the means to develop a general theory of citizenship in a modern urban setting. In addition, it displayed a disturbing upper-class-reformer's habit of mistaking citizenship for personal hygiene or, in the case of the religious missions, Christian salvation. This movement, like the others, lacked an understanding of citizenship's political dimension and thus was liable to be co-opted by groups whose interest in citizenship was doubtful at best.

Gradually these scattered efforts succeeded in molding a more or less precise image of the "good citizen." The model citizen's loyalty was evidenced by his recognition of the nation's symbols and his adherence to an extremely vague set of principles which changed from year to year. ("Free enterprise," for example, was sometimes an "American" idea second to none; at other times, it was merely a good idea.) He was an efficient and happy worker (in that order), and he did not join labor unions. "To be a good citizen," Teddy Roosevelt declared, "a man must first be a good bread-winner, a good husband, a good father. . . . " Woodrow Wilson told a group of newly naturalized citizens that "the good citizen must be physically, vocationally, and culturally competent . . . He must be an efficient, right-thinking, right-acting individual." In 1928 a popular civics text declared: "We can conclude therefore that vocational and civic education must be judiciously combined, so harmonized as to produce a citizen who is an effective worker, and a worker who is an effective citizen."

But it didn't work. Attempts to reform the immigrants and clean up the slums, whatever their motives, failed to address the problem of citizenship in any but the most superficial sense. By 1917, in any case, even superficial efforts were abandoned. In that year Congress passed a restrictive immigration law that required a literacy test for applicants and, more important, established national quotas. The end of the First World War, however, did not bring with it an end to the insecurities caused by mass immigration. The Palmer raids of 1919–20, the anti-union drives sponsored by industrial organizations, and the popularity of new "patriotic" organizations like the American Legion all attest to the persistence of widespread anxieties about American loyalty and identity.

Pessimism moved in respectable circles as well. Scholars saw much to disturb them in postwar America. In 1925 Walter Lippmann captured this mood with *The Phantom Public*, in which he argued that the "common man" displayed little of the informed opinion upon which democracy was supposed to rest. Walter Shepard, in his presidential address to the American Political Science Association in 1934, was even more pessimistic than Lippmann, and while we can assume that his was an extreme view, his fears were shared by much of the educated public:

> The dogma of universal suffrage must give way to a system of educational and other tests which will exclude the ignorant, the uninformed, and the antisocial elements which have hitherto so frequently controlled elections. . . . There is a large element of fascist doctrine and practice which we must appropriate.

The time seemed ripe for a reappraisal of American citizenship. What conception of citizenship might be appropriate for a mass, industrial, urban democracy? What institutions might provide the kind of civic education required for such a citizenship? What political experiences should be made more widely accessible as a way of replacing older ways of learning?

These would have been useful questions—but they were not, with a few exceptions, the kind of question posed by those who studied the problem. They were not the questions, for example, that appealed to political scientists. By the 1930s, civic education had become an outmoded interest among the members of the APSA, replaced by a fascination with scientific technique. In any case, there were more urgent research problems—those raised by the Depression and the New Deal seemed most urgent of all.

By the time the emergency had passed, the moment of opportunity seemed to have passed as well. In the 1950s, American political science put its formidable research energies to work in the collection of data which showed that the fears of men like Shepard and Lippmann were more than justified: American citizens were not an impressive lot, unless they were compared to citizens in some rustic backwater like southern Italy or Mexico. They were ill-informed, indifferent, sometimes intolerant, unskilled in the art of politics and unwilling to learn. Fortunately— and it seemed at times as if this were the greatest of America's many fortunate circumstances—Americans were also, by and large, willing to leave political participation to others. The active political class was, on the whole, a more impressive group—better informed, more tolerant— and if American citizenship could have any real meaning at all, the meaning would have to be found in the elite.

In the 1950s, consequently, political science rediscovered Madison. Separation and division of powers, the use of faction to balance faction, the tying of interest to the high moral purpose of stability, a citizenship that was restricted, for most, to providing occasional "inputs" into the "system"—these and other distinctly Federalist conceptions found their way into a hundred texts and monographs of the time.

It is probably no accident that during the same period American political science rediscovered Alexis de Tocqueville. The nagging doubts left after the Madisonian argument was done—and there is no denying its brilliance or its appeal—found echoes in Tocqueville's appraisal of the Framer's work. Thus, it is with Tocqueville—and not Madison—that any reconstruction of American citizenship must begin.

Although the First Amendment protected freedom of religion, it also provided that the new American nation would not support a state church. Professor Steven Pepper argues that the religion clauses, when taken to their logical conclusions, contradict each other and that the Framers provided little information to resolve this conflict. For a variety of reasons, it was not until the twentieth century that the controversy surrounding the religion clauses truly ripened. In surveying the Supreme Court's treatment of these clauses in the twentieth century, Pepper finds the Supreme Court invariably reluctant to protect conduct based on religious beliefs, other than that involving speech and press—which is already protected by other clauses of the First Amendment. In turning to the establishment clause, Pepper writes that Court doctrine is controversial and confusing. Pepper, however, is sensitive to the difficulties faced by the Court in these areas. He recognizes that the Court has been a victim of historical discontinuity. The Framers simply could not anticipate the diversity of religious beliefs in the twentieth century, the secularization of society, or the intrusive nature of bureaucracy in American lives. When these are added to the inherent conflict between the religion clauses and American misconceptions about the Bill of Rights, one can begin to appreciate the enormous complexity of the issues faced by the courts. Pepper concludes by offering some interesting suggestions to help the courts and Americans through this maze. But, essentially, he observes that there will probably never be a settled meaning of the religion clauses. The most he hopes for is that the courts can intelligently mediate between the various objectives of American society in this part of its culture.

STEPHEN PEPPER

The Constitution and Religious Pluralism

I. Introduction

This was the problem: how to design a single government for people with fundamentally different beliefs about things they considered very important—for many, things they would claim most basic to their lives. Hence, one of the difficulties of Constitution building for the Framers was that of encompassing groups with differing religious identifications within one government. In one sense—in some areas—that problem remains present and familiar to us. Upon leaving colonial status in 1947, India was wracked with religious civil violence; two nations—one Hindu, one Muslim, with immense human displacement across new borders—are the result. Almost forty years later, Indira Gandhi, India's prime minister, was assassinated by Sikhs as a result of religious division within Hinduism. Religious violence is endemic in Northern Ireland and institutionalized by the ayatollahs in Iran. In Ireland the split is between different strands of Christianity; in Iran much of it involves various strands of Islam.

In another sense, however, such violence seems very far removed from us, as Americans—either far across oceans and cultural chasms or far across centuries, deep in our past. At least part of the reason for this distance is the principle of separation of church and state. The success of that American experiment has insulated us from the strife of religions contending for and exercising the power of the state. Separation of the two contending powers, the Framers' answer to the problem, is found in the first words of the first amendment they made to their new constitution: 'Congress shall make no law respecting an establishment of religion, or prohibiting the free exercise thereof . . . " What follows is a look at the history behind those words, their development as constitutional law, and some of the issues they present for the future as we approach the the two hundredth anniversary of our Constitution.

II. History

A. The Colonial Background

Distance from the problem of the relationship between church and state was not the experience of the colonials creating the new American nation. Their longer term historical background was several hundred years of armed conflict concerning the religious identification of the various European nations. From Israel and ancient Greece until the American experiment, the assumption was that uniformity of religious practice and belief were essential to civil peace; thus, dissent from the state church was tantamount to treason. The more direct background for most was the English background of constant strife and suspicion over issues of religion and state: first, the break from Roman Catholicism under Henry VIII, second, the attendant fear of both external and internal Catholicism, and third, the Anglican-Puritan conflict. As is well known, many of the early colonists were braving the New World in order to practice their religions in a manner free from the interference of the state and the controversies of England.

Their practice of religion, however, included the continued use of the government for the ends of the church or vice versa. The colonies replicated the Old World's alliance of church with state, altering only the identities of the "ins" and "outs." Puritanism (later known as Congregationalism) was the established religion in the New England colonies, at times limiting citizenship to the elect of the church, at times persecuting dissenters. Rhode Island, the one exception, will be discussed briefly later. Pennsylvania's Quakerism resembled Rhode Island's freedom in some ways the Massachusetts's establishment in others. Anglicanism (the Church of England) was the established church of the southern colonies. The middle colonies all had experience, also, with established churches.

These disparate colonial religious establishments tended to share a common historical trend in the period before the American Revolution: the formal governmental establishment of, and identification with, a religion loosened, and the persecution of minority religious believers likewise slackened. Toleration of dissenters grew more rapidly and was more common than disestablishment of the preferred sect. The reasons for this are complex. England had opened up the colonies to dissenters and schismatics; as a result the colonies had a large multiplicity of sects. The Great Awakening, a widespread evangelical movement which began in the middle colonies in 1734 and quickly spread to New England, stressed a direct relationship between the believer and God. This deemphasized the significance of the church and led to a further proliferation of sects, churches, and ministries, thus decreasing support for any established church. Also, mixed in with this diversity of sects, there were many unchurched in the colonies. Commerce and economic competition tended to force colonies to make themselves at least tolerable, if not attractive, to devotees of sects other than that established. The Revolutionary War itself tended to promote cooperation and tolerance between colonies with antagonistic religious establishments. The revolution against England also tended to undermine the power of, and support for, Anglican establishments such as that in Virginia.

Two contrary but significant strands in the history of ideas also supported the trend toward disestablishment. In Rhode Island, Roger Williams initiated a "lively experiment" in toleration of all Christians and a separation of church and state. He, and the radical Protestants who followed him and proliferated throughout the colonies, perceived in an alliance of church and state a threat to the purity of religion and the church. Protection of religion (the garden) from the state and secular concerns (the wilderness) was the goal of separation. Conversely, protection of the state from the church was the benefit of separation from the Enlightenment-deist-rationalist view. Exemplified by Jefferson, this view rested on the Enlightenment view of traditional Christian religion as a shackle on the mind of man. Free inquiry was a key to progress, and a church formally connected to the state inevitably would be hostile to such freedom. Thus, many of the intellectuals who favored disestablishment did so from a hostility toward religion.

Finally, the extent of progress toward disestablishment and toleration should not be overemphasized. Past the middle of the eighteenth century, all but one colony restricted the public exercise of Catholic rites. As Leo Pfeffer has noted, even in relatively progressive Virginia:

> up to the time of the Revolution, denial of the Trinity was punishable by imprisonment for three years, and a Unitarian or free thinker could be adjudged an unfit custodian of his own children. Baptists, particularly during the "period of the Great Persecution," 1768 to 1774, were whipped, beaten, arrested, fined, and imprisoned, sometimes on bread and water. In 1774 Madison wrote to a friend: "There are at this time in the adjacent county not less than five or six well-meaning men in close jail for publishing their religious sentiments, which in the main are very orthodox."

B. The First Amendment

The Constitution said nothing about church and state except for prohibiting any religious test for holding federal office. Many state ratifying conventions were concerned about the silence, and the first Congress, as a result, presented the First Amendment to the states for ratification. What was meant by prohibiting the "establishment of religion" and guaranteeing the "free exercise thereof"? The clauses seem to have been directed at the familiar church establishments in the colonies: the establishment clause aimed at governmental acts favoring a preferred religion (subsidy or other enforced financial support, official declaration of dogma or faith, enforced church attendance, etc.) and the free exercise clause aimed at governmental acts disfavoring other sects (limitation of the franchise, citizenship, or property rights; banishment, imprisonment, or physical punishment for advocating or practicing disfavored religious views). Beyond this, there is very little known of the specific intention of the Framers and adopters.

Along with the disparate support for separation of church and state coming from the radical Protestants on one side and the Enlightenment-deist-rationalist group on the other, support for the Amendment also came from those who favored the establishment of their sect in their state—but feared that a national contest for federal governmental support might end in some other religion claiming the prize. The Amendment clearly did not affect state establishments; it limited the federal government, not the state governments.

Let us pause for a moment to return to the problem as stated at the beginning of this essay—the abstract problem facing the Framers: how to construct a governmental order from first principles when (1) a substantial portion of the citizenry recognizes the validity of a spiritual authority and (2) there is substantial diversity amongst them as to the requirements of that spiritual authority. Conflict between spiritual and temporal authority can be anticipated, as can conflict between differing visions of the spiritual authority. The radical position taken by the Founding Fathers was the conclusion that any attempt to combine spiritual and secular authority (whether to strengthen one or both) was likely to do more harm than good. But the severing of an official link between spiritual and secular authority leaves significant problems. Assuming that the government cannot aid any religion either affirmatively (singling it out for special benefits) or negatively (imposing burdens on the nonfavored groups), what of those conflicts between the secular authority and spiritual authority, between the government and the individual with religious beliefs placing him or her at odds with the law?

Three alternatives seem possible. First, the government can claim superiority of the secular allegiance over the spiritual. Such a view is likely to alienate that substantial portion of the citizenry recognizing the spiritual power. Second, the governmental order may attempt to demarcate jurisdictional lines between the two powers. This was the Lockean tradition voiced by Jefferson and a strong element in the Enlightenment-deist-rationalist stream of American separationist thought. It, too, will alienate that significant portion of citizens with allegiance to a spiritual authority who view the demarcation as incorrectly drawn. (The power to draw the line implies superiority for the line drawer, the secular authority.) The third alternative is to have a "free exercise" clause—a recognition by the government of the superiority of the spiritual in the lives of some individuals. When combined with the decision to separate the two powers (an establishment clause), the conflict among differing understandings of the spiritual authority is relegated to the private realm. While the state has recognized the superiority of the spiritual authority, the limits of the individual's right to follow that authority await resolution of conflicts among individuals and between individuals and the state in which someone claims to act under the authority of religious belief.

C. The Nineteenth Century

The first significant religion clause case to come to the Supreme Court presented such an individual with a spiritual allegiance in conflict with the commands of secular government: in *Reynolds* v. *United States* (1878) the defendant had committed the crime of bigamy, pursuant to the dictates of the Mormon faith. How was the separation of church and state to be applied? From the radical Protestant point of view that the separation protects the garden of the church from invasion by the state, an exception to the criminal law based upon sincere, genuine religious belief makes sense. From the Enlightenment-rationalist view of separation protecting the state from invasion by the church, the criminal law is a primary tool of the state which cannot be subordinated to religion. The Court took the latter approach, elevating the Enlightenment view to constitutional doctrine. It did so by adopting the Jefferson-Locke jurisdictional approach, finding bigamy laws to be within the realm of civil authority rather than in the area of religious belief. Action was regulable by civil authority; beliefs could not be regulated.

Because the Bill of Rights limited the federal government and not the states, *Reynolds* was the only major development in the constitutional law of the First Amendment in the nineteenth century. For interesting historical reasons, *Reynolds* arose under federal law and in a federal jurisdiction, one of the territories. Since almost all governmental acts dealing with religion came from the states, there was relatively little federal law that might be challenged. As public education grew, for example, it tended to be vaguely Protestant in character, but the states were creating this preference, not the federal government. Catholics resorted to the creation of their own school system—and to the effort to gain public support for it—rather than to constitutional challenge of the public schools.

The general trends of the eighteenth century toward disestablishment and greater toleration continued through the nineteenth. The last formally established church was in Massachusetts, where disestablishment occurred in 1833. Blasphemy statutes remained in many jurisdictions, and there is at least one appellate opinion upholding a blasphemy conviction for declaring that the Holy Scriptures were mere fable and contained a great many lies. A few questionable matters arose in which argument was made that the religion clauses applied—for example, in disputes as to whether the federal government should have formal diplomatic relations with the Vatican and whether post offices should be open on Sunday. In the main, however, the meaning of the First Amendment's religion clauses applied, as binding constitutional law awaited twentieth-century development.

III. Twentieth-Century Religion Clause Doctrine

A. Incorporation

The First Amendment begins "Congress shall make no law . . . " As noted above, the limits to be placed on the government by the free exercise and establishment clauses are unclear, but it is clear that the intention was to bind the *federal* government only; some at least of those favoring the Amendment wanted to protect state establishments of religion from federal interference. While the language in the remainder of the Bill of Rights is less specific as to the government whose power is restricted, the initial interpretation was that all of the Bill of Rights, including the religion clauses of the First Amendment, restricted only the federal government, not the states.

The foundation of the role of the federal courts (preeminently the Supreme Court) in the development and protection of individual constitutional rights has been the reversal of this position: most of the first ten amendments (the Bill of Rights) are now held to limit the states as well as the federal government. The process by which this has occurred, through interpretation of the Fourteenth Amendment (ratified in 1868), is beyond the scope of this article. Here, it is sufficient to note that modern constitutional law is built upon an interpretation of the Fourteenth Amendment under which it incorporates and applies most of the Bill of Rights against the states. While there is a strong argument that, given its history, this is inappropriate as a general matter and particularly so in the case of the establishment clause, there is also a strong contrary argument which perceives the free exercise and establishment clauses as different faces of a unified principle protecting individual rights in the area of religion from interference by government at any level—local, state, or federal. We will not elaborate on the contending arguments as to either the establishment clause, the First Amendment, or the Bill of Rights as a whole. As constitutional law, the arguments are settled, and both the establishment and free exercise clauses have repeatedly been held to limit the states as well as the federal government.

B. The Free Exercise Clause

Beginning law students are usually surprised at the large degree of uncertainty in the law. Finding whatever law there may be in the books is usually just the first step. In many situations much remains to be determined; a large area for manipulation and argument exists. After many cases elaborating and applying both clauses, First Amendment religion law is a paradigmatic example: the more the Court speaks, the larger the areas of uncertainty and confusion.

With the *Reynolds* belief-action dichotomy, the law may have been clear, but there was little protection for the exercise of religion. Beginning in 1940, the Court pulled away from that dichotomy, announcing that action was protected as well as belief. The cases (usually involving Jehovah's Witnesses) tended to focus on behavior that could be seen as protected by the free speech and press clauses of the First Amendment as well as free exercise. As a result, although *Reynolds* was left behind, the question of whether the free exercise clause was redundant—that is, whether it provided protection for conduct other than speech and press—remained unclear. In 1963 with *Sherbert* v. *Verner* and again in 1972 with *Wisconsin* v. *Yoder*, the Court clarified that conduct beyond speech was protected. Sherbert could not be denied unemployment compensation benefits when she lost her job due to her voluntary conduct of refusing to work on Saturday, her Sabbath. Yoder could not be punished for his violation of the criminal law in refusing to send his child to public school in accordance with the Amish religious mandate to live a life "separate and apart from the world and worldly influence."

In these cases the Court's interpretation of the free exercise clause seems expansive in its protection of religiously motivated conduct. If a legal provision burdens religious action to a significant degree—even if that law is religiously neutral on its face, in its application in the vast majority of cases, and in its motivation—it can be justified only if the government's reason for the law is extremely important, that is, only if the provision is directly instrumental to a "compelling interest." Even if the governmental interest in general is compelling, an exemption still must be granted to religious objectors unless there is some equally important (compelling) interest in refusing such an exception. If a "less

drastic means"—such as exemption of a minority of religious dissenters—will sufficiently serve the government's compelling interest, then
the Constitution's guarantee of free exercise of regligion protects the
dissenters. In *Sherbert*, while unemployment compensation insurance
was an important state interest, the state had shown no threat to its
insurance scheme from a practice of considering refusal to work on a
Saturday Sabbath as an acceptable reason for unemployment. In *Yoder*,
while compulsory schooling is a paradigmatic compelling governmental
interest, the state could show no significant damage to this interest from
an exemption for Amish children after the eighth grade.

But the Court has not been consistent. In *Sherbert* it refused to
overturn a recent prior opinion holding that the First Amendment did not
require a "free exercise" exemption from a Sunday closing law for
Saturday Sabbatarian merchants. They could be required to conform even
though closure on Sunday (mandated by law) and Saturday (mandated by
religion) put them at a significant financial disadvantage. The *Sherbert*
Court claimed it saw a compelling state interest in having a uniform day
of rest, without exceptions. Also, in a recent case parallel to *Yoder* the
Court came out with a result contrary to *Yoder*. Following the same
mandate to live "separate and apart," an Amish owner of a small
carpentry shop refused to comply with his obligations under the Social
Security Act. (Statutory exemption from Social Security benefits and
obligations is provided for self-employed Amish, but not for employees
and employers.) For some reason, the Court chose not to focus on the
effect of an exemption limited to the Amish, as it had in *Yoder*, and
instead ruled against the Amish on the basis of the extremely important
but also extremely broad general governmental interest in a functioning
tax system. (The Court refused even to narrow its focus to the Social
Security tax system.)

With such conflicting precedents to guide them (even *Yoder* itself
contains inconsistent strains), the lower courts have had great latitude in
decision. One court, for example, holds that certain Alaskan Indians must
be granted a religiously based exception to moose hunting season
limitations which remain applicable to all others, while another court
refuses to allow religiously motivated Indians similar preferential access
over the public in general to sacred sites on government property. The
Biblical Second Commandment to refrain from making "any graven
image or likeness of anything that is in heaven above, or that is in the
earth below . . . " is understood by some small denominations to include
a prohibition of all photographs, including those most states require for
drivers' licenses. Some courts have found in the Supreme Court's free

exercise doctrine a requirement to allow such persons licenses without photographs; some courts, to the contrary, find a compelling state interest in allowing no exception to the photograph requirement.

In what promises to be an important decision elucidating application of free exercise protection, the Court should announce by the summer of 1985 its decision in an appeal of one of these driver's license cases. Should it retreat from the *Sherbert-Yoder* doctrine, as many fear it will, the free exercise clause may be relegated to redundancy, providing little protection for religious conduct beyond that already provided for nonreligious activities under the free speech and press clauses. As long as a law was religiously neutral (that is, not aimed at religion or motivated by religious bias*), it would constitutionally bind even those whose religious practice it significantly burdened. This would be a clear triumph for the Enlightenment view of the clauses as protection for the state from the danger of religion. The equally valid, if not more basic, view of the clauses as protecting religion from the power of the state or as protecting minority practice or idiosyncratic individualism in religion—would be lost.

C. The Establishment Clause

Establishment clause doctrine has developed on a separate track and may be even more confused than that for free exercise. The primary articulation is a three-part test. The legal provision must (1) have a secular purpose, (2) have a principal or primary effect that neither advances nor inhibits religion, and (3) *not* foster an excessive government entanglement with religion.

The secular purpose test, in the main, has been rather easy to pass, for the courts have not pressed too deeply beyond the purpose expressly manifested by the legislature or the legislation. "Primary effect" has been the more frequent basis for decision, and it is problematic because of the difficulty of determining the level of generality at which to evaluate primary effect. For example, a municipality's fire protection or sewer facilities or sidewalks would obviously have both a secular purpose and primary effect. But what of including church property in such service? Focusing on that specific aspect of the service might yield the contrary

---

*A requirement of such neutrality is contained in current establishment clause doctrine, and the free exercise clause seems unnecessary for this purpose. As noted above, the *Reynolds* Court based its decision on the nonreligious nature of the bigamy law, yet in fact the *federal* antibigamy statute was aimed at, and the result of hostility toward, the Mormons. Thus a neutrality approach honestly applied might have protected the Mormons.

result. Refusing such services to churches, on the other hand, would seem to reveal a principal effect (and purpose) of harming or inhibiting religion. Such difficulty in analysis is not fanciful. Recently the Supreme Court of Washington, dealing with a law providing vocational assistance to the visually handicapped, found such assistance to a person studying for the ministry unconstitutional under the primary effect test.

What about various tax benefits (property tax exemptions, tax-exempt status, nonprofit status, deductibility of contributions from donor's income, etc.) typically provided to a large class of "religious, charitable, scientific, . . . literary, or educational" institutions? Should the primary effect test be applied to the entire mixed bag of beneficiaries, with the result of a finding of constitutionality, or to the legislative decision to include religious institutions on the list, which might well result in a finding of unconstitutionality? In 1973 the Supreme Court held unconstitutional a program of tax credits for parents of students in nonpublic schools on the basis of a primary effect of aiding religion. In 1983 the Court held a similar tax deduction plan constitutional because it covered parents of students attending public as well as nonpublic schools. This was the result in the 1983 case despite the fact that the overwhelming bulk of the benefit had been received by those with children in religious schools (96 percent of those eligible to receive the tuition deduction had children in such schools)—about as clear a primary effect benefiting religion as one might imagine. As a final example, consider Sunday closing legislation, which the Court has found constitutional as a secular labor regulation (like minimum wage, maximum hour, and overtime laws). Requiring one day of rest per week for all employees makes sense as a labor regulation, but how justify the requirement that the day be Sunday for all workers without exception without finding a religious purpose or primary effect?

"Entanglement" is merely an antonym for separation, and the third part of the establishment test, prohibiting "excessive" entanglement, has proven difficult to apply. Under one conception, it has referred to laws which create administrative involvement in religious affairs. In the school funding cases this has seemed a "Catch 22." The more a state attempted to regulate and police use of funds to ensure a primarily secular effect, the more it was found to have entangled itself. Under another conception, entanglement has meant a tendency to foster political divisiveness along sectarian religious lines. Such a rule, if applied, would involve a troubling censorship of acceptable motives which citizens and legislators could bring to the legislative process. It also would appear to discriminate against citizens and legislators who wish to act politically on the basis of religious beliefs in a way which implicates the establishment clause, both in the clause's underlying values and in the primary effect prong of the current tripartite test.

The three-part test primarily has been developed and applied in disputes involving religion and education, and these arise in two main forms: public financial aid to private parochial schools and religious practice or instruction in the public schools. In the former situation the fungibility of money creates a real roadblock. A dollar given to a religious school for some "secular" function it performs obviously allows another dollar formerly allocated to that secular function to be transferred to the religious function.

From a historical perspective, the Court's application of doctrine here has been comprehensible. In two early cases, it allowed state provision of secular goods and services (bus transportation and books) on the analytical ground that these were more like provision of fire protection and sidewalks than like direct subsidy of religious education. Later on, however, the court became quite stringent in limiting financial aid. Since the first two cases were not overturned, this has had the anomalous effect of allowing state funding of bus transportation to religious schools, but not for field trips from such schools to a museum or the state capitol; of allowing funding for secular books, but not for recording equipment, maps, or laboratory materials. Even a stringent limit on state funding for parochial schools requires a line, and as all law students know, distinctions become very difficult on the margin. Just within the line—that is, constitutional—is a state's use of its own employees in nonpublic schools to *diagnose* illness or educational disability; but *treatment* or *remedial* services are only constitutional if done at a site other than the parochial school. Funding may not be given for preparing and administering tests required by the state in certain required subjects, but funding to distribute and score standardized educational tests is constitutional. Capping and complicating this historical perspective is the most recent tuition tax deduction case, mentioned earlier, which seems to have reversed the Court's strict limitation approach and may signal the beginning of a new view allowing more financial aid.

It is in the second situation, religion in the public schools, that the Court's decisions have been the most controversial. Here again, the Court has been strict in keeping most overtly religious material presented as religion (that is, for example, prayer as prayer, rather than a prayer as a piece of literature to be analyzed in English class) out of public schools. This general issue, as well as the controversial prayer in the schools issue, will be taken up later.

Before moving on, however, a second line of establishment clause doctrine should be mentioned, which has an unclear relationship to the main tripartite test. Beginning with the property tax exemption case (the same case in which the entanglement test originated), the Court occasionally has relied on the long history and traditional wide usage and acceptance of a practice as constitutional legitimation. Thus, the use of a particular sectarian minister over a long period as a paid legislative chaplain was recently approved by the Court on the basis of the long American tradition of legislative chaplaincy. This was the result despite the unlikelihood that the particulars of the Nebraska practice at issue could pass muster under any of the three prongs of the tripartite test. Also, this alternative approach has emerged despite the fact that it would certainly have justified prayer and Bible reading in public schools, as well as many other practices already held unconstitutional under the tripartite test.

IV. Two Pervading Difficulties

A. The Conflict Between the Clauses

The First Amendment forbids both laws "respecting an establishment of religion" and those "prohibiting the free exercise thereof." Each of these limitations when extended to the limits of its logic conflicts with the other. Assume that the establishment clause forbids laws which favor religion (in modern doctrinal terms, laws whose purpose or primary effect is to benefit or advance religion). The free exercise clause itself is a law which does just that and hence is forbidden under the establishment clause: the clause singles out religion for the special legal benefit of shelter from other law. There is no clause protecting the free exercise of science, sports, philosophy, or sex; only religion, speech, and press are granted this special exemption from legal restraint. The Amish can keep their children out of school after the eighth grade, but someone who desires to do so from a genuine philosophical belief in home education has no such constitutional shelter from mandatory education laws. A Jehovah's Witness who quits work in an armaments factory for religious reasons cannot constitutionally be denied unemployment compensation; if I quit work in the same factory because it doesn't leave enough time for my running training, the Constitution allows denial of unemployment compensation—no matter how important that running is to me. Such governmental discriminations would seem to clearly and primarily benefit religion over other aspects of human life.

Contrariwise, assume that the free exercise clause shelters all religiously motivated conduct which does no clear, concrete harm to other persons. Many religions, including the Catholic church, believe in using the government to support and enforce religious practices. Such use of the law to enforce financial support or prayer, or to punish blasphemy would seem a violation of the establishment clause—despite the fact that it might be a genuine exercise of religion. Again, there is no clause prohibiting an establishment of science, philosophy, or speech; this seems a special governmental burden on *religious* conduct.

School prayer provides a useful example. For many, prayer in public schools—as long as it is voluntary and involves no coercion of those who do not desire to participate—involves a simple exercise of religion. For many others, however, the irreducible core of the establishment clause is the principle that the majority cannot use the government to exercise their religion. From this latter perspective, the group which supports prayer in school overlooks the unavoidable fact that public education is run by governmental bodies, usually elected school boards. Thus, prayer in public schools inevitably involves the majority in using the government (school boards) for the exercise of their religion. Authority for such prayer—who will say it and when, who will choose it and how—must rest in the end with a governmental body. The majority can exercise their religion through prayer in their homes, churches, parks, or streets but not in what is probably one of the most convenient places, the local public school.

This frustration of majority will—the simple desire of a local group for its children to say seemingly harmless prayers in school—makes sense in constitutional terms. The Bill of Rights protects the minority from the majority. The Bill of Rights is and was meant to be a list of limits on what the majority (or a coalition of minorities, if you wish to be more technical) can do *through the government*: it cannot limit the minority's (or the individual's) expression through speech or press; it cannot invade the privacy of the home through an unreasonable search or seizure; it cannot take life, liberty, or property without due process of law; and it cannot restrict the minority's practice of religion or support its own practice of religion.

At the time of the framing, the conflict between the clauses may have been easy to overlook or defer because government was involved in so little. The past two hundred years have seen fundamental changes from the minimal to the bureaucratic state: (1) government at all levels has grown exponentially in size and in areas of involvement and (2) there has been a drastic legalization of both public and private life. From income tax to Social Security tax and benefits, OSHA regulations and inspections, vehicle emission limits, labor relations law, consumer product safety laws, real estate licensing, employment contracts, and on apparently without end—government and legal rules are involved, it seems, in everything. Religion in the schools is a good example. At the time of the framing of the Constitution and the Bill of Rights, virtually all education was private, religious, and sectarian. Now most education is managed by government, and even private education is extensively regulated by government. Dealing with the rights and often conflicting limits created by the religion clauses in this extremely important context was simply beyond the conception of those who framed the basic rule. The First Amendment comes from an old world and must be applied in the new.

The underlying issue is one of pluralism. As noted at the introduction of this piece and again in the history section, our Constitution makers confronted plural religious establishments and beliefs. The potential citizens of the potential nation frequently perceived their fundamental identities and allegiances as Congregationalists, Quakers, Baptists, or Anglicans as much or more than as Georgians or Pennsylvanians, let alone as "Americans"; those differences in belief were fundamental and important to them. In confronting the conflict between the clauses, it is useful to remember the two conflicting motivations for the religion clauses: protection of religion from the state and protection of the state from the power of the churches. The latter view will emphasize the establishment clause at the expense of free exercise if there is a conflict; the former will prefer free exercise. In the intervening two hundred years, religion has become less frequently a primary identification (more persons would consider themselves Americans first and Presbyterians, Jews, Catholics, or Baptists second); the majority will often see more of a threat than a promise in those minority groups for whom religious matters are dominant and demanding. This view is concordant with the dominant modern social scientific objectification of religion and the modern intellectual discomfort with the root irrationality (the leap of faith) of much religious thought and many religious movements.

Such a modern view can easily submerge the issue of pluralism and perceive religion as something not inherently valuable, vulnerable, or worthy of special protection, but rather as something similar to race—of no intrinsic importance, but historically subject to abuse and persecution—and therefore a bad ("inherently suspect") basis for governmental action or classification. This stance has often led contemporary scholars to a "neutrality" interpretation of the clauses, suggesting that they prevent government from acting either favorably or unfavorably toward religion—from classifying in religious terms, to use "equal protection" terminology—and thus to an establishment clause that dominates the free exercise clause. Other contemporary scholars see in pluralism the modern meaning of the religion clauses; they are a fundamental protection of individual and group liberty. From this view, the problem is to protect minority and individual views of the world from the dominant bureaucratic state; the free exercise clause liberty is the predominant value, and the establishment clause is merely an attendant provision to assist in preventing the government from impinging on individual liberty in religious matters.

These two contrasting views lead to significantly different interpretations of the clauses and to differing resolutions of the inherent conflict between the clauses. The Supreme Court has recognized the conflict but has found no approach for resolving it. As discussed above, the Court has developed two independent strands of doctrine, one for each clause, and has not created consistency within even one of those strands.

B. Definition of Religion

The past two hundred years have also changed fundamentally the scope of the question: What is the meaining of "religion"—what is it which is both limited and protected in the First Amendment? While religious differences were more intense and divisive in eighteenth-century America, they were also within a narrower scope. The slowly developing toleration and disestablishment—the issues of church and state—were mainly confined to varieties of Christian Protestantism, with lesser degrees of toleration spreading (and growing in the nineteenth century) for Catholics, Jews, and even unbelievers. (Theoretically, the Enlightenment view associated with Jefferson was expansive, including freedom for Jews, heathens, and unbelievers. But this was the view which saw religion as a threat to a rational, scientific world view and to the enlightened, democratic state, and therefore wished to confine the power and scope of religion: its freedom was in the realm of belief only, not the concrete realm of action, which was what really mattered. In the late twentieth century, the religious diversity of the nation is vastly greater, with Buddhism, Islam, and a plethora of diverse, lesser known sects well represented. Of perhaps even more significance, the dominant secularism of the century, combined with contemporary theology (perhaps itself an aspect of the dominance of the secular), has blurred the line that once demarcated the religious from the nonreligious. When Paul Tillich, a significant modern theologian, suggests that if you have trouble finding meaning in the word "God," translate it to "your ultimate concern, . . . what you take seriously without any reservation," it ought not to be surprising that the Supreme Court quite reasonably has concluded that a young man's opposition to war was "religious," even though that young man had expressly claimed it not to be religious.

The difficulty is real and goes to the heart of the values underlying the clauses. Denominational identification was a primary form of personal identification, which competed with political allegiance to the states and their union—it was the primary problem of pluralism at the time the Constitution and Bill of Rights were drafted, aside from the underlying issue of federalism (discussed elsewhere in this volume). In contemporary America, religious identity for most is less fundamental and intense, yet the problems of pluralism remain in serious sexual, political, professional, ethnic, and racial identifications that fragment the body politic. Add in the worldwide explosion of activist religious fundamentalism in which America is taking its part. How does one determine which of these ought to fall within the term "religion" in an eighteenth-century document governing a late twentieth-century society?

In the nineteenth century—as well as in many eighteenth-century documents of religious liberty—the constitutional term was seen by many as applying only to Christianity. The freedom of religion was only for Christians, and the prohibition on establishment only applied to preferences or disabilities amongst the varieties of Christianity. (In cases following *Reynolds*, this view was expanded to the holding that Mormonism was not a religion protected by the First Amendment, thus avoiding the *Reynolds* belief-action dichotomy and allowing, among other governmental restrictions, disenfranchisement merely for Mormon beliefs.) This "content of belief" definition for religion works to make the clauses complementary. But, in an age of widely diverse belief and unbelief, such a definition appears to be a violation of the establishment clause, for it singles out what we now see as only one variety of religious belief—Christianity—for the special benefits and burdens of the First Amendment. American Indians would have no free exercise protection; Secular Humanists could establish their religion with no constitutional impediment.

At the other extreme, some contemporary commentators suggest that any judicial definition of religion is an establishment of religion: it is law which favors some (those whose practices are defined in) and imposes on the freedom of others (those whose practices are defined out). Two observations are important in response. First, this view merely restates the conflict between the clauses. The Framers meant *something* when they used the word religion, and whatever it was, they meant both to favor it (the free exercise protection) and to hobble it (the establishment limit). Second, while the "no definition" view may seem liberal, it drastically devalues religion and the religion clauses (and thus is consistent with the modern dominant intellectual view of religion). If the term "religion" can be given no limit, then any individual can claim the shelter of the free exercise clause for any conduct virtually without challenge. In such a situation, the scope of protection of the clause, its power, is likely to be very narrowly circumscribed. No sensible court will grant an unlimitable power. Similarly, no court would cripple government with an infinitely expandable understanding of religion that, under the establishment clause, would forbid the government from involvement in just about everything. A legally binding provision with an unlimitable content is not likely to become anything other than a dead letter.

At this point, it should come as no surprise to learn that the Supreme Court has provided no consistent answer, that it has given conflicting signals. At one time—interpreting religion as used in the conscientious objection provisions of the draft law and quoting modern theologians such as Paul Tillich and John Robinson—the Court created a comparative criterion that focused on the intensity and function of the belief in the life of the individual. But later, in an apparent effort to narrowly circumscribe access to the broad free exercise freedom it was creating, the *Yoder* Court implied that both theistic belief and some organized "church" might be part of its definition of religion.

Consistent with most commentators, the Court has tended to perceive religion differently for the two clauses. If the free exercise clause is a protection for the religious practices of minorities and the individual, it makes sense to allow substantial room for diverse and even idiosyncratic beliefs to qualify as religious. To enforce a narrow majoritarian understanding of religion upon the dissenter would entail the very oppression the clause appears designed to prevent. On the other hand, to allow each minority sect or idiosyncratic individual to define religion for establishment clause purposes might well paralyze the government. Almost everything the government supports or regulates could be sincerely viewed as religion by someone. There are very different consequences involved in a declaration that one will not believe in evolution or will not have evolution taught to one's child (a free exercise claim) and a declaration that evolution may not be taught in the public schools or portrayed in the Smithsonian (an establishment claim). The former creates a space for the individual to be free from government intrusion, but leaves government otherwise free to go about its business; the latter generally disables the government from acting in an area, not just as applied to an individual or a minority, but as applied to everyone. In *Yoder* the Amish successfully avoided compulsory education after the eighth grade; they did not disable the government from enforcing it for everyone else.

V. A Concluding Problem: the Public Schools, Religion, Values, and Secular Humanism

Before concluding, let us draw together some of the threads of the prior discussion on a contemporary problem. In the nineteenth century, American Catholics found the bland Protestantism of the public schools (including readings from the Protestant King James version of the Bible) unacceptable and withdrew, making the creation of their own system of parochial schools a major priority. In the early twentieth century, the public schools became identified as the prime inculcators of the American culture. Their task was the assimilation of the vast numbers of non-Anglo-Saxon immigrants. Following World War I, Oregon took this task to the extreme of requiring public school for all; private schools, including Catholic, were not to be allowed. But the Supreme Court held that such "standardization" of children was not an option for the state; private schools were a matter of constitutional right. By mid-century, for complex reasons, values, religion, and moral education had disappeared as explicit topics from public schools. In the sixties, the federal courts removed organized prayer from the public schools. The new Christian fundamentalists claim that the result is a religion of Secular Humanism in the public schools, a violation of both the establishment clause and their free exercise rights. A quite different, broader constituency finds in the absence of values in the schools a reflection (and perhaps a partial cause) of the decline of community and social cohesion in an urbanized, mobile, anomic society. From this more general perspective, when church, community, and family have all declined in power as transmitters of values, a demand on the public school to be at least a partial answer is inevitable.

To put the problem a different way, a primary task of any culture or tradition is the transfer of that tradition or that culture to the next generation. If the task is not accomplished, that culture or tradition has ended. A society that (1) encompasses significantly different plural cultures and traditions and (2) has a strong history of a successful public school system, clearly has a major ongoing problem. When a significant portion of those diverse cultures and traditions identify themselves in religious terms, that problem implicates the First Amendment, and application of the religion clauses will be part of the solution, for better or worse.

To understand the complaint of the fundamentalists, begin with two premises. First, it is impossible to have a system of education which does not convey morals and values. An avowed absence itself conveys a message. Further, the message of example and practice—how the system works, what teachers and administrators do—cannot help but convey ethical and value lessons. (This first premise is shared by that broader constituency which perceives a need for a more explicitly thought-out transfer of values and ethics in the school.) The second premise is that morals and values are inherently matters of religion; they cannot be religiously neutral. Thus, the morals and values taught in the public schools necessarily involve governmental support of religion—that religion of which those values and morals are a part. If the supported religion is antithetical to my religion, then compelling me to send my children for indoctrination in that religion is a highly significant burden on my free exercise of religion. Compulsory education in someone else's religion— when I cannot afford to create, and send my child to, the alternative of a private school—is exactly the kind of abuse the religion clauses were designed to prevent. Seen and felt from the inside, such complaints have considerable substance.

Let us first approach an answer from the free exercise side of the complaint. The Bill of Rights places certain areas in the realm of *private* freedom: the state cannot interfere, but there is no guarantee of the means to exercise the freedom. Implicit in the liberty protected by the Constitution is the freedom to travel: government can't forbid travel, but it need not provide you the air fare to France, or even to Des Moines. Likewise, one's right to free speech doesn't include a governmental obligation to provide you with the funds to buy television air time. The same would seem to be true regarding funds to freely exercise religion through the medium of a private school.

But if one is compelled to send one's children to public schools due to the absence of funds and one believes that religion and education cannot be separated, does one not have a free exercise right to select the religion that will be conveyed? Here we run into the conflict between the clauses. What the free exercise clause can be seen to mandate, the establishment clause prohibits. As with school prayer, the answer which leaves meaningful content for the establishment clause is that one cannot use the government (in this case the public school) as a mechanism for the practice of religion. Thus, no one—neither majority nor minority— can dictate a religious content or component for public schools. Nonetheless, the free exercise clause can provide some relief. Returning to the Supreme Court's present doctrine (at least one stream of the conflicting precedent), it would seem that compulsory public education is clearly a "compelling" governmental interest in general (and has been so identified in *Yoder*). Exempting some students from some of its aspects or components, however, does no major harm to this interest. Thus, exempting dissenters from required physical education or biology classes if they offend religious principles, or accommodating yarmulkes (skullcaps) on the competitive basketball floor, would appear to be an arguable requirement of the free exercise clause.

Such remedies, of course, are no answer for those who find the pervasive moral and value atmosphere of the public school to be hostile to their religion. For them, *Yoder* itself is of some value: under certain circumstances the free exercise clause requires total exemption from compulsory public education. (As a caution, remember that *Yoder* only involved post–eighth grade education, and the Court made much of the excellent at-home education provided by the Amish culture.) But this is not the solution sought by the fundamentalists. Religion acceptable to them must be part of the public schools, or religion must be removed from the public schools. This returns us to the perception of secular humanism as a religion in the public schools, to the establishment clause, and to the underlying issue of a definition of religion for First Amendment application.

The controversy results from a confusion of Secular Humanism with capitals and secular humanism without capitals. With capitals, the reference is to a small organized group with a creed and other attributes characteristic of religious organizations. Although one cannot predict what definitional approach the Supreme Court will settle on, under some tests currently in use in the federal courts and under the functional test articulated in the draft cases, this group and its creed could accurately be termed a religion. But this is not the secular humanism which is in the public schools. No evidence has been brought forward to support a claim that this organized group has any particular influence in public education, and its small number of adherents (15,000 on the mailing list of its publication) suggests that it could not have a major influence.

Secularism and humanism without capitals, to the contrary, are among the strongest and most persistent currents in contemporary Western thought, and as such are probably pervasively reflected in the public schools. The word "secular" simply means the absence of religion, and secularization is perhaps the dominant historical process in the period immediately preceding the drafting of the Constitution and continuing for the past two hundred years. Secularization occurs when attention is turned away from other worlds and the supernatural and focuses on this world and the natural. To say that something is secular is to say that it is *not* concerned with religion. To say that secular humanism is religion is a contradiction, unless one is speaking in a code. Humanism is a philosophy concerned primarily with human beings, their problems, and the betterment and enrichment of their condition. It focuses on man rather than God but not necessarily to the exclusion of God. There is a long and honorable tradition of religious humanism. Thus, *secular* humanism is a focus on mankind *in this world*, and this would appear to be a perfectly appropriate subject matter for the public schools. For those who wish to connect man in this world to God and to other worlds, education in the home and the church remain appropriate adjuncts to public school. For those who perceive a focus on man in this world as necessarily contrary or hostile to an understanding of man connected to God and to a world beyond, the private school remains the difficult and expensive alternative. The Catholic parochial school system, developed in the late nineteenth and early twentieth centuries, is a model.

To allow a minority to equate secular humanism with Secular Humanism and, calling it a religion, to remove it from public education would (1) amount to a religious censorship of major underlying trends in Western thought and (2) be an establishment of that minority's religion. On the other hand, to allow the majority to define secularism and humanism as general nonreligious philosophical trends that must be taught in all schools, including the private schools of the fundamentalists, would appear to constitute a real impingement on the free exercise rights of the minority. Thus, the tendency toward a majoritarian understanding of religion for application of the establishment clause and a minority or individual understanding for application of the free exercise clause would appear to make sense.

We are left, finally, with the problem of values, ethics, and the public schools from the perspective of that broader constituency mentioned earlier. It would seem that it is only from a minority perspective that values and morals are inherently religious; to explicitly convey them

without a reliance on a religious or theistic authority need not rule out
the possibility of such authority or convey hostility toward it. To believe
that theft is wrong, that intentionally hurting others is wrong, that
respect for all persons is right, that being a productive person is good—
these attitudes can all be conveyed without choosing amongst the many
possible sources for such belief. Surely, then, the state can adopt and
promulgate these opinions without establishing religion. If pluralism
means that the state is unconstitutionally sectarian in taking such
positions, then not only is the concept of public school unworkable but
the democratic polity itself may be an anachronism.

VI. Conclusion

"Almost two hundred years old, and still in the middle of adoles-
cence" may be the best description of the religion clauses of the First
Amendment. During the last several decades they have drawn a lot of
attention and been involved in a great deal of controversy, but they still
have not achieved a stable identity or purpose. While the general
intentions have always been clear—separation of church and state,
freedom of religion—the specific intentions and meaning were unclear at
the beginning, and neither society as a whole nor the Supreme Court has
since given the clauses clarity or consistency. Thus, these major constitutional provisions await maturity and stability.

In moving toward that end, the issues sketched above must be
traversed. The scope the clauses will have in a secularized society must
be decided; what will be defined in, what out, of the protections and
restraints of the First Amendment's religion provisions? In dealing with
the conflict between the manifest logic of each of the clauses, we will be
forced to determine the goals, and compromises between the disparate
goals, of the clauses. How will we accommodate plural religious communities in one polity? In cases such as that dealing with the driver's
license photograph, we will decide how much respect the majority—
those governing—must give to a small number of citizens whose religious
beliefs seem strange and are inconvenient. In our public schools, we must
decide how to accommodate basic differences while restraining the
government from sponsoring particular religious positions and, at the
same time, transfer the values of our shared culture.

It is perhaps illusory to believe that a mediating constitutional
provision such as the First Amendment can reach maturity and have a
settled understanding. It may be, as discussed elsewhere in this volume,
that the role of the Constitution is to remain an adolescent, to maintain

that ability to adapt, to mediate in the sense of meaning and promising different things to different people. If this is so, the religion clauses may be a model. As long as the issues discussed above are considered important and in dispute, the meaning of the religion clauses may always be in the process of being determined, never settled.

It is clear that the framework of government provided by the Constitution left much for subsequent generations to fill in for themselves. In no area is this more important than in the conduct of the bureaucracies which govern much of American life. In fact, Professor Michael Nelson provides evidence that, in the opinion of many Americans, one or more of the government's bureaucracies have a more direct bearing on their lives than the traditional institutions of electoral politics. Unfortunately, the evidence also suggests that many Americans are not pleased with their experiences with bureaucracy. Nelson exposes the weaknesses of the models used to explain or guide bureaucratic behavior but concludes that it is very difficult to pin the blame on either the bureaucrat or the client. Here again, American diversity is partially the culprit. Bureaucracy depends on rules which work best in a homogenous society and become difficult to administer in a pluralistic society. Nelson closes with some suggestions for making bureaucracy more effective. One of these is that education in government should begin to devote more time to teaching students how to deal effectively with bureaucracies. He offers no evidence that one solution to the problem of bureaucracy will be that Americans will ask less from their government.

MICHAEL NELSON

Holding Bureaucracy Accountable: The Search for a Model

The United States may be the only nation in history whose constitutional plan of government can be read in the map of its capital city. The Constitution's separation of powers, for example, was expressed physically when the Capitol and the White House were "separated by a considerable distance, and situated so as to command different aspects, avoiding mutual confrontation." The idea that Washington's sole reason for being was to represent the rest of the country was displayed by the city planners in the wide avenues that radiate from the city in all directions, symbolically inviting citizens to come and be heard. No space was left for the construction of large commercial enterprises: as constitutional government was to rest on the consent of the governed, so would Washington survive as a city only through their financial support.

Yet the plan of the city was somewhat hazy about where the administrative departments were to be housed. John Adams, who as Vice President served as President of the Senate, had wanted them near Congress; George Washington argued that they should be close to the White House, where the President could administer them conveniently. Another reason, Washington explained, was that during the government's residence in Philadelphia, "the universal complaint of [the department secretaries was that] while the legislature was in session, they could do little or no business, so much were they interrupted by the individual visits of members" of Congress.

The vagueness concerning the place of the departments in the otherwise specific community plan reflected the Constitution's own failure to specify the place of the administrative agencies in the new government. In the absence of clear constitutional guidance, three models of bureaucratic accountability developed in the early years of the republic. None have been either theoretically or politically satisfactory, but all have endured. For the sake of verbal consistency, one can think of these models as "top-down," "inside-out," and "bottom-up."

MODELS OF BUREAUCRATIC ACCOUNTABILITY

Top-Down

Whatever else the intent of the Framers may have been, it was certainly their purpose that the actions of administrators be governed by, and held accountable to, officials who owed their positions, directly or indirectly, to the people. But what few references to the departments there are in the Constitution are distressingly unclear as to how this is supposed to happen.

Article II, for example, says that the President "may require the Opinion, in writing, of the principal Officer in each of the executive Departments." But the political history of the Philadelphia Convention shows this to be less a mandate for Presidential control than the residue of the anti-Presidentialists' unsuccessful proposal for an executive council. It gives the President power to nominate executive officers, with Senate approval, then adds: "but the Congress may by Law vest the Appointment of such inferior Officers as they think proper, in the President alone, the Courts of Law, or in the Heads of Departments." Beyond these two specific references, there is the Article's oracular first sentence: "The executive Power shall be vested in a President of the

United States of America." Was this merely preface to the list that follows, or did it suggest the existence of administrative and other executive powers undefined in the Constitution? And how was Article II's charge to the President to "take Care that the Law be faithfully executed" to be interpreted in light of Article I's grant to Congress of the power to create and define the departments by statute and appropriate the money that sustains their activities?

Thus, although the Constitution mandates "top-down" accountability, it does not say who is on top—nor have two centuries of political experience under the Constitution. The direction of change, starting with the First Congress's decision in 1789 to recognize the President's implied power to remove department officers, has been toward Presidential primacy, but only the direction. Although Congress has placed most executive agencies under the supervision of the President, it also has created a host of independent regulatory agencies such as the Interstate Commerce Commission and the Federal Communications Commission. In 1921 Congress gave the President power to propose agency budgets, but it continues to review and revise those budgets through its substantive appropriations and, most recently, budget committees. Recent Presidents have been extended the right to reorganize executive departments— subject to congressional approval.

Virtually all descriptive theories of American national government view the agencies as, if anything, more responsive to the congressional committees that are charged to oversee them and the interest groups that are affected most directly by what they do than to the President or to Congress as a whole. Few applaud this situation, but prescriptions for change range from Presidential primacy through management to congressional dominance by means of clearer statutory control. The public seems to share this ambivalence. It wants Presidents strong enough to do good but a Congress strong enough to prevent harm.

Inside-Out

Political stalemate between President and Congress had a curious effect on the departments in the early nineteenth century. Having two bosses turned out to be not much different from having no boss. The politics of personnel illustrates the consequences. Presidents could remove a public employee from office unilaterally, but only at the risk of alienating the employee's friends in Congress. Congress, in turn, could refuse to confirm the nominations of Presidential appointees, but could make no appointments itself. Stalemate ensued—few were appointed, fewer removed. Civil servants grew proprietary, feeling in some cases that they not only had a right to their jobs, but a right to pass them on to their sons. More important, an ethic developed that the primary mechanism of accountability in administration should be trust in the professional responsibility of administrators.

This model, like the first, has received periodic reinforcement in American history. In the late nineteenth century, the Pendleton Act replaced politics with "merit" as the basis for hiring and firing in the federal executive branch; a host of agencies, boards, and commissions was given virtually independent discretionary power in rule making; and expertise and professionalism were the reigning rhetorical symbols. The argument of the distinguished German sociologist Max Weber early in this century that, "under normal conditions, the power position of a fully developed bureaucracy is always overtowering" because "the 'political master' finds himself in the position of the 'dilettante' who stands opposite the 'expert'" suggested that, desirable or not, agency power independent of political control was a condition of modern society. Accepting this analysis, the political scientist Carl Friedrich went on to argue in 1940 that we should make a virtue of necessity and encourage bureaucrats to develop norms of responsibility that would serve as inner checks on their behavior and keep them voluntarily attuned to policies enacted by elected officials. Contemporary scholarly exponents of a "new public administration" take this argument one step further: they want "a public service which is unabashedly aware of its great power and determined to commit its total sources to the ceaseless struggle for the maintenance of the dignity of man"—as defined by public employees.

If the problem with the first model was an absence of constitutional clarity, the problem with the second is a lack of constitutional fit. The "letter" of the Constitution permits no administrative power independent of political-branch control; its spirit contemplates no unchecked power anywhere in government, least of all in its unelected departments. Personal responsibility in government was certainly a desirable mechanism of accountability, but not a trusted one.

At one time or another, of course, almost everyone finds himself applauding the actions of bureaucrats who assert their independence. Liberals, for example, were cheered when J. Edgar Hoover, the longtime director of the Federal Bureau of Investigation, thwarted the Nixon administration's "Huston plan" of wiretaps and break-ins by his obstinate refusal to cooperate. Conservatives invariably applauded military leaders who spoke out on the need for more armaments when Carter administration policy was different. Scholars are happy to know that their National Science Foundation grant applications are evaluated by peers—and almost everyone is glad that the Bureau of Labor Statistics is free to publicize its economic indicators even when the findings are harmful to whoever is in power.

Still, modern experience confirms the wisdom of much of the Constitution's stance toward administrative power. Expertise born of long and professional study of weapons systems, social work, or educational theory may qualify bureaucrats for their jobs, but it is likely to cloud their judgment about how important their individual areas of expertise are to government and society or as to what ends such expertise should be put. The agencies they work for also will have an inflated, if sincerely held, view of their importance and act in ways that will advance their own organizational well-being. Beyond that, experience suggests that agencies with the most discretion in applying the laws—regulatory boards, contracting agencies, even judges sentencing convicted criminals—tend to do so in ways that favor socially and economically advantaged groups.

Bottom-Up

In form—citizen participation in bureaucratic decision making, block grants to local governments, and so on—the bottom-up model of bureaucratic accountability is the newest of the three; in American political philosophy, however, it may be the oldest. The theory of the Anti-Federalist supporters of the Articles of Confederation, drawing largely on Montesquieu, was that governmental power should be as close to the people as possible, both geographically and institutionally. There was, in fact, strong and enduring resistance to the very creation of administrative departments in the Continental Congress, for fear that a locus of national power two steps removed from the citizenry ultimately would become independent of public control.

Within a century, the sense that such a locus indeed had evolved led powerful groups in society to start demanding direct representation in the executive branch. "Client" departments were created to represent the interest of farmers (Agriculture), business (Commerce), labor (a bit too bluntly, perhaps, union leader Samuel Gompers hailed the new Department of Labor as "Labor's Voice in the Cabinet"), and, most recently, professional educators (Education). In the 1960s and 1970s, the drive for bottom-up accountability took the form of added demands for decentralization of power within client agencies. Liberals emphasized direct citizen participation in agency decision making; conservatives called for the consolidation and devolution of federal categorical programs into block grants to state and local governments.

The bottom-up model of bureaucratic accountability, like the inside-out model, takes it for granted that agencies inevitably will exercise political power in government and seeks to develop extra-constitutional mechanisms of control that are independent of the President and Congress. As such, it has the inside-out model's problem with constitutional fit: Is it anywhere contemplated in the Constitution that departments should be responsive to the policy wishes of their clientele rather than to the people as a whole? The bottom-up model also has a problem all its own. In practice, its effects appear to be different from those that are intended. Citizen participation in agencies that allow or even encourage it tends to be small in extent and unrepresentative in character, even of agency clientele. In block grant programs, write Erwin Hargrove and Gillian Dean, "[i]t has proven difficult to create, as intended, institutional arrangements at the grass-roots level that allow programs to be planned in a comprehensive way."

BUREAUCRATIC ACCOUNTABILITY AND POLITICS

Although no model of bureaucratic accountability has proved satisfactory to the American people, as long as the federal government's administrative apparatus remained small in size and scope, this did not seem a matter of great political urgency. As the political scientist Herbert Kaufman notes, at the turn of the twentieth century, "[w]hile European scholars . . . were observing and analyzing the development of bureaucratic power in political institutions, the subject drew scant attention in America." Through the period of its blossoming in the 1930s, bureaucracy had few enemies, and almost all of them were on the political right. Prominent liberals like Paul Appleby and Alben Barkley defended it unblushingly even in the 1940s; Appleby dedicated his book *Big Democracy* "To John Citizen and Bill Bureaucrat," and keynote speaker Barkley quipped to the 1948 Democratic National Convention that "a bureaucrat is a Democrat who holds a job a Republican wants." During the 1960s, however, antibureaucratic sentiment began to spread leftward across the political spectrum. The first rhetorical shots of the student rebellion were fired against anonymous, "computer-card education" at Berkeley; urban rioters often raided the welfare office before the loan company. By the mid-1970s, Americans—so recently polarized by race, the Vietnam war, and other issues—seemed united as seldom before in their anger about the ills of bureaucracy.

I began to find this out in 1975 and 1976, after I decided to try to learn what politics and government look like from a "citizens'-eye" view—

what people think about when they think about the political system and how they feel about what they see. I did so by going to three towns to talk with families from three classes of people—poor whites in Augusta, Georgia, professionals and business people in Towson, Maryland, and blue-collar workers in New Milford, New Jersey. I drew people's names randomly from the phone book, wrote to tell them I was interested in finding out what was on their minds concerning politics, and asked to come visit for a couple of evenings with them and a few of their friends. I did not bring a long list of questions; instead, when I got to their homes, I repeated my interest in hearing about their concerns—then sat back and listened as they talked, partly to me, but mostly with each other. Unlike a pollster, I was as interested in what people chose to talk about when they talked politics as in the opinions they expressed.

As the conversations rambled along, people began to paint a verbal landscape of the political world as they saw it. To my surprise, what loomed largest in that portrait was not Presidents, elections, policy issues, or the rest of the things that scholars, educators, and journalists usually think of as "politics." In fact, when people spoke of current affairs and the like (mostly, I suspect, because they thought it would please me), they usually did so stiffly, with uncomfortable pauses and lags in the conversation. The subject that they warmed to with raised-voice, table-thumping intensity was the bureaucracy—not bureaucracy in general, but rather the specific agencies of government they felt intruding into their personal lives.

As one perhaps would expect, each class of people related experiences with somewhat different groups of agencies—the well-off with, for example, the Internal Revenue Service (IRS), the blue-collar families with the unemployment food stamp office, the poor with the Social Security Administration or Veterans Administration (VA). But regardless of their class, almost everyone found "politics" to be remote from their personal lives and concerns, and bureaucracy to be intimate.

Further, they did not like that intimacy, those intrusions. It meant dealing with organizations that not only were large and impersonal, but whose actions sometimes seemed to defy all reason. For example, Frank, a prosperous middle-aged lawyer, told of trying to find out from the IRS how his purchase of a condominium would bear on his taxes. "I went all the way to the IRS district director before I could get anybody to listen to what I was saying. The district director finally says, 'Well, I can't help you; you have to talk to the agent of the day'—you know, call a number and agent so-and-so answers. So when I finally reached him, he says, 'Does your company subscribe to Prentice-Hall and Commerce Clearing-

House and different tax services?' I said yeah. He says, 'Well, you better look it up there because that's more help than we can give you.'"

Martha, a retired single woman, had been supporting herself with a small social security check. Ordinarily, that would have entitled her to get additional Supplemental Security Income (SSI). But because she had saved over the years for her burial, she told me, she had accumulated more in the bank than SSI recipients were allowed to have. Thus, the local office turned down her application, although a sympathetic caseworker advised her that if she spent her savings, she would become eligible.

Bureaucrats' behavior also seemed random and arbitrary, although, for those who were shrewd enough, it could be gotten around. A real estate agent explained, "It's very difficult to get the right information out of the government in my business. Trying to get a decent appraisal out of a government official—the VA or the FHA (Federal Housing Administration)—is unbelievable. The red tape. If he appraised it, that's the last word—that's it. And the only way we could rectify two of the things that came in grossly under-appraised was to go to our congressman, who used to be a neighbor. He helped us out."

All too often, though, an inept agency action gave the appearance of being malicious. Many of the poor whites were certain that the government now practiced racial discrimination against them, using evidence like Homer and Viola's. "I know a black man who used to work at the truckstop," complained Homer, a young, part-time school janitor. "His wife went down there and said him and her was separated and had two young 'uns. And at that time she'd been drawing welfare and food stamps for two years and she said they [caseworkers] never had so much as come to her house." "And that woman came down here and went through every cabinet I got, that welfare woman," added Viola.

For some, the inherently complicated nature of bureaucratic procedures was a source of anger and confusion. After Willie's husband, Fred, a mechanic, broke his arm, she went down to the food stamp office. "I had a note from the doctor saying he'd have to stay out of work for ten months. But they told me I could get them, but I'd have to wait 30 days. I told her that in 30 days I'd be starving and she could forget about it." Ron, an unemployed landscaper, dreaded going down to the unemployment office. "You have to get on one line for this and another line for that, and the people behind the counter—they're busy, I know—but they treat you like you're probably a rip-off artist or something. You know, guilty until proven innocent."

The impersonal nature of agency contacts further incensed people.

The IRS had sent an impersonal letter demanding a meeting at a specified time, complained Dianna, a university press editor. "Computerized courtesy, a friend of mine calls it. And we go down and everything is fine. Well, good Lord, I've been paying taxes for thirty years now and everything's been fine. Why do they need to call me now?"

Even worse was having to rely on a large, anonymous, and hence unpredictable organization for basic sustenance. Gene and Ella, who live off his VA disability check, got very upset when "some bureaucrat" waited too long to get the checks out. "If a man is depending on that check," said Gene, "he could be sitting out in the street with his family maybe for ten days if his landlord wants his rent on the first of the month. You can get pretty hungry from the first to the tenth waiting for that check, and they should take that into consideration. Some of them wait until the last minute and foul everybody up, and it can be real costly to people."

One thing that was striking about these complaints, and the scores of similar ones I heard, was their nature. As Max Weber states it in his classic "Essay on Bureaucracy": "Precision, speed, unambiguity, knowledge of the files, continuity, discretion, unity, strict subordination, reduction of friction and of material and personal costs—these are raised to the optimum point in strictly bureaucratic administration." Yet not only did these qualities—efficiency, rationality, uniformity, and courtesy of treatment—manage to conceal themselves from the people I talked with, it was their very opposites that seemed more characteristic. People of all classes felt that their treatment had been bungled, not efficient; unpredictable and bizarre, not rational; discriminatory or idiosyncratic, not uniform; and, all too often, insensitive or downright insulting rather than courteous. Equally curious, the agencies that drew the most fire were, on the whole, those whose business is supposed to be that of providing benefits to people—social security, food stamps, welfare, tax counseling, and so on.* It is not surprising, of course, that when the

---

*This finding was underscored by a 1977 report to President Carter from Richard Pettigrew, a Presidential assistant working on reorganization. Pettigrew sent out a letter to every representative and senator asking them which federal programs their constituents thought were "administered least efficiently," "most confusing," "least successful in achieving their stated objectives," involved the most "excessive paperwork," and, finally, were "most responsive." Although members of Congress, who are at the receiving end of almost all citizen complaints against the government, were the logical ones to ask, evidently no one ever had before. More than two hundred of them replied, often in great detail. Their answers, interestingly enough, were quite uniform, spanning party and

government exacts its burdens—taxes, fines, jury duty, and the like—people grumble. It is something else when the government makes them mad in the process of doing something for them.

Given the small size and unrepresentative nature of my sample, it was hard to conclude anything confidently from these findings. Indeed, the conventional wisdom of the political science profession was that, aside from the draft and taxes, "the impingement of government on daily lives is invisible" and that, if anything, "Americans love their bureaucrats."

There were straws of supporting evidence, however, to be found in breaking events. In 1976, for example, voters in the two parties' Presidential primaries nominated a Democrat who was antibureaucracy, even though the modern welfare state is essentially a Democratic Party creation, and a Republican who was antibureaucracy, even though, as President, he was its head. When the winner of that election, Jimmy Carter, held his first series of radio phone-in programs and town meetings in 1977, the responses included many pleas for help like that of the Cleveland woman who could not get her mother's GI Bill benefits straightened out, complaints such as that of the Lanham, Maryland jobseeker who felt she had been frozen out of civil service employment, a California man's protest about letters the Post Office seems to take forever to deliver, and so on. Most obvious, there was the growing volume of congressional mail from constituents asking for ombudsman-style interventions in their dealings with federal agencies—so much of it that members of Congress increased the size of their staffs and assigned nearly half of them to district offices.

---

ideological lines. (The author of a call for "less government involvement in the 'daily lives' of individuals and businesses," for example, was George McGovern.)

Two agencies ranked high in all four "bad" categories: the Department of Labor's Office of Workers' Compensation Programs, which administers the black lung program and workers' compensation for federal employees, and the Social Security Administration's disability insurance, Medicare, and Aid for Families with Dependent Children programs.

The Veterans' Administration was next on the list; it scored badly in three categories. The IRS, Immigration and Naturalization Service, and Small Business Administration showed up in two. Among the others that were singled out frequently: the Occupational Safety and Health Administration, the Department of Housing and Urban Development, the Civil Service Commission, the Farmers Home Administration, the Postal Service, the Economic Development Administration, and the Employment Retirement Income Security Administration.

Aside from the IRS and, perhaps, OSHA, all of these are, supposedly, "benefits" agencies. The patterns of complaints Pettigrew found—unnecessary delays in processing cases, the agencies' failure to provide people with information, and "outright rudeness"—were very similar to the ones I heard.

But these were straws. Then, in 1978, a more "research-able" event that bore on the bureaucracy question took place, and, fortunately, the depths of its meaning were plumbed thoroughly. Several hundred thousand Californians signed petitions to place an initiative on the June 6 ballot that would reduce property taxes by more than half; several million more voted for it, enough to carry Proposition 13 by a margin of approximately two to one. The "tax revolt" spread to other states that November. A nationwide poll sponsored by the *Washington Post* found that some three-fourths of those surveyed thought that they too would vote for a Proposition 13-style proposal in their state if they had the chance.

The initial reaction of most political analysis to this wave of events was that the public was calling for a reduced government role in society or simply for lower taxes. Subsequent studies found something quite different. Everett Carll Ladd, for example, reported on a national survey that asked people whether they thought "the amount of our tax money now spent" for various government activities should be increased, maintained, reduced a bit, or reduced entirely. The activities included aid for the poor, the black, the sick, the elderly, and the unemployed; rebuilding rundown cities; and providing adequate housing where needed. Before answering, people were admonished to "bear in mind that sooner or later all government spending has to be taken care of out of the taxes you and other Americans pay." Yet, in no case did less than 63 percent favor increased or continued spending; indeed, support for all but one (welfare) ranged from 72 percent to 97 percent. Remarkably, this support was nearly uniform across class lines.*

This information, placed alongside the *Post* poll, put the "tax revolt" into some perspective. An even higher percentage than the three-fourths who said they would have voted for Proposition 13 also told the *Post* that it wasn't the taxes that bothered them so much as the way the money was wasted. When given a choice between a hypothetical "Candidate A [who] says we should cut spending on government programs and reduce taxes" and "Candidate B [who] says we should keep taxes the same but make government programs more efficient so that they do what they are supposed to do," more than two-thirds chose B—again, this was true among all classes. Ladd noted a poll taken on the eve of the Proposition 13 vote that discovered 88 percent of California's voters insisting that "if

---

*Gallup reported similar findings in a poll taken in early 1981. *Newsweek* (February 23, 1981), p. 19.

government services were made more efficient, the current level of service could be provided even though budgets were reduced."

What did all this mean? It seemed to indicate that Americans were not engaged in a tax revolt at all, any more than they were repudiating the welfare state. "Their real concern," concluded the *Post*, "is that it is the bureaucracy, not the public, that benefits from taxes." To use the oversimple analogy of a church food drive, the parishioners support it in principle and are willing to support it in deed. But that willingness is likely to vanish if they get the impression that a healthy share of their donations is being eaten by the church staff and another share is carelessly left to rot.

Equally important to the substance of public dissatisfaction with bureaucracy in California and elsewhere was the primary form it took: initiatives. An initiative is a device by which—in the twenty-three states that allow it—citizens can draft a piece of legislation, place it on the ballot by petition, and have their fellow voters decide on election day whether it should become law or not. Historically, reports Austin Ranney, intiatives have been used more often to alter governmental processes than for any other purpose. Presidential primaries, direct election of United States senators, woman suffrage, and poll tax repeal were reforms first instituted by initiative. The 1970s were marked by a whole host of ethics, disclosure, and "sunshine-in-government" initiatives aimed at bureaucracy, even before the wave of tax proposals. As an index of popular dissatisfaction with the ordinary processes of government, initiative use is probably as helpful as any other.

As Figure I shows, the 1970s saw an astonishing rise in initiatives: there were almost twice as many as in the 1960s, a decade when voter turnout in candidate elections was higher. What's more, the rate of initiative use accelerated through the decade, from fourteen in 1970–71 to more than forty each in 1976–77 and 1978–79—and forty-one in 1980 alone. In the past, an average of around one-third of all initiatives on the ballot have passed; since 1978, virtually one-half have passed.

In terms of our models, this may seem to be the full flowering of bottom-up accountability: citizens seizing the legislative power away from legislative institutions and using it to club administrative agencies into a state of willing responsiveness. In truth, though, the history of the initiative shows that usually it is used to strengthen the connection between elected officials and the public or to remind officials of their responsibilities. Supporters of the tax-cut initiatives were not so much telling bureaucracy how to become more efficient as telling their elected representatives to grab hold of the reins of administrative power. They

Figure I: Initiative Use, 1960–80

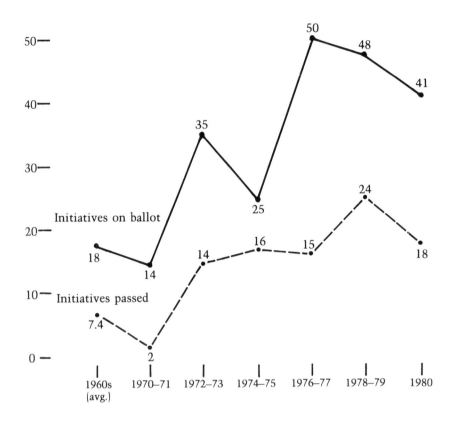

Source: 1960–76: Virginia Graham, A Compilation of Statewide Initiative Proposals Appearing on Ballots through 1976 (Washington, Congressional Research Service, 1978). 1977–80: Initiative News Service, Washington, D.C.

were not asking for new policies but for the successful implementation of existing ones, so that they would receive what those policies entitled them to. This is clearly as much, or more, an affirmation of the top-down model as of the bottom-up.

WHERE IS THE PROBLEM?

The preceding discussion raises a question about which one can only speculate: Where is the source of the pathology—in bureaucracy itself or in people's response to it?

Perhaps no one has made the case for bureaucracy more vigorously or strenuously than the political scientist Victor Thompson. As he sees it, people who can't get along with bureaucracy are suffering from "bureausis," which he defines as "immaturity, the dysfunctional persistence of childish behavior patterns." Thompson explains:

> The child cannot bind time. . . . He must have the object immediately; tomorrow he will have forgotten. The child has little skill in taking on the role of others, in putting himself in someone else's place. He experiences himself directly and immediately and expects others to experience him in the same way. Consequently, to have to explain himself . . . frequently makes him furious . . . [children] grow accustomed to receiving love without a price . . . simply because they are there, not for what they do . . . They carry into adulthood the habit of receiving gratification without a corresponding return or effort on their part.

What all this adds up to, in Thompson's view, is that people act like children when they come into contact with bureaucracy, and that it is up to them to grow up because bureaucracy is here to stay. Yet, looking at the excerpts from conversations reported in this essay, it is hard to find more than a few situations where either the citizen or the agency seemed unarguably in the wrong, where people were clearly childish or bureaucrats malicious. In most cases, one could easily imagine two approximately equal sides to the question.

This brings us to a point not yet made: the simple difference in perspective between agency and client, a difference that can make it difficult for the two to interact in a mutually satisfying way. Perhaps it is best understood by starting with the desk or counter set between them.

On one side of the desk is the citizen, a unique individual with a unique set of circumstances. Think of Martha, the woman who, because she had saved all her life for a decent burial, had more money in the bank than the SSI law allowed its beneficiaries to have. She is, of course, a whole person, and wanted to be treated as a whole person. Special consideration? Of course. Bend the rules a little? Certainly; I'm different. And she is different, as is every person who sits on her side of the desk.

Across from her is the bureaucrat. He is there not as a friend or neighbor but purely as the representative of his agency. As much as possible, that agency is supposed to execute the law as written, that is, to function as an efficient machine. It is not supposed to do whatever it—or one of its employees—wants or feels is right. This means that the bureaucrat, sitting at the bottom of the agency ladder, must function as a cog in the machine. He is empowered only to do certain limited things and only for those clients who are eligible. By definition, he must not look at the whole person but only at those features that enable him to transform her into a "case," a "file." His first job, then, is to categorize this woman who sits before him as eligible or not eligible; if so, for what and on what terms. Once classified, she becomes subject to the same treatment as all the others in her category. So Martha does not get her SSI check. The fact that her savings are for burial purposes, not high living, cannot even be considered.

This simple difference in perspective explains why what looks like fairness, rationality, and efficiency from the bureaucrat's side of the desk can come across to the client as insensitivity (You're not treating me like a person), irrationality (What do you mean, those are the rules? the rules don't make any sense in my case), idiosyncracy (I got a mean one; maybe the next clerk will be nice), and inefficiency (Why does it take so long?).

Assigning blame in such a situation is pointless, a truth of which citizens seem at least partially aware. Thus, most people express generally favorable attitudes toward government employees. And even though only 46 percent of a Harris survey said they had been satisfied by their most recent experience with a federal agency, 73 percent said that the federal employees that they had dealt with had been helpful in that experience.

WHAT IS TO BE DONE?

It should be clear by now that what the public seems to want in the way of bureaucratic accountability, although not unharmonious with constitutional principles, cannot be achieved fully. It wants top-down accountability in the sense that bureaucracy takes its cues from elected officials (but that does not solve the problem of lack of clarity in the Constitution). It also wants bottom-up accountability, at least to assure that agencies are responsive to citizens' individual needs in particular cases. It even wants some elements of the inside-out model, as we noted earlier, although by and large it is excessive control over the actions of bureaucracy by public employees that the public is most upset about.

To a great extent, these desired ends could be served by an added measure of simplicity in government programs, with no real reduction in government's role in society. Although there are limits to what can be done to change bureaucracy, there are ways it could be cut down to size, minimizing the number and complexity of contacts between citizens and agencies while simultaneously clarifying the relationship between agencies and elected officials.

For example, the vast array of government programs that are designed to give people sustenance (Aid to Families with Dependent Children, workers compensation, social security, disability insurance, food stamps, unemployment insurance, and so on) really are addressed to one basic need: money to live on. A guaranteed annual income, with poverty the only measure of eligibility and family size the only determinant of benefit level, would address that need far more simply than the present system. The legislation passed by Congress and signed by the President that would establish this program could be sufficiently plain to provide clear top-down instructions to the administering agency. This simplicity also would make it easier for citizens to understand their rights when they dealt with that agency and could reduce the sheer number of grating citizen-bureaucracy contacts. "The desk" between them still would be there, but it would be clearer to both parties what was involved on either side of it. The advantage of this shines through in the experience of the Social Security Administration. The administration of the old-age pension, whatever one may say about its conception, is simple and popular— I heard practically no complaints about it, nor did the members of Congress who reported to Pettigrew. Rather, the highly complicated SSI, disability, and welfare programs spawned the problems.

One reason that this kind of simplicity is not more widespread is that the government's intentions are, in a way, too good—it cannot bear to give away money without making sure it is well deserved. Mayors testify that if they want federal money for some useful project, they have to put up with reams of forms designed to insure that the construction company does not discriminate in its hiring, that the plans are perfectly sound, that the "environmental impact" of the project will not be adverse, and so on. These are all worthy goals, but they create a lot of bitterness and kill a fair number of projects. Sometimes it may be better for the federal government just to give the money to the state or local government, itself elected, trusting its recipient to spend it in reasonable ways and accepting that there will be some who do not. A strategy of consolidating as many of the hundreds of federal categorical programs for the states and localities into block grants even more flexible than those presently in effect for manpower training, community development, and social services could help to achieve this end.

A variation on this theme is offered by Charles Schultze, former chairman of the Council of Economic Advisers, in his call for more "market" mechanisms in various regulatory programs. Water pollution abatement provides his major case in point. A 1972 law requires the Environmental Protection Agency (EPA) to fix specific limits, based on current technology, on water-borne pollutants for every type of industrial process and to apply those limits to every industrial firm—taking into account the age of the firm's equipment, engineering and process variables, "economic achievability," energy-use side-effects, and other criteria.

If that sounds complicated, it is. Compounding the problem even more, there are 62,000 point sources of water pollution in this country. To have developed sound standards in the first place for each one of them, taking into account all the variables the law specifies would have required an "omniscience" that EPA does not have; to revise standards as the variables change in value is equally impossible. The result so far has been that thousands of lawsuits have been filed before judges who know little about technical environmental issues, at immense cost and delay to EPA. Further, since the law ties the pollution limits to "best available" technology, businesses have no incentive at all to develop new pollution-control devices—that would just make EPA crack down harder.

What Schultze would have us do in lieu of regulation is to try a kind of economic jujitsu on water polluters, using the market system's virtues to defeat its weaknesses. The great strength of the market, of course, is that it can achieve almost anything if the money is right. So, instead of telling firms that they can only pollute up to some specified (and by definition, artificial) limit, Schultze proposes that we simply tax polluters heavily for each unit of pollution they generate. The same market system that has always encouraged pollution because it does not cost firms anything would then discourage pollution because it would cost them a great deal. They would have every incentive to come up with new technologies to reduce pollution (and pollution taxes) instead of hiding behind present technologies.

The same principle could be applied widely in government. Instead of the Occupational Safety and Health Administration hopelessly trying to write regulations to prevent every conceivable industrial accident, it could impose a stiff tax each time a worker is injured, thus placing the burden on each business to develop safety practices that will keep it from going broke. Air pollution could be attacked in the same manner as water pollution. Another advantage of the market—that its transactions are voluntary—could be put to use in certain nonregulatory policies, such as education. "If government is to assist higher education," Schultze asks, "should it aid individuals who can 'buy' education where they choose or should it directly subsidize colleges and universities? Should federal manpower training subsidies take the form, as they do now, of grants to institutions or of vouchers to individuals, a la the GI Bill of Rights?"

Others have made easy extensions of this idea. For example, housing vouchers have replaced public housing construction to some extent.

In addition to these reforms of bureaucracy, we need to learn and teach better about its functioning. For learning, the tools already are partially at hand. As we have seen, every day thousands of letters and phone calls come into congressional offices from citizens who need help in their dealings with government agencies. These are serious pleas almost by definition; the physical and emotional effort required for such a letter or call is evidence enough in most cases that it reflects more than simple grousing. Thus, the obvious self-serving electoral dividends aside, it is not inappropriate that many members of Congress devote much of their staff to the task of investigating these grievances.

The system works well as far as it goes; unfortunately, it does not go far enough. Few, if any, of the 535 representatives and senators know what the other 534 are hearing from back home—if there is a pattern to the complaints about a program that citizens are sending in, it rarely is detected. Not only is Congress consequently blind to the forest, many offices are organized so as to obstruct its view of even the trees. An increasingly popular practice on Capitol Hill is to palm off all casework on the district office so that the legislative staff in Washington will not be bothered by it. As cases are resolved one by one, the symptoms are treated, but the disease—the legal or organizational aspect of a program that may be spawning many of the complaints—is left undiagnosed.

The solution may be quite uncomplicated: an office to monitor the cases that come into House and Senate offices, to sort them out according to agency, program, region, and other variables to see what the recurring complaints are, and then to investigate the legal or administrative sources of discontent and make recommendations for action if improvement is possible. In Hawaii, where all this is done by an ombudsman's office, 181 reforms of administrative procedure were effected in the first seven years.

In this regard, former Representative Henry Reuss's proposal for an Administrative Counsel of Congress seems sensible. The Counsel would be appointed by congressional leaders every two years to perform ombudsman-style functions. Citizens' complaints still would come first to the legislator, who would, if he chose, forward them to the Counsel. The Counsel's office would investigate, then send the member of Congress a report describing what it had found. The legislator could decide where to take it from there, and he, of course, would be the one to reply to the constituent.

The advantage of such a plan for members of Congress is obvious:

they would continue to get whatever credit there was to be gotten and with considerably less effort. The public probably would benefit even more. For one thing, the Administrative Counsel's staff would be more expert and experienced at their particular tasks than the staffs of most members of Congress; they also would have the power of subpoena, which individual legislators do not. Most important, at last someone would have the whole picture.

We also need better teaching about how bureaucracy works. Our present system of civics education, sticking as it does to explications of the Constitution and perhaps of the electoral process, tells people almost nothing about how agencies work. Nor do newspapers and television help very much; bureaucracy seems too difficult a story to cover, much less dramatize. This explains a startling finding by the authors of *The Civic Culture*: although Ameicans ranked first among the five democracies they studied in "civic competence"—the feeling that they could do something to prevent an unjust law from being passed—they ranked only third in "subject competence"—the "ability to appeal to a set of regular and orderly rules in their dealings with administrative officials." We do not teach those things, in school or out, so we should not be surprised that people feel ignorant and overwhelmed when they have to deal with as many agencies as they do.

None of these proposals will solve the problem of bureaucratic accountability. They are offered primarily for purposes of discussion. It is to be hoped that the result of that discussion will be a simplification of the programs administered by bureaucratic agencies and that wider public understanding of their workings will enhance and harmonize the values of top-down and bottom-up bureaucratic accountability.

In tracing the history of the amending process, David Kyvig examines one method offered by the Constitution to Americans for exercising political citizenship and democratic consent. In providing for a less stringent mechanism for amending the Constitution than found in the Articles of Confederation, Kyvig shows that the Founding Fathers gave their approval to a relatively new idea. Prior to the eighteenth century, as Kyvig relates, rulers claimed divine inspiration and considered it a heresy for men to suggest that they could alter governments. By the time of the American Revolution, political theorists and politicians no longer accepted this view of government. By 1787 eight state constitutions reflected the new politics by providing a method for amendments. Although the Founders embarked on a new direction, they acted cautiously. The Constitution required three-fourths of the states to ratify an amendment coming out of Congress. As a result the Constitution has been very difficult to amend, as evidenced by the fact that there have been only twenty-six amendments in almost two hundred years of American constitutional history. In comparison to some contributors to this volume, who fear constitutionalizing policy issues, Kyvig is more optimistic about the Constitution's capacity to withstand such pressure. He acknowledges that the Prohibition Amendment damaged confidence in the amending process, but emphasizes that amendments abolishing slavery, protecting civil rights, and expanding suffrage have stood the test of time. Kyvig concludes by urging Americans to approach the amending process with care. If a mistake is made, however, his survey suggests that unwise amendments can be repealed or be modified by interpretation.

DAVID E. KYVIG*

Alternative to Revolution: Two Hundred Years of Constitutional Amending

How remarkable it is for the United States to observe the two hundredth anniversary of the creation of its Constitution. The American people can celebrate the fact that the nation still operates under a charter of government rights, responsibilities, and structures drawn up when animals provided the fastest transportation and greatest power; when farming employed the vast majority of the population; when the three greatest urban centers in the country, New York, Philadelphia, and Boston, contained 49,000, 28,000, and 18,000 people respectively; when the distance from foreign nations and threats could be measured in weeks or months; when the latest military innovation, the rifle, was only

*The author would like to thank the American Council of Learned Societies, Project '87 of the American Historical Association and the American Political Science Association, and the University of Akron faculty research committee for their support of the research project upon which this essay is based.

beginning to replace the smooth-bore musket; and when governments in Britain, France, Russia, China, Japan, and other states were headed by hereditary monarchies. The United States, in other words, can celebrate the survival of an eighteenth-century scheme of government into a twentieth-century world so radically different from their own that the Founding Fathers could scarcely have imagined it.

The American Constitution has survived far longer than its creators could have anticipated. It has endured in part because people ceased to think of it as merely a set of operating rules for the conduct of the public's affairs. They began instead to regard it as an inspired work of political genius and the embodiment of timeless ideals. For the most part it gained this status after the Civil War, viewed by many as principally a heroic defense and bloody vindication of the Constitution. No longer considered merely a frame of government, it came to be treated as the sanctified embodiment of immutable principles, a hallowed document worthy of civic worship—a latter-day secular version of the Ten Commandments, with the drafters a committee version of Moses. Americans endlessly quoted British Prime Minister William Gladstone's praise of the Constitution: "The most wonderful work ever struck off at a given time by the brain and purpose of man."

The Constitution's longevity can also in large part be attributed to its very vagueness. Because the Founding Fathers made its provisions so broad and general, the courts, the Congress, and the executive could interpret it in such a fashion as to legitimatize innovations in governance. When, for instance, the Civil War affirmed central national authority distinctively different from the state-national balance struck by the Founding Fathers, justification for the new order was sought and supplied from the original Constitution. Later, in the twentieth century, the original list of Presidential duties could be claimed as sufficient basis for broader and greater exercise of executive authority. Each branch of government could find constitutional validation as it adapted to meet new and unexpected circumstances.

To a perhaps lesser, but nevertheless still critical extent, the Constitution has survived for two centuries because it could be amended. Formal changes in the government's charter could be made by a method which bore the endorsement of those revered Founding Fathers. At various pivotal moments in the nation's history, the Constitution might have shattered if it had been unable to bend before the demands of reform (one thinks particularly of the initial state ratification debates, the Civil War, and the Progressive era). The power of amendment gave the Constitution the flexibility required to resolve tensions. Furthermore, the promise of permanence associated with the installation of reforms in the Constitution itself helped persuade crusaders for change that their victory was complete and secure. In reflecting upon the longevity of the American charter of government, therefore, it is well to consider its often overlooked or misunderstood amendment feature.

Any consideration of amendments must begin with an examination of what the Founding Fathers had in mind in drafting Article V, the Constitution's amending provision. Indeed, it can be said that the 1787 Constitution owes its very existence to the failure of its predecessor, the Articles of Confederation, to contain an adequate amendment mechanism. After only a few years, the Articles were found wanting, and demands for change arose. To alter the Articles of Confederation, however, required the approval of every state. In drawing up the Articles in 1776–77, the second Continental Congress wanted to be certain that liberty was safeguarded, that a central national government could not acquire too much power. Therefore, the Congress defined the powers of government narrowly and made changing the Articles exceedingly difficult. The Philadelphia Convention of 1787, ostensibly called to revise the Articles, instead took the radical step of disregarding them altogether. The delegates decided that the prevailing requirement of unanimous state approval would make revision too difficult. The necessity to compromise would be too limiting. The Founding Fathers therefore proposed different, less stringent terms for the acceptance of the new Constitution and for its further amendment. Indeed, it is this overriding of the Articles more than any other facet of its law making that earns the Philadelphia Convention of 1787 the label "revolutionary."

Formal prearrangement for altering the fundamental charter of government was a new idea in the eighteenth century. Governments of an earlier day claimed divine inspiration, sanction, and guidance. To suggest a plan which openly anticipated that those governments would not function perfectly and that mere mortals would need to make organic changes in their structure and authority would have been outright heresy. None of England's seventeenth-century Cromwellian constitutions, for instance, provided for amendment. Among American colonial charters, only William Penn's Pennsylvania Frame of Government of 1682 contained even an oblique and negative reference to altering the terms of government.

Not until the era of the American Revolution did the idea start to take hold that governmental charters were never perfect and must be capable of formal modification from time to time if they were to avoid being simply disregarded as conditions changed. Post-Independence

American state constitutions began to contain provisions for their own revision. By 1787 eight state charters contained amendment provisions, with three giving the power to the legislatures and five to state conventions.

Delegates to the Philadelphia Convention discussed the desirability of an amending provision early in their deliberations. When Edmund Randolph first presented Virginia's plan for a federal union, he included a call for an amending procedure. Virginia delegate George Mason called attention to the American Revolution's principle that governments were founded by the people and thus could legitimately be altered or abolished by them. He asserted that "Amendments therefore, will be necessary and it will be better to provide for them, in an easy, regular and Constitutional way than to trust to chance and violence." Alexander Hamilton agreed that "an easy mode should be established for supplying defects which will probably appear in the New System."

Problems arose, however, over the method of amendment. The delegates showed no enthusiasm for the English system of allowing Parliament to make changes in the framework of government in the same manner and by the same majorities as used in approving ordinary legislation. Such a system appeared too unstable and sensitive to a temporary majority or whim. Constitutional change in the emerging U.S. federal system should require, the Founders thought, broader participation and a greater degree of agreement, a higher level of consensus.

The drafters first considered a plan which would obligate Congress to call a constitutional convention at the request of two-thirds of the states. Delegates were determined to avoid placing the power of amendment exclusively in the hands of the national legislature. Some thought that the national legislature should not be involved in the process at all. George Mason argued that requiring the consent of Congress to an amendment would be improper. If Congress found a way to abuse its power, that body would naturally refuse to agree to corrective action at its own expense. "The opportunity for such an abuse may be the fault of the Constitution, calling for amendment," Mason reasoned.

On September 10, 1787, near the end of the Philadelphia Convention, delegates finally hammered out the details of an amending provision. After securing the right of two-thirds of the states to initiate the amending process by obligating Congress to call a national constitutional convention at their request, the Framers were willing to grant Congress nonexclusive power to propose amendments as well. In any case, they saw state approval of all amendments, however initiated, as essential. A proposal to require ratification by two-thirds of the states was rejected on a six-to-five vote, but when the requirement was raised to approval by three-fourths of the states, it passed unanimously.

Constitutional change would have been easier, of course, had the lower two-thirds ratification standard been endorsed. For example, the Equal Rights Amendment would have taken effect when the thirty-fourth state ratified in 1975. But although they had rejected the unanimous consent standard of the Articles of Confederation, the Founding Fathers were determined that amendments not be adopted without extremely wide support. By setting the standard at three-fourths, they were insisting upon an even greater degree of state approval to alter the Constitution than the nine-thirteenths they agreed would be sufficient to put it into effect initially. Minority positions were to be protected until a very broad consensus among the states had been achieved in favor of amendment.

As a last step in defining the amending process, the Philadelphia Convention approved a provision offered by James Madison and seconded by Alexander Hamilton that states might ratify amendments either by legislative action or through conventions. Congress could choose between the two methods without restriction. This provision was apparently slipped into Article V at the last moment without much discussion. In presenting the alternatives of legislative ratification or action by specially elected convention delegates, the Founding Fathers were tempering their usual preference for representative government and making possible a ratification method which, as it turned out, would prove to be much closer to direct democracy.

The existence of the amending provision helped insure the acceptance of the new Constitution. At one time or another as each state debated the proposed charter, critics raised objections to practically every one of its provisions. Defenders of the Constitution offered reassurance by pointing to Article V. In the North Carolina ratifying convention, for instance, James Iredell soothed fears by saying, "There is a remedy in the system itself for its own fallibility, so that alterations can without difficulty be made, agreeable to the general sense of the people." In fact, the promise of prompt amendment to remedy the most serious objection to the Constitution, the absence within it of a bill of rights, proved crucial to the Federalist victory in several state conventions.

The demand for immediate addition of a bill of rights forced the first Congress to face one question not addressed by Article V: Where should amendments be placed in the Constitution? When James Madison introduced a series of amendments, he proposed that they be woven into the charter at appropriate places. Roger Sherman of Connecticut and others protested any alteration of the original text and argued for adding amendments as supplements. Sherman's proposal prevailed, setting a precedent which has been followed ever since and fostering the image of the original Constitution as sacrosanct. Furthermore, with amendments treated as supplements, no obligation existed for their proponents to remove or clarify possibly contradictory constitutional language. On the contrary, the need would arise for the Supreme Court to determine which of the Constitution's provisions applied.

A major concern of the Founding Fathers was that amendment not be made too difficult, as it had been under the Articles of Confederation. By the start of the twentieth century, however, this appeared very much the case. Of the fifteen amendments adopted before 1900, twelve had come during the first years of putting the federal government in operation. The Bill of Rights, the first ten, had been adopted within two years of the ratification of the Constitution. The Eleventh Amendment followed in 1795 and the Twelfth in 1804. Since then, only three more amendments had been adopted, all during a five-year period at the close of the Civil War. Many politicians and political observers had come to believe, therefore, that amendment was impossible except under extraordinary circumstances.

Early in the twentieth century, however, a stream of amendments began to win approval. The stream was not large, but it was rather steady. Dealing with a variety of subjects and drawing on different bases of support, these twentieth-century amendments demonstrated that the Founding Fathers' intention could be realized: the Constitution could be amended, not easily, but successfully. In the course of the adoption of these amendments, more would be learned about the amending process itself.

In the decade before 1920 came four amendments which implemented major goals sought by Progressive reformers: a graduated federal income tax, direct popular election of U.S. senators, woman suffrage, and national prohibition of alcoholic beverages. In order to implement a direct tax on personal income, constitutional change was necessary after the Supreme Court declared such a system of taxation unconstitutional in 1895. Specific provisions of the Constitution allowing state legislatures to choose senators and to define the franchise had to be overturned if national policies of direct election and female voting rights were to prevail. Adoption of the prohibition amendment, in itself an effort to gain a permanent national solution to the long-standing dilemma of alcoholic beverages, proved particularly interesting in terms of the amending process.

Ohio Senator Warren G. Harding wished neither to see liquor

abolished nor to lose the votes of Anti-Saloon League and Women's Christian Temperance Union supporters. Believing that only the two dozen states which had adopted statewide liquor restrictions were prepared to ratify a national prohibition amendment in the foreseeable future, he proposed a plan whereby he and others would vote for the amendment in Congress provided there was a seven-year time limit on ratification. He figured that they could thereby appear to support the amendment, while at the same time effectively killing it. To Harding's surprise and horror, it took only thirteen months for more than the required thirty-six states to ratify the Eighteenth Amendment.

Since then, seven-year time limits have frequently been attached to amendment proposals, though never to such ironic effect. A 1938 Supreme Court case addressed the question of how long a proposed amendment remained alive if Congress did not place a specific time limit on ratification. In *Coleman* v. *Miller* the Court held that Article V spoke solely of the power to ratify amendments, saying nothing about previous rejection or time limits. Suggesting that ratification was like a ratchet wheel, capable of turning freely only in one direction, and that a state legislature's rejection of an amendment did not bar it from subsequently ratifying, the Court held that the validity of ratification was ultimately not a legal question, but a political question to be determined by Congress. The 1924 Child Labor Amendment still seemed alive after thirteen years, since the conditions of labor which gave rise to the proposal had not changed and since twenty-two states had decided to ratify the amendment between 1933 and 1937. But in the absence of a specific time limit, Congress, not the Court, must decide whether a reasonable time for ratification has expired.

National prohibition raised other questions about the amending process as well. Anticipating congressional submission of prohibition and other amendment proposals, the state of Ohio had adopted a law allowing public referendums on their ratification. When the Ohio legislature overwhelmingly ratified the prohibition amendment in 1919, citizens petitioned for such a referendum. In November 1919, Ohio voters rejected national prohibition, if only by the slender margin of 479 votes out of a million cast. Ohio's was the only ratification referendum held in 1919, but others were in prospect, as opponents of not only the Eighteenth but also the Nineteenth Amendment sought to overturn legislative ratifications.

The U.S. Supreme Court quickly rejected the Ohio referendum in *Hawke* v. *Smith* (1920). The Court declared that Article V gave Congress sole power to choose the means of ratification, saying, "The determination of the method of ratification is the exercise of a national power specifically granted by the Constitution, and is limited to two methods, by action of the legislatures of three-fourths of the States, or conventions in a like number of States." The Court, dismissing the argument that referendums were part of the legislative process, held that the Ohio referendum had no effect. The Eighteenth Amendment was upheld, and other proposed referendums on the Eighteenth and Nineteenth Amendments were never conducted. But a widespread public feeling arose that national prohibition had been put over by special-interest-dominated legislatures against the will of a democratic majority.

The Supreme Court continued to rule in support of national prohibition throughout the 1920s. Among other things, it approved expanded police powers of search and seizure, allowed both state and federal governments to punish a single liquor violation (a system which appeared to some as constituting double jeopardy), and permitted police wiretapping of telephones. Under the leadership of conservative Chief Justice William Howard Taft, the Court clearly felt obligated to take every possible step to insure the success of the Constitution's new provision— even when to do so led the government into unfamiliar, perhaps even dangerous territory.

The widespread and highly visible disregard for prohibition, together with the implications of the law's enforcement, alarmed and alienated some Americans who had initially thought a national ban on liquor was a good idea. For several years, however, prohibition's critics despaired of remedying the situation. After all, no amendment had ever been repealed. To do so required a massive shift of support to reverse the margin of a two-thirds congressional vote and a three-fourths state ratification. Quite understandably, most people accepted the assessment of one of prohibition's Senate sponsors: "There is as much chance of repealing the Eighteenth Amendment as there is for a hummingbird to fly to the planet Mars with the Washington Monument tied to its tail."

Nevertheless, opposition to national prohibition continued to increase. The 1932 Democratic Party platform called for the amendment's repeal. Viewing the Democrats' sweeping election victory as a mandate to end the liquor ban, Congress voted in February 1933 for a new amendment to abolish the Eighteenth.

Leading antiprohibitionists, recalling the 1919 Ohio episode, insisted that Congress not send the repeal amendment to state legislatures for ratification. Repeal advocates successfully argued that the new amendment should be submitted to state conventions so that in selecting delegates the public could decide the liquor issue. While each state set the rules for its own convention, in most states voters were provided a simple choice between one statewide slate of wet convention delegates and one slate of drys. Nationwide, 73 percent of those voting preferred the wet slates. Of the thirty-eight states to vote in 1933, only South Carolina rejected repeal. The conventions themselves quickly confirmed the public choice. No convention took more than a day, and New Hampshire's lasted a mere seventeen minutes. By December 5, 1933, nine and one-half months after Congress approved the new Twenty-first Amendment, the entire ratification process had been completed. This time, no one argued that the outcome did not reflect the popular will.

Given the speed, relative ease, and unquestioned democracy of convention ratification, it is noteworthy that 1933 marked the only use of this method since the original Constitution was approved by state conventions in the 1780s. In recent decades, the procedure has not even been given serious consideration. When, for instance, the Equal Rights Amendment won congressional approval in 1973, its Senate sponsor assumed that the greatest hurdle had been cleared and that state approval would follow automatically. No thought was given to requiring convention ratification, thereby taking the matter out of the hands of state legislatures and giving the public a direct voice in deciding the issue. The heavy majority of public support for the measure which opinion polls repeatedly indicated then existed was not called into play. One can only speculate, therefore, what the results of convention delegate elections might have been. It seems worth noting, however, that the organized opposition to the ERA, which helped stall legislative ratification three states short of the necessary thirty-eight approvals, did not fully emerge until 1975, long after a convention ratification process would likely have run its course.

The national prohibition episode made politicians cautious about further constitutional amendments, but not unwilling to consider them. After the Supreme Court twice blocked congressional efforts to prohibit child labor, an amendment granting Congress such power was submitted to the states in 1924. It encountered stiff resistance, but eventually won twenty-eight state ratifications. The amendment died only when it became clear in 1938 that the Court's thinking had changed enough to permit Congress to accomplish its purpose through the passage of ordinary legislation, the Fair Labor Standards Act.

Amendments were adopted in 1933 to transfer authority to a new President and Congress in the January rather than the March after an election (reducing the "lame duck" period by six weeks) and in 1951 to limit a President to two terms (which Republicans championed after losing four elections to Franklin Roosevelt, but soon came to regret when Dwight Eisenhower was barred from a third term). Furthermore, in the early 1950s Congress gave serious consideration to a proposed amendment which would have curtailed Presidential power to enter into international executive agreements without Senate approval. After a heated discussion of Presidential authority in foreign affairs, this so-called Bricker Amendment failed by one vote to achieve the necessary two-thirds approval from the Senate.

By the 1960s, amendment was coming to be viewed as a normal and manageable, if still infrequently used, part of the law-making process. When civil rights developments and the death of John Kennedy suggested the need for changes in suffrage and Presidential succession arrangements, amendment was regarded as a practical solution. The prompt and seemingly easy adoption of amendments allowing the District of Columbia to participate in Presidential elections (1961), outlawing poll taxes (1964), and establishing a new system of Presidential succession and Vice-Presidential replacement (1967) seemed to dispel doubts about the workability of amendment procedures.

A surge of confidence in the amending process as a means of changing both laws and social attitudes was evident, especially among political liberals, in two separate episodes in the early 1970s. Concern about the disdain of Vietnam-era youth for the American political process generated enthusiasm for encouraging their participation by lowering the voting age from twenty-one to eighteen. Among legislators, support grew for an eighteen-year-old suffrage amendment. A Supreme Court decision supporting eighteen-year-old voting in federal elections and the specter of differing state and federal suffrage requirements led Congress to ignore the decisive rejection of lower voting ages in seven of eight state referendums on such proposals in 1970. Early in 1971, an eighteen-year-old suffrage amendment was rushed through Congress. Its ratification by thirty-eight state legislatures followed in only one hundred days.

The next year, 1972, Congress passed an amendment to insure equal rights for women. This proposal had been around since 1923, but the sudden growth of congressional support was linked to the surge of public interest since the mid-1960s in full legal equality for women. Within twenty-three months, the Equal Rights Amendment won ratification in thirty-three states, but then the process slowed. Two more states added their support by 1977, but they were the last to ratify. Even a controversial modification of its joint resolution proposing the amendment—by which Congress extended the original seven-year time limit on ratification by three years, to 1982—could not generate the necessary thirty-eight state endorsements. Four state legislatures even reconsidered their initial action and voted to rescind their ratification of the amendment. It seems doubtful, on the basis of their earlier interpretations of Article V, that either Congress or the Supreme Court would have held these rescissions to be valid, but neither body had to face this interesting and problematical question since the required three-fourths of the states never ratified the ERA.

The ERA episode served as a dramatic reminder that state approval of constitutional amendments is not automatic, despite a two-thirds Congressional endorsement and public opinion polls showing a substantial majority of popular approval. States retain enormous power in the amending process. A handful of states, even those most sparsely populated, can block ratification. In the 1980 census, the combined population of the thirteen smallest states was 9,800,000, or 4.3 percent of America's 226,500,000 people. Either directly or through the actions of their legislative representatives, a bare majority in those states—slightly more than 2 percent of the nation's population—could conceivably prevent an amendment's adoption. In the case of the ERA, the fifteen nonratifying states contained 28 percent of the U.S. population, a much more sizeable minority, but a distinct minority nonetheless.

While ERA advocates called the support which the amendment received a sure sign of a national preference for equal treatment of women, opponents claimed that the amendment's defeat reflected continued commitment to traditional values. Proponents and detractors alike regarded the amendment as a symbol well worth fighting over, both before and after the battle. Although ERA supporters might have a more logically sound interpretation of the voting, their adversaries found plenty of solace in the failure of the amendment to obtain the degree of national consensus required by the Founding Fathers.

In recent years, other interest groups, in a quest to place symbols of their beliefs in the Constitution, have also sought amendments. These efforts often represented responses to congressional or Supreme Court action to which the group objected. Such feelings have led to proposals for amendments to require a balanced federal budget, permit school prayer, prevent legal abortions, and end imposed racial integration through school busing. The very obstacles to amendment allow the discontented to keep preaching the need for their proposal without having to face the consequences of success. The repeated calls for a balanced budget amendment, for example, rest on the assumption that this would force federal spending cuts, although such an amendment might just as plausibly compel tax increases.

As this is being written in December 1984, the United States faces a situation in which thirty-two states have requested a constitutional convention to consider a balanced budget amendment. Many observers expect that two more states will join the call and that the convention will be held. Many express concern that, like the 1787 Philadelphia Convention, such a convention could not be held to a narrow agenda but would propose sweeping and radical changes in the American political system. Some worry that, if it came to that, Americans would not be sufficiently tolerant to renew the Bill of Rights. What seems likely? A strong, if rather legalistic argument contends that state requests for a convention have been neither identical in their language nor closely timed in their adoption; thus, Congress could legitimately ignore them. Congress would be perhaps more inclined to propose an amendment of its own design than to either dismiss the calls or allow an uncontrollable convention to be held.

Questions about the wisdom of an actual balanced budget amendment—as opposed to symbolic calls for consideration of the idea in order to discourage government spending—make it doubtful, though hardly impossible, that thirty-eight states would ratify such a measure. If a balanced budget amendment were to be adopted, however, other efforts to amend the Constitution would be likely to follow. In contemplating such a possibility, we might draw certain observations from this brief review of the history of constitutional amending:

1. The amending article has thus far been an important component of the success of the constitutional system. It has permitted enough change to mollify extreme discontent. At the same time, it has proven sufficiently resistant to change to insure a great degree of stability in American governmental arrangements.

2. Given the Founding Fathers' intent to make amending difficult, the odds against any proposal succeeding are rather long, though not insurmountable. Of the more than five thousand proposals for amendment introduced in Congress since 1789, only thirty-three have obtained two-thirds congressional approval. Of these, twenty-six have been ratified (one of those repealing another), six have failed, and one (granting the District of Columbia voting representatives in the Senate and House of Representatives) is still pending before the states.

3. Although constitutional provisions ostensibly deal only with the powers and procedures of the federal government, various innovations, from the 1790s to the 1960s, have brought about important policy changes. Amendments abolishing slavery, imposing taxes in proportion to wealth, prohibiting alcoholic beverages, and expanding the suffrage all

had immediate and profound impact. Amendments, in other words, do offer a means of fundamentally altering the policies as well as the procedures of American government.

4. Amendments, once adopted, are both powerful and inflexible. The Supreme Court regards them as directives which it must respect; witness the prohibition episode. The Court reconsiders other constitutional provisions and sometimes modifies its interpretation of them in light of a new amendment. The reform or repeal of amendments is far more difficult than the alteration of ordinary legislation found to be unsatisfactory. Yet, it is not impossible to put second thoughts into effect, to abolish provisions which have come to be thought unwise. The Civil War amendments ended the constitutional protection of slavery. Prohibition repeal also overturned prior policy. The Constitution can be reversed. Avoiding imprudent amendments is clearly best, but if they are adopted, they do not create a hopeless situation.

5. The symbolism of an amendment, once it has gained the required approval, can encourage the political process to set off in new directions on a broad front. The wave of Progressive-era amendments provides one example of this phenomenon, the burst of amendments during the 1960s another. The impact of an amendment can, therefore, be great and unexpected, extending far beyond the subject matter of the amendment itself.

In sum, amending provides the opportunity to modify the Constitution so as to prolong the effectiveness of our two-hundred-year-old charter and avoid its wholesale abandonment. This is as the Founding Fathers intended. At the same time, however, amending poses risks. The opportunity to make unwise decisions is, of course, a necessary aspect of the right of free choice. But in the case of constitutional change, the consequences of imprudence can be extremely wide ranging and long lasting. Treating every amendment proposal with utmost seriousness and considering its consequences very carefully is the responsibility of each generation of Americans to those who will live under the Constitution in the years to follow.

CONTEMPORARY
CONSTITUTIONAL
TENSIONS

Today, according to Harvey Mansfield, the Constitution is in trouble. His evidence for this claim is that Americans no longer enthusiastically celebrate their Constitution and regardless of their political persuasion seem determined to amend it. He accounts for this development by arguing that it is the result of a fundamental change in the American view of the Constitution over the past two hundred years. Specifically, Americans have transformed the Constitution into an instrument of change rather than maintaining it as a form of government. Mansfield traces this new conception of the Constitution to a novel redefinition of constitutional rights in the twentieth century. Mansfield contends that, unlike eighteenth-century Americans, who sought the right to act without government interference, modern Americans believe the Constitution guarantees them the right to government assistance. In pursuing this new vision of the Constitution, Mansfield believes that Americans have departed from the Framers in two other important ways. First, rather than resting on the reasoned judgment of the people, law now rests on the demands of factious majorities. If consent, which Mansfield considers the most important American right, is not properly established, law and policy are and will remain whatever is convenient for those in government. Second, Mansfield criticizes government, especially the judiciary, for responding to these factions by satisfying their passions, in a bid for popularity, rather than appealing to their reason. He notes that there has been, ironically, an inverse relationship between government's desire to please and its popularity. The only alternative to this constitutional dilemma, Mansfield concludes, is for people to voluntarily make fewer demands on an overburdened Constitution and for government to summon up enough courage to temper the passion of the people.

HARVEY C. MANSFIELD, JR.

Our Constitution Then and Now

As the Constitution's bicentenary approaches, we find that Americans no longer speak of their Constitution as frequently and as enthusiastically as they once did. Once notorious for reciting without any prompting the excellences of our Constitution, we no longer praise it as we used to. Conservatives have a series of constitutional amendments they seem to favor more than the Constitution itself. They believe that the Constitution has been abused and perverted by a liberal judiciary, but they seem to have lost interest in what the Constitution might embody when not mistreated. Liberals, for their part, have been pushing for one amendment, the ERA, but mostly they have profited from the discovery by the judiciary of several new rights, hitherto unknown, such as the rights to abortion, to self-expression, and to an equal weighting of one's vote. Liberals are fearful that if they leave the Constitution as it is, it will become out-of-date. They seem to have lost any sense that a Constitution should embody principles, procedures, and institutions that do not go out-of-date.

Without entering into the merits of these proposals, we can take note of their common characteristic. The social movements of our day, both right and left, regard the Constitution not as a *form of government* but as a *means of getting what they want.* They both seem to believe, therefore, that popular government is a means of getting the people what they want. If the Constitution has this effect, follow it; if it does not, then amend it—either in the regular way or by judicial, executive, or congressional reinterpretation.

What does it mean to consider the Constitution as a form of government? This, I will argue, is the intent of the Framers of the Constitution, as it is set forth most authoritatively in *The Federalist.* There, it is explained that the American Constitution is popular government, but of a new kind—it is an "experiment." An experiment is needed because all previous popular government outside America had failed (as we learn from *The Federalist* Nos. 9, 10, 14) when the majority of the people behaved tyranically as a faction hostile to the rights of others or to the interest of the community. The problem of majority faction—for an example we have only to think of slavery in America—is what we forget when we suppose that popular government is a means for getting the people what they want.

Two new remedies for the general failure of popular government were found, according to *The Federalist,* and put into our Constitution. These were the principle of representation, by which government is delegated to a small number elected by the rest, and the idea of an extensive republic, in which the imperial size that had previously been thought fatal to a republic is deliberately embraced as a means of its salvation. If you "extend the sphere" or "enlarge the orbit," you include many more "fit characters" to serve as representatives, who are more likely to be elected from large constituencies; most important, you take in a greater variety of parties and interests, that are less likely to combine in a majority faction than a homogeneous majority would be.

This "wholly popular government" is derived in all its parts from the people, on the one hand—but on the other, being wholly representative, it never allows the people to rule directly. In *The Federalist* No. 49, James Madison advises against a proposal by his friend Thomas Jefferson for an appeal to a convention of the people whenever breaches of the Constitution might occur. Madison objects that government that has its origin in the people cannot recur to the people if it is to maintain its authority over the people. Although—indeed, *because*—the Constitution must originate in the people, it must be elevated above the people if they are to respect it. Popular government needs not only legitimacy or credibility, as we would say today, but "veneration" and "a reverence for the laws." To recur to the people on the occasion of a breach of the Constitution would invite a partisan quarrel followed by a partisan decision. It would encourage the will or the passion of the people to dominate. But, Madison says, it is the *reason* of the public alone that ought to control and regulate the government. The passions ought to be controlled and regulated *by* the government. Popular government cannot dispense with the necessity of keeping reason paramount over the passions.

Thus, in the new Constitution there were two other innovations besides representation and extensive size. Although we take them for granted today, they were not proclaimed as innovations in *The Federalist* because they were generally thought to be undemocratic. These features are a strong executive branch and judicial review. In considering each of these, *The Federalist* maintains that in popular government the reason, not the passions, of the people ought to prevail. A strong, energetic executive is needed for sound administration of the government and for developing long-term plans to direct it. The people are not merely to be *led*, as we would say now; they are to be *directed*. "Leadership" is a pejorative term reserved for demagogues who try to ride to power on popular passions. Similarly, judicial review of breaches of the Constitution is justified because judges will not have "too great a disposition to consult popularity" (*The Federalist* No. 78). Instead, they will consult "the intention of the people" as it is revealed in the Constitution and the laws. Judges must have "firmness and independence" so that they can help ensure that popular government is exercised not by popular will alone but through the rule of law. The separation of powers that we are so familiar with has, indeed, the purpose of dividing power—but not so much to diminish power as to cause it to be prudently and lawfully exercised.

So far I have spoken of the Constitution as a form of government without mentioning *rights*; yet surely the Constitution is intended to secure our rights. To see how it does so, we must distinguish between natural rights and civil rights. Natural rights are the ones on which civil society is founded; civil rights are the ones it secures. Natural rights are to life, liberty, and the pursuit of happiness, according to the Declaration of Independence. They are the rights for the sake of which we establish a Constitution. But the rights actually secured under this Constitution are civil rights, and their hallmark is that you cannot be deprived of them without due process of law. Civil society secures rights precisely by *depriving* of their rights those who violate them, providing, of course, that this deprivation occurs only by due process of law.

Due process of law refers primarily to procedural rights in trials (such as immunity from self-incrimination), but also to the rights of habeas corpus and protections against ex post facto laws and bills of attainder. Ultimately, due process of law depends on the rule of law as it is established in the Constitution understood as a form of government. In this way, the right to due process of law depends on the right of consent, since the Constitution is a form of popular government. The right to consent is our most fundamental right because all other rights are unsafe without it. Without this right, all other rights exist merely at the convenience of the government. When we consider whether governments maintain the human rights of their peoples, we should be concerned with the right of consent above all others. But it also matters very much how the right of consent is established. In our Constitution that right establishes the rule of a majority, to be sure, but (as I have argued) the rule of a *constitutional* majority, not of a factious majority. Since all rights depend on the people's right to consent, all rights depend on the form of government through which they exercise their consent.

It may seem that I have spoken in homilies and have described a perfect Constitution made by perfect men. To the contrary: one reason that the Framers spoke of our Constitution as an "experiment" was that there was no guarantee of success. Despite our high hopes and our best contrivance, popular government may degenerate once again into majority faction. The Framers were not complacent. It is we who take our Constitution for granted, supposing that we can use parts of it for partisan purposes while refusing to live under it as a form of government.

Today, the Constitution, as the framework that stands above and behind government to connect it to the reasoned intention of the people, has almost been lost to sight. Government has come to be equated with bureaucracy and, as such, to be considered too big and too remote. This is the way it looks to both parties: Carter in 1976 and Reagan in 1980 both successfully ran their campaigns against government. They attacked government for having the faults of bureaucracy. The faults have no hidden virtues, for bureaucracy is large but petty, meddlesome but unconcerned, stupid but complex, flighty but inconsistent, and forgetful but inflexible. Our politicians—and we, too—regard government as unreason with the outward manners of reason.

In this view, the main problem for government becomes government itself. Nothing the government has to do is more important than overcoming its own bureaucratic nature. To do this, some believe, government cannot turn to reason and try to make the reason of the American people control their passions, as the Framers did. Too much reliance on reason, they think, is what makes government heavy, cold, and remote; reason in the sense of bureaucratic formalism is precisely the problem rather than the solution. The solution, we seem to believe, has to be a new resort to passion. Government can recover its lost connection to the people by appealing to the passions—in America recently, the passion of compassion. (But less lovely passions are also possible.)

Thus, government, it is supposed, can overcome its unfeeling bureaucratic nature by showing that it cares. Showing compassion makes a direct and informal appeal to the people which is quite different from the formal connections between government and people established in our constitutional system. It is as if all government can and should behave to the people in the manner of a passerby who sees an accident in the street and rushes to see if he can be of any assistance. Our politicians, when they run for office, do not promise to act like the responsible bureaucrat but like the compassionate passerby.

In the mood of compassion, the regular, constitutional departments of government no longer regard their job to be that of controlling the people's passions with their reason. Instead of refining popular feelings by transforming the people's will into a settled intention, they seek to make direct contact with the people. The executive branch, rather than using its constitutional strength to set an unpopular course, looks for popular strength through charisma. Although the Founders spoke of "leaders" pejoratively as demagogues, today everyone looks for executive leadership. In the same vein, Congressmen have increasingly given themselves over to the service of constituents and have become "fixers" for the people when the regular channels do not work, as often happens. The bureaucracy has undertaken the role of ombudsman against itself, as bureaucrats try to show, however clumsily, that they too have hearts.

The greatest change, however, has come in the judiciary. Activism is not confined to the judiciary, but it is concentrated there. What is activism? It is the same aggressive compassion on behalf of the people, to do their bidding—or more often, to do them good—without regard for the integrity of legal or constitutional procedure. The result is not always to reduce the amount of procedure, because the judiciary is as ready to erect new legal obstacles to what it regards as evil as it is eager to circumvent the law when it seems to get in the way of good. The very institution traditionally most attached to the forms of the law and the Constitution now seems the least devoted to them except as instruments of expert, activist manipulation.

Yet it would be unfair to the constitutional branches of the government not to mention the extraconstitutional medium in which they work. That medium, presided over by the "media," relentlessly demands and provides direct contact between the people and their government. It forces government to be charismatic whether it wants to be or not, on pain of being exposed as insensitive bureaucracy. The least departure from the simplistic morality of compassion is punished without compassion. Besides this, government must contend with a plethora of surveys, many originating from the government, which imply that people ought to have what they want and right away.

Somehow, though, the new requirements of exposure do not make government more honest, the new demands for compassion do not make it care, and the new techniques for measuring popularity do not make it more popular. The reason is that our capacity to fool ourselves easily surpasses any advance in technology or social science. The more popular government tries to be, the more unpopular it becomes, because popularity is not a standard any government can live by—even, or especially, a popular government like ours. No government can govern without imposing duties and asking for sacrifices, but duty and sacrifice must be called forth by a higher ideal than popularity.

When government seeks popularity, it seeks more than consent. With the right of consent, the people call government to account and give it scope to govern within the limits of the Constitution, constrained by the need to maintain a constitutional majority. To do this, the people put aside their desire to rule directly but retain, at least in principle, their right of independent judgment. When government seeks to do what is popular, however, it must claim to know what people will consent to in advance of elections. Popularity as determined by surveys becomes a substitute for consent in elections, and we have the paradox of a popular government seeking popularity under which many people do not even bother to vote. The right to consent to government becomes the right to have government do popular things.

Indeed, unnoticed by many Americans and most intellectuals, there has been a general transformation in thinking about rights which is at least partly responsible for our view of the Constitution now. We have turned away from rights of individuals and the people *to do* certain things and begun to believe in rights to *have things done for us* by government. As long as we insist on our right to have the government act for us, we shall have bureaucracy; as soon as we have bureaucracy, it will seek popularity. Our Constitution deserves to be celebrated and admired, but if we are to continue living under it, we must rethink our present understanding of it.

Edwin Yoder joins Harvey Mansfield in lamenting the failure of Americans to view the Constitution as a framework of government containing such important neutral values as due process, liberty, equity, and order. Single-issue interest groups and widespread public ignorance of constitutional values are some reasons cited by Yoder for contemporary constitutional confusion. The passage of two hundred years, in Yoder's view, confirms the wisdom of the Framers' work. Unlike some modern statesmen outside the United States who have produced lengthy constitutions, the Framers wisely avoided grandiose promises and recognized the difficulties of constitutionalizing public policy. Yoder does not shy away from describing the Framers as an elite, although not in the terms of Charles Beard. He sees the Framers as a public-spirited elite, which was succeeded by generations of talented men who have cared for and preserved the Constitution. In preparing his paper Yoder was asked to respond to the question, Is the Constitution mine or yours? His answer is simple: the Constitution belongs to no one group but is a legacy between generations. Yoder concludes that the future viability of the Constitution rests on the ability of Americans to see this and, consequently, to make fewer demands on the government.

EDWIN YODER

My Constitution Or Yours?

My own answer to the question posed for this discussion is "neither." None of us owns the Constitution. As a disciple of Edmund Burke, I see the Constitution as a trust between the generations. We are bound as temporary stewards not to bend it to self-serving or transitory advantage.

From this principle, it follows that "popular perceptions" of the Constitution are of distinctly secondary importance. The Constitution is not a subject of frequent referendum; that seems to me a good thing.

According to a recent poll, some 80 percent of Americans say they favor a constitutional amendment guaranteeing the right of organized prayer in public schools. But here, numbers seem to me unimportant, if not utterly irrelevant. Surgery on the First Amendment, however popular it may seem, is too delicate to be performed by plebiscite.

When I was in college thirty years ago, a survey was contrived to discover the depth of public attachment to the basic principles of the Bill of Rights—a pertinent subject at the time, which was the era of so-called McCarthyism. Without exception, the respondents declared their dedication to the Bill of Rights in principle. But many did not know what rights it guaranteed, because in practical terms they overwhelmingly repudiated them.

Even today—and I suppose eras do not differ much in this—I find surprising gaps in public knowledge of the Constitution. Many associate it with Thomas Jefferson, a confusion doubtless arising from Jefferson's authorship of the Declaration of Independence. How many people in the street today could say whether the idea that "all men are created equal, and endowed by their Creator with certain unalienable rights" is in the Declaration or the Constitution? The casual attitudes toward our basic instruments of government are depressing—a reflection, I suppose, of our failure to teach our own history well, to say nothing of the history of the wider world.

What it comes down to, then, is that the Constitution is inescapably an "elitist" document, to use a term that today carries some negative overtones. In my book, however, this is no condemnation. The Constitution was the work of an elite, less of birth or wealth than of public spirit and talent, the natural "aristoi" of whom Jefferson often spoke. An elite, if you will, has remained its guardian and interpreter; it has done a fair job, too, considering the cruel vicissitudes that have befallen so many nations and political systems over the past two hundred years.

It does not follow, however, that the Constitution was written to serve, or does serve, only the few. Had that been the case, the Constitution of 1787 would long ago have proved insufficiently flexible to accommodate the robust growth of twentieth–century democracy.

The belief that the Constitution is elitist in the negative rather than the positive sense has persisted throughout our history. It was articulated in the state ratifying conventions by the able men calling themsleves, or known to historians as, "Anti-Federalists." In the modern era, in the 1920s, the distinguished historian Charles A. Beard popularized a theory that men of property had written the Constitution primarily as a bulwark of property values. He provided elaborate tables to support the theory that the Constitutional Convention of 1787 had staged a sort of bloodless coup d'etat, by and for the rich.

Most historians today view Beard's famous theory as a period piece which, like most materialist explanations of history and human behavior, rests on very selective evidence. In truth the propertied classes of the 1780s were sharply divided over the virtues of the Constitution, many seeing it as a threat to their wealth, not a reinforcement of it. Indeed, the Beard theory told far less about the origins of the Constitution than about the political climate of Beard's own time. The Progressives, to whom Beard the citizen was devoutly attached (sometimes pulling Beard the historian in tow), believed that a conservative legal system, rooted in the Constitution, was holding back overdue reform. There was some substance to this belief. But the Constitution, or even the Fourteenth Amendment, wasn't the problem. It was a political, not a constitutional, problem. Attitudes needed changing, not constitutional articles.

To be sure, the Progressives were right about one thing: The Constitution was designed to temper and delay change. It explicitly acknowledges that the people are sovereign, not government—and popular sovereignty was a daring idea when the Framers embraced it. They were sufficiently fearful of democratic excess to draw up complicated rules of political procedure. The underlying doctrine was liberal, especially for its time; the structure was conservative. Lord Macaulay, the popular nineteenth century British historian, reflected the Whiggish misconceptions of the day when he declared it "all sail and no anchor"— a spectacular misjudgment. Many have found it the reverse.

Our topic leads me to still another fundamental reflection. The Constitution of the United States is now among the oldest written constitutions still in force, if not the very oldest. Its nearly two-hundred-year lifespan is the more remarkable when you consider that most constitutions have not been durable. Most constitutions (like most nation-states) are very new, post–World War II or later; many are so prolix, so catalog-like in their guarantees, that the human mind can hardly master them, even in a lifetime of study. Our own, at some seven thousand words, is not simple. Yet its main lines may be grasped rather easily at a reading.

The contrast suggests a vital point. The reason why many recent constitutions are prolix is that they take an expansive view of the obligations of government. Many of them, for instance, incorporate, at one gulp, the U.N.'s Universal Declaration of Human Rights and make other encyclopedic pledges and promises. But since government is always flawed, many of these high-minded pledges are fated to be mere wallpapering. The more grandiose the promises, the farther the performance is likely to fall short of them. Many recent constitutions, for example, guarantee a human right to work, even as the U. S. Constitution guarantees rights of speech, press, assembly, and religion. Obviously it is easier to place limits on what government may do than to guarantee what it will do. That is where more recent conceptions of constitutionalism stumble and flounder. Indeed, a title to a job for everyone who wants to work is an ideal and an obligation in American statutory law. But it is not a constitutional right, and trying to declare it as such is an invitation to disillusionment and cynicism.

From time to time—and ours may be such an age—Americans grow restless with the modesty of our Constitution and long for something a bit racier—a bit longer on the sort of modern promises and entitlements at which the Brazilian and Argentinian constitutions beat ours all hollow.

Underlying this impulse, there is a certain failure to understand the teachings of historical experience. The Framers of the U. S. Constitution omitted social and economic policy from the document for both practical and philosophical reasons.

Nonetheless, issues of policy do occasionally become constitutional battlegrounds. Slavery, the income tax, the consumption of alcoholic beverages, and more recently, the chronic insolvency of the Treasury, are familiar examples. But please note that the turmoil and confusion that have usually marked the incursion of social and economic policy into the constitutional arena dramatically demonstrate why such incursions are wisely avoided. Often enough—the fiasco of the Eighteenth Amendment is the classic example—an attempt to make policy constitutional causes more trouble than it cures.

There are historians who believe that the Civil War might have been prevented but for the "constitutionalization" of the issue of slavery extension between 1854 and 1857. I am not sure they are right, but whether they are right or not, the consequences of this development were catastrophic.

Less explosive, though similar in some ways, was the growing belief that measures taken to revive business prosperity during the Great Depression of the 1930s threatened constitutional values. By 1935 or so, President Roosevelt and the Congress had reached accord on the need for an experimental program aimed at economic recovery. But the Supreme Court majority of that day remained wedded to the view that certain economic doctrines had been embedded in the Constitution: "sanctity of contract," for example. Invoking these doctrines, the Court precipitated a crisis by blocking a number of congressional policies and frustrating the President's popular mandate for experiment. At issue here, as we can now so plainly see, were not systemic issues but issues of policy. The Court was levering proximate social and economic arrangements into ultimate issues. Instead of guarding the rules, it sought to shape the outcome of the game. The impasse was abruptly broken by retirement, and the Court withdrew—none too soon—from an attempt to regulate economic life under the mystique of "substantive due process." Today, we are surprised to recall that many eminent judges and scholars of that time saw issues of constitutional dimension in farm price manipulations or legislative regulation of the gold content of the dollar.

The capacity of the Constitution to shed the barnacles of substantive due process is, to my mind, a vindication of the wisdom of the Framers—specifically, their wisdom in regarding economic and social issues as political, not constitutional. What so many of the slick latest model constitutions view as entitlements, we usually view as political questions, to be settled to the rough satisfaction of each generation by voting and debate.

But are we not in some danger of drifting away from this fundamental of American constitutionalism? I see some warning signals.

One notable trend today is what one might call, not very originally, the atomization of American society. We are becoming a nation of claimants. Far more than in the past, or so it seems, Americans are sensitive to ethnic, social, class, racial, and other group distinctions—and the claims that flow so readily from them. The occasion for this trend is not, or is not usually admitted to be, conflict or strife. It is, rather, the popular idea of group entitlements—rights that belong to us not as persons or individuals, but as members of some group.

A former colleague of mine, Anne Crutcher, once summed up the idea brilliantly: *E pluribus plus*—a witty pun on the national motto. Not "one from many," but "more from many." She was summarizing an interesting development—the addition to the 1980 census forms of questions about ethnic background. For the first time Americans were asked to identify themselves by ethnic origin: a minor but significant symptom of the new atomization.

At an earlier time in our history, all this bother about group rights and group claims would have been regarded as discreditable, going against the American ideal of the melting pot. "Hyphenated Americanism," as Theodore Roosevelt called it, was frowned upon. But the melting pot ideal has fallen, at least temporarily, into some disfavor—perhaps because it melted some more easily than others. Now it is an accepted practice to assert rights and claims not as citizens or individuals but as members of various unmeltable groups. My Constitution or yours? You take your part, and I'll take mine.

Thus the self-consciousness of youth, at first a function of mere numbers as the "Baby Boom" generation came of age, helped get the vote (rarely exercised) for eighteen-year-olds. The assertiveness of women as women, blacks as blacks, Hispanics as Hispanics, Asians as Asians, or Aleuts as Aleuts is historically understandable; but the outcome of all this scrambling is yet to be seen. Whether the outcome is wholesome or not, this group-consciousness can hardly fail to have a decisive effect on our view of the Constitution, what we owe it and what it owes us. It will no doubt influence "popular perceptions" of the Constitution. For good or for ill?

If the new vogue of group-based rights and claims fosters an assertive parochialism, a tendency to see the Constitution as a grab bag of promises and entitlements rather than as a modest charter of liberty and self-government, it could do great harm. Our political parties, once an inducement to coalition politics, have been enfeebled by television and other forces. Coalitions are harder to form and hold together, surely one reason why so many Americans are playing "single-issue" politics. Occasionally, our basic institutions seem almost too feeble to reach principled, timely, and effective resolutions of urgent problems—problems like the solvency of Social Security, or the integrity of the federal budget. The "E pluribus plus" idea is part of the problem, though certainly not all of it.

We know from the sad experience of some Third World and Latin American nations that the more numerous and exalted the expectations encouraged by a constitution, the greater the room for—indeed, the certainty of—disappointment, and after disappointment, cynicism is bound to follow.

Those who wrote the Constitution of the United States viewed it primarily as a rule book. It enshrined and promoted wholesome, even noble, values. But the crucial and central values are procedural and neutral: order, continuity, liberty, and equity. A good constitution, the Framers thought, should declare the rules of the game and tell us how the players qualify to play it. But, except for the grand generalities of the Preamble ("the general welfare"), it does not attempt to draw a blueprint for society. Had it done so, it would have been a blueprint that cramped succeeding generations, weighing them down with the dead hand of the past.

For the sometimes frustrating way in which the Constitution slows and tempers change, even desirable change, it compensates with a wonderful tensile strength. Its recent monument is the great revolution in civil rights. It is only 88 years since "separate but equal" was declared to be the rule of the Fourteenth Amendment and only 127 since the egregious *Dred Scott* decision held that blacks never had been, and could not be, citizens. Ours is another and immeasurably better world on this score. Yet the Constitution was not wrenched out of shape or recognition by the change.

Indeed, "popular perceptions" of the Constitution may matter in one respect, even when misguided. They galvanize the discontented to attempt improvement. Thousands of amendments are thought of, hundreds presented, a handful ever passed or ratified. Yet times do change; things do move.

I think it is just as well that the Constitution does not undertake to settle, let alone entrench, what passes in a passing age for social and economic wisdom and justice. We leave that wisdom to the statute books, which, by majority vote, are more easily blotted and rewritten. Our constitution is a promissory document only to the extent that it promises liberty and representative government—neither yours nor mine, but a deed of trust between generations.

Ira Glasser, Executive Director of the American Civil Liberties Union, accepts the idea of the Constitution as a set of rules, but he rejects the claim that social movements have converted the Constitution into a political football. According to Glasser, the Founders designed the Constitution to preserve majority rule and to protect individual liberty. Mr. Glasser stresses that the Bill of Rights represented the Founders' recognition that personal liberty required explicit protection from potentially tyrannical majorities. But the Bill of Rights was not, and is not, self-executing. Moreover, as it was then understood, Glasser suggests two flaws in the original Bill of Rights. In practice it protected only white males, and in law it applied only to transgressions committed by the national government. It was not until the twentieth century that the Bill of Rights protected individual liberty from state action and covered groups other than white males. Glasser applauds this expansion of the Bill of Rights and credits it to the efforts of organized associations and to the relative independence of the American judiciary. He denies that such organizations as the American Civil Liberties Union are bent on creating new principles or carving up the Constitution. Instead, Glasser believes, civil libertarians seek to apply old principles to new situations and to extend their application to groups not yet conceived in 1787. The success of these efforts, Glasser concludes, helps to account for the long life of the Constitution.

IRA GLASSER

"The American Civil Liberties Union and the Completion of the Bill of Rights"

While I agree that the Constitution establishes a set of ground rules, I think it is an oversimplification to talk about the Constitution as the plaything of social movements. Instead, I believe that a good way of looking at our legal culture is to suggest that our country is built on two ideas. One is deeply embedded in our culture, and that is the idea of democratic majority rule. The second idea, less well understood and much more fragile, is that the majority does not always rule. This is a concept that the Framers of the Constitution clearly understood. They realized that what was necessary to protect democracy was quite different from what was necessary to protect the liberty of those people who would never be in a majority. It is true that one method of dealing with tyrannical or factious majorities was Madison's idea of the extended republic. Contrary to conventional eighteenth-century political wisdom, which held that a democracy could only work in a small state, Madison believed that democracy would flourish in a large country. He reasoned that in a sprawling nation politicians would have to appeal to a broad array of the voting public, preventing the formation of a factious majority capable of tyrannizing the people.

Some people thought this would not be enough and demanded the addition to the Constitution of a Bill of Rights, which would set explicit legal limits on the Congress. Some of the leading Federalists argued that a Bill of Rights was unnecessary since Congress's powers were already limited to those delegated by the Constitution. Congress, they argued, would have no powers beyond those delegated and could not therefore legislate against the rights of the people. The Anti-Federalists won this argument, and history has sustained the soundness of their position. It is difficult to argue that the rights we enjoy today would have been possible without the Bill of Rights. Surely most of the U.S. Supreme Court's landmark decisions protecting individual rights would have been hard pressed to locate sufficient authority in the original Constitution. In fact, our Bill of Rights is the envy of the world, and the lack of one is still an issue even in other countries that respect liberty. In Great Britain, for example, there is deep division over the question of parliamentary supremacy, and many people are worried over the ultimate consequences of the fact that no British law limits what Parliament may do. In principle, for example, Parliament is supreme and thus could pass laws interning Jews or enslaving blacks. In practice, Great Britain has a tradition that so far has prevented such outrages. But we all know how ephemeral mere tradition can be, and many British legal scholars worry about the absence of a Bill of Rights.

The Bill of Rights is essentially a list of restrictions placed upon the government. The major challenge posed historically by the Bill of Rights is how to interpret its meaning. Although the First Amendment states that Congress cannot abridge the freedom of speech, Congress has in fact passed laws restricting free speech. The Fourth Amendment prohibits unreasonable searches and seizures, yet the government has disregarded this prohibition. The mere existence of these legal limitations upon the government does not automatically ensure that the government will comply with, or respect, the restraints placed upon it. The history of civil liberties shows that one way to keep the government honest is by going to court and trying to persuade judges that the law prohibits what the government has done. An explicit set of such prohibitions (the Bill of Rights) and an independent judiciary have enabled the United States to exceed all other nations in the institutionalization of individual rights.

In my view of rights, the fact is not simply that your rights cannot be taken away from you without due process of law. Certain rights cannot be taken away from you, period. Freedom of speech does not mean that your speech can be taken away from you after a trial. The right to live in the United States without being subjected to racial discrimination similarly cannot be taken away by a trial. Where people disagree, and will continue to disagree as long as there is a Constitution, is about the content or definition of constitutional rights. What is speech? The Supreme Court has often found itself divided on whether free speech embraces picketing and nonverbal forms of communication. What is racial discrimination? One of the most divisive issues in today's society is whether affirmative action is a form of racial discrimination or whether, as I believe, it is a remedy for racial discrimination. But the fact remains that the Bill of Rights created both procedural and substantive limits on democratic power. The Framers of the Constitution were not satisfied with simply making it difficult for factious majorities to monopolize political power in the United States. They realized that even in a democracy that successfully limited factions power would have to be limited. Those who advocated a Bill of Rights recognized that tyrannical majorities could take many forms. By limiting the power of Congress and providing for a Bill of Rights, the Framers supplied the textual limits upon majorities. In providing for an independent federal judiciary with the final authority to interpret the Constitution, the Framers created a referee relatively independent of the political process to resolve disputes between majorities and minorities.

This history is important to understand when we approach the study of twentieth-century social movements. We must recognize at the outset that some people were left out of the Constitution. Women were left out. All of the Framers were white men of property. Not until 1920, with the ratification of the Nineteenth Amendment, did women win the right to vote. The current effort to ratify the Equal Rights Amendment is in many ways analogous to the struggle for woman suffrage. Today, no one would seriously argue against the Nineteenth Amendment. But for over a century, serious arguments were made in behalf of denying women the vote. Many of these arguments were similar to those we hear today against the Equal Rights Amendment.

The original Constitution also left out blacks. To win the support of slave states for ratification, the Framers agreed to protect the institution of slavery. The men who wrote the Constitution were very much the products of their time. All of us are trapped in the culture of our time. As recently as twenty years ago, men fought to advance the rights of blacks without considering the plight of women. Time helps to identify the people who will come under the umbrella of the Constitution's protection. Today, there are new groups of people who are seeking their rights under the Constitution—such as persons in the military services, mental patients, prisoners, homosexuals, and the disabled. These people were not explicitly written out of the Constitution. They just were not considered.

Eventually this changed as various social groups organized to bring themselves within the protections of the Bill of Rights. Such social movements have a contagious quality. The successful struggle of one group serves as a model for another still seeking its rights. As the civil rights movement evolved, women claimed that their history was analogous to that of blacks and that their grievances required similar attention. Similar parallels have been drawn to mental patients, prisoners, soldiers, homosexuals, children, and the disabled.

Parenthetically, it is useful to point out that these movements did not arise spontaneously but were the result of organized associations of people coming together around a common goal. The study of American social movements reveals the special place of voluntary associations in our history. America is unique in this; there is no other country with so many voluntary associations. As far back as the early nineteenth century, Alexis de Tocqueville noted with approval the singular role of associations, in his widely acclaimed *Democracy in America.* He knew of no place in the world where associations were used so effectively in such a variety of causes. Given his sensitivity to the tyranny of the majority in a democracy, Tocqueville believed that associations were especially needed in this kind of political society. Before the Civil War, Americans belonged to such associations as the American Anti-Slavery Society, the American Peace Society, the American Temperance Society, the American Tract Society, the Anti-Dueling Society, and countless others. Modern America has witnessed the organization of such associations as the National Association for the Advancement of Colored People, the National American Woman Suffrage Association, the National Organization for Women, the Sierra Club, Common Cause, the Moral Majority, the National Rifle Association, and many others. Some groups, organized around a single issue, have sought to maximize their effectiveness by making the support of their single issue a political litmus test for their support. To what degree this has distorted our political system is the subject of much debate. Nevertheless, it is more important to recognize that the people who create these organizations and direct their policies are participating in an important part of the American political tradition.

One of the most interesting shortcomings of the Bill of Rights was its failure to apply to the states. The debate over the Constitution focused on the fear of consolidated national power. Those leaders who demanded a Bill of Rights wanted assurances against a grasping national government. They failed to anticipate that state governments could be just as insensitive to minority rights as the national government. Accepting the prevailing eighteenth-century notion that democracy worked best in small units, the Framers saw the states as part of the solution rather than part of the problem. In 1833 the Supreme Court, with John Marshall writing, endorsed this position in the case of *Barron* v. *Baltimore.* Given Marshall's nationalism, his opinion that the Bill of Rights applied solely to the federal government carried great weight. Despite Marshall's opinion, the slavery controversy kept alive the issue of the Bill of Rights' application to the states. The Fifth Amendment prohibits the deprivation of life, liberty, or property without due process of law. Slaveholders, viewing slaves as property, attempted to persuade courts to apply the Fifth Amendment to states in order to protect their investment. Abolitionists countered by arguing that slaves were people, and therefore the Fifth Amendment protected their liberty against slavery. The Supreme Court failed to resolve this issue prior to the Civil War. After Appomattox, the Republicans abolished slavery (Thirteenth Amendment), attempted to protect the rights of blacks as citizens (Fourteenth Amendment), and tried to secure black voting rights (Fifteenth Amendment). Many nineteenth-century Americans and twentieth-century historians believed that the Fourteenth Amendment had a broader purpose. Specifically, they believed that the purpose of the privileges and immunities clause was to make all the prohibitions of the Bill of Rights applicable to the states. In the *Slaughterhouse Cases* (1873), the Supreme Court, in a narrow five-to-four ruling, held that the Fourteenth Amendment did not alter the meaning of the Bill of Rights in our society. The Court feared that it would be overwhelmed with civil liberties and civil rights cases if it decided otherwise. From the Court's perspective, the result would be a nationalization of the Bill of Rights and a destruction of federalism. The result was immediately disastrous for blacks and subsequently unfortunate for other minorities—sexual, political, and religious.

It was not until 1925, in a case supported by the American Civil Liberties Union, that the Supreme Court began to reconsider the scope of the Bill of Rights. In *Gitlow* v. *New York*, the ACLU asked the Supreme Court to void New York's criminal syndicalism law, on the theory that freedom of speech and freedom of press were among those rights considered so fundamental to our constitutional order that they were protected by the due process clause of the Fourteenth Amendment. Although the Court held that New York did not violate the First Amendment, it ruled that the due process clause of the Fourteenth Amendment did apply to state violations of speech and press. At this point, the selective incorporation of the Bill of Rights through the Fourteenth Amendment was born. Over the next fifty years, practically all of the rights found in the Bill of Rights would be incorporated, with the effect that the prohibitions of the Bill of Rights applied equally to the states—and indeed to all local governments as well as the national government.

After incorporation, rights were enlarged in other important ways. During the last two decades, many cases have been brought in attempts to apply the limits of the Bill of Rights to school administrators, welfare officials, mental health officers, housing officials, and prison wardens. In *Goldberg* v. *Kelly* (1971), the Supreme Court ruled that due process required an evidentiary hearing before welfare officials could terminate welfare benefits. In *Tinker* v. *Des Moines School District* (1969), the Supreme Court ruled that high school principals were barred by the First Amendment from penalizing students who wore black armbands to protest the war in Vietnam. In *Cooper* v. *Pate* (1964), the Supreme Court ruled that an Illinois federal court could not dismiss a Black Muslim's claim that his religious freedoms were being denied when prison officials refused his request for religious material and religious counsel. After a retrial, the federal district court ruled that Mr. Cooper should be permitted to buy the Quran and meet with a Black Muslim minister. In all of these cases, the questions were new, the advocates were new; but the principles were the same. This kind of litigation took traditional rights and applied them to nontraditional people in nontraditional settings. Over the past twenty years, the volume of this kind of litigation rose exponentially.

Still another example of the dynamics of fitting an eighteenth-century document to the conditions of twentieth-century life involves the privacy of personal financial records. In the eighteenth and nineteenth centuries, most people kept these records in their house or place of business. The Fourth Amendment protected them from scrutiny by the government unless there was good reason to believe people were committing a crime; it established a reasonable right of privacy against government by requiring the government to obtain a warrant and demonstrate sufficient reason to a judge before it could search the places where private records were kept. Today, such records are no longer kept at home. They are held by banks, telephone companies, insurance companies, and employers. Third parties control an immense amount of private information about us, which is generally available to the government. In the case of *United States* v. *Miller* (1976), the Supreme Court dealt with a case in which a United States Attorney subpoenaed from a bank the records of a person suspected of a crime. The Court ruled that this person did not have a right to know about or challenge this subpoena because the records belonged to the bank rather than the customer. The Court has taken the position that the Fourth Amendment protects places, not privacy. The ACLU believes that the Fourth Amendment protects privacy, not just the places where private records used to be kept. Is this effort to apply old principles to new settings an attempt to create new principles? I think not. If you do not make the effort to apply the principles of the eighteenth century to the conditions of the twentieth century, you are left with a document that will gradually become lifeless. You cannot limit the principles in the Bill of Rights to the facts of the eighteenth century. You have to apply the principles to new conditions. This is where the tension exists.

The ACLU vision of the Constitution is that it is more than a collection of abstract principles. Our goal is to complete the Constitution so that it protects those who were left out and so that it adjusts itself to modern conditions. We will not discontinue our efforts until that day when the rights of Americans no longer depend upon who you are or where you live. The American Civil Liberties Union is a conservative organization in the sense that we seek to conserve the unique foundation of American tradition—the Bill of Rights. The defense of this noble eighteenth-century document is a deeply and truly conservative undertaking.

In studying the Constitution and social change, Professor Vincent Harding of The Iliff School of Theology celebrates the role of the people in taking the Constitution and making it into a more equitable document. Professor Harding believes that in studying constitutional development, scholars have spent too much time analyzing cases and opinions, especially those of the Supreme Court. Behind these cases, as he illustrates with civil rights law, were masses of courageous people willing to risk their lives for justice. Although almost anonymous, these people helped make the Constitution a living document. Professor Harding laments the depoliticization of the American people since 1975 and suggests that there is a significant agenda waiting for their revitalization.

VINCENT HARDING

"We The People: The Constitution and Its Creators."

My response to the issue of the Constitution and social change is shaped by the poet Langston Hughes, who has influenced much of my intellectual development. In 1937, in a period of his life when he was filled with visions of an America with new possibilities, Hughes wrote a poem entitled "Let America be America again." The poem ended like this:

> O, let America be America again—
> The land that never has been yet—
> And yet must be—
> The land where *every* man is free.
> The land that's mine—
> The poor man's, Indian's, Negro's, ME—
> Who made America,
> Whose sweat and blood, whose faith and pain,
> Whose hand at the foundry, whose plow in the rain,
> Must bring back our mighty dream again.

Sure, call me any ugly name you choose—
The steel of freedom does not stain.
From those who live like leeches on the people's lives,
We must take back our land again,
America!

O, yes,
I say it plain,
America never was America to me,
And yet I swear this oath—
America will be!
An ever-living seed,
Its dream
Lies deep in the heart of me.

We, the people, must redeem
Our land, the mines, the plants, the rivers,
The mountains and the endless plains—
All the stretch of these great green states—
And make America again!

This is, for me, the starting point. The assumption of the poem is that neither America nor its Constitution belongs to any elite group—that the land in its fullness must belong to its people. He assumes, of course, that the American people must come to a new understanding of their rights and responsibilities. Only in that development of the fullest possibilities of Americans can the Constitution be what it was meant to be.

In examining the Constitution and social change, some Americans have had a tendency to exaggerate the role of the Supreme Court. For example, in the desegregation case of *Brown* v. *Board of Education*, some commentators have exaggerated the role of the Supreme Court as a vehicle of social change. One could get the idea that there were nine wonderful wise men who were just waiting around for a marvelous opportunity to let the Constitution go free.

No, it did not happen that way. It happened because people, generally nonintellectuals and undereducated and black, saw a vision of a nation that did not yet exist. In South Carolina, Kansas, Virginia, Delaware, and Washington, D.C., these people rejected the way they were being educated. They saw a vision of the Constitution that was beyond the perception of most of America's elites. Then, risking their own lives, these people in the 1940s and 1950s began to challenge the Constitution as it was generally perceived by this society. They were the ones who reversed *Plessy* v. *Ferguson*, which in 1896 had permitted public segregation to be constitutionalized. They somehow sensed, somehow knew that America had not yet been America for them. They somehow sensed, somehow knew that America could be more than it had been for them.

It was through the initiative of the people, not the Supreme Court, that the Constitution was set free to open up new possibilities for us all. I think it is ahistorical to speak about the Constitution and the activities of the courts without a sense of the tremendous struggle, even sacrificial struggle, on the part of very ordinary human beings who at some point in the 1940s and 1950s determined that this Constitution must mean more than it had up to then. They supplied the initiative which the Supreme Court had not taken and, perhaps, was constitutionally unable to take. I think that we ought not to forget this story. It is easy to simplify the study of the Constitution by concentrating on cases, doctrine, and abstractions. But this separates the Constitution from the life, struggles, and blood of the people and separates the Constitution's being from those who made America. I also want to suggest that the reason why men and women can now think seriously of watering down constitutional rights is because ordinary people are not moving actively and responsibly in the same way they were in the 1945–1975 period. It is the people and not the elites who must guarantee constitutional rights. *We* are the keepers of the Constitution. We must keep the Constitution if we believe America is a democratic society—a society in which the people are sovereign.

There is a wide range of issues waiting for the attention of the American people. They might begin to look at the lives of the handicapped, the poor, and the elderly and ask themselves if society has an equal responsibility to them. My hope is that women will spend less time fighting for the right to be drafted and more time working for peace. It seems to me that the primary issue is not which of us has the right to fight and kill, but which of us will help to create a society in which war is not necessary.

Given my views of the relationship between law and society, I think those who emphasize the irrelevance of public opinion are mistaken. I think popular perceptions of the Constitution are absolutely crucial. The point I just made was that black perceptions of the Constitution and its potential have changed all of our lives. Therefore, I cannot, at any point, become too enamored and impressed with a Constitution that wrote my slavery into its very core. Because of the insufficiency of vision of those who wrote the Constitution, it seems to me that we must do what slaves and abolitionists did prior to the Civil War, which is to insist that the elites who created the document were wrong on critical issues. I do not trust elites. It seems to me that they have been proven in many cases as wrong as the wild mob. It is only in a dialectic between the so-called public (the so-called uninformed) and the so-called elite that we can solve our problems. I agree that there is great public ignorance about the Constitution. But I am unwilling to sit by and let the elite handle America's problems. I have seen the elite mishandle too many situations—such as in Vietnam. My question is, how does the public become less ignorant? How do we create a new public, one with a new consciousness? Such an effort seems to me a better idea than deferring to elites on all issues of significance. I have no confidence that elites—by themselves and without constant pressure from the public—will ever lead us in the way we need to be led.

Some scholars and journalists are worried about demands made by groups that claim they are entitled to certain benefits of the society. It does not seem to me that entitlements are automatically a bad thing. The first Constitution certainly had its share of attractive promises, but they were made to elites. For example, the Constitution included a fugitive slave clause which guaranteed to return my ancestors into slavery if they ran away. The Constitution promised to guard other kinds of property held by elites. But where did the wealth of elites come from, and at whose expense did they acquire the time and leisure to write and interpret the Constitution? If we conclude that wealth, time, and leisure came from the suffering and sweat of other people, then we must conclude that those people have a claim to some of the benefits of our society. Perhaps the problem before us is to determine who should have entitlements and who should not. How do we move from a society which benefited white males of wealth to one which speaks to the needs of all the people? But as we address this question, we must always remember that we have had constitutional entitlements before and that they benefited the guardians and keepers of the Constitution.

I would not be frightened by the possibility of playing with the Constitution in the best sense of the word "play." I would like to see us explore where we can go with the Constitution, because I think it is crucial that we develop new perceptions. For example, I want to mention three ideas that seem worth exploring. The first is to see if we can find some way to move from a system based on white supremacy to one based on pluralism, a majestic goal which should be affirmed by and written into the Constitution. The second is to give more thought to the question of economic democracy. For instance, can the Constitution speak to Youngstown, Ohio, where the lives and jobs of 20,000 people are fundamentally affected by a group of mostly white men in a board room? At stake here is a decision which has no bearing on freedom of speech or assembly, but on the self-respect which comes from having a job. Is not the right to work at least as important as the right to freedom of speech in this world? Of what value is free speech if you have no ground upon which to stand?

Finally, I would like to discover some way that we can move from the seventeenth- and eighteenth-century emphasis on rights and enter the twenty-first century by stressing an interdependency in which we acknowledge our responsibility for one another. Can we find a way of expressing in the Constitution our mutuality, our sense of need for one another as "the people?" For me, the answer is fairly obvious. The Constitution is ours, but not in any simple-minded sense of being handed down from elites. The Constitution is created by our actions, out of our perceptions, hopes, dreams, and sacrifices. Maybe this will be the set of resources that will help renew our Constitution as we approach a new era in our history.

Professor Wilson Carey McWilliams joins other contributors to this volume in portraying the difficulties faced by the Constitution in modern America. His point of departure is that the rule of law or constitutionalism works best in a homogenous, relatively slow-paced society—hardly a description of contemporary America. Change and diversity simply undermine the legitimacy of the law. To fill this void, McWilliams urges Americans to pay closer attention to the education of their statesmen and citizens. He believes that in the future more of government's decisions will be made upon the prerogative of American leaders. Citizens, in turn, must be equipped to identify those men and women who have the quality of statesmanship. Unfortunately, McWilliams finds that the institutions responsible for the political education of Americans are not working well. Because of this failure of the media and political parties—the principal sources of political information—McWilliams concludes that American citizens are progressively more "on their own, so many faces in the crowd." Complicating the problem of constitutional democracy is the continued growth of private power. Without a government willing to exercise its power to regulate corporations as well as itself, McWilliams fears even greater problems for our Constitution. He extends his belief in the necessity for strong government to freedom of speech. Given American pluralism and the uninhibited nature of speech in America, McWilliams wonders whether "good manners and social pressure" are enough to avoid bloodshed and mistrust caused by "fighting words." McWilliams recognizes that there are risks inherent in what he recommends. His willingness to place restraints upon business and speech conjures up fears of repression. But the argument unifying his theory of democracy is that Americans must recapture the belief that a republican society depends on the subordination of private to public interest.

WILSON CAREY McWILLIAMS
The Embattled Constitution

The American Constitution is an antique surviving from a slower paced, less threatening political world—much friendlier than ours to the rule of law. All the more reason to cherish it: the Constitution, like many antiques, grows more fragile, but also more valuable, with the passing of time.

Establishing a constitutional government is never easy. Our own constitution could not have been founded without great statecraft and a measure of good luck. Yet the Framers did not doubt that America, in the years after the Revolution, enjoyed something close to the best of circumstances for the founding of a constitutional republic. When Hamilton wrote that Americans had the opportunity "to decide . . . whether societies of men really are capable or not of establishing good government from reason and choice," he implied that if America, so uniquely favored, failed in the attempt, it would be necessary to conclude that the task was beyond human power.

Our situation today is by no means favorable to constitutional rule, and the very things that make the Constitution seem "outdated" make it unlikely that we could replace this constitution with a better one. We do not need a new constitution; we need new ways of caring for our old one.

The Challenge to the Rule of Law

Any government of laws finds itself embattled in the twentieth century. Law, as we ordinarily understand the term, is a *general* rule which prescribes *stable* or *predictable* forms of conduct. Constitutional government is an extreme form of the rule of law, characterized by very general rules which are hard to change. Under the American Constitution, moreover, even ordinary statutes—the result of complex deliberation and bargaining—are enacted slowly and changed with difficulty.

The rule of law, consequently, is threatened or undermined by *diversity* and *change*. Change unsettles the relation of means to ends, transforming the meaning of rules and laws. In effect, change makes new laws out of old ones. In a small town, for example, leaving the care of the needy to their "friends and neighbors" is likely to result in a humane and personal form of assistance. In a metropolis, on the other hand, whatever friends the needy have are likely to share their need, and thousands have no friends at all. Applied to a large and mobile society, the "friends and neighbors" principle—which Ronald Reagan, a small-town boy, once suggested as the basis for welfare policy in California—results in hardhearted indifference rather than respectful compassion. In modern regimes, the needy depend on public rights that give them a claim to care by strangers. In changed circumstances, just as old rules take on new meanings, the defense of old meanings requires new laws.

The rule of law presumes that law can anticipate and direct change or, at least, that the law can keep pace with change. In our times, however, change has become so radical that it baffles and outruns prediction. In fact, the future *itself* has become contingent in a way the Framers never anticipated: in the 1930s, Lord Keynes was apposite in remarking that we will all be dead in the long run; today, we can feel fortunate if we survive the short run. The perspective of politics is more limited to the present. Events outpace law, which must struggle to catch up; more and more, it is change, and not law, that rules.

Similarly, diversity reduces law to a crude approximation of justice. Since general rules treat us as though we were all alike, law is just to the extent of our likeness, and it will seem oppressive to the extent that we are preoccupied with our differences. Civil equality is the first principle of the rule of law.

Since the Framers based the Constitution on the doctrine that protecting the "diversity in the faculties of men" is "the first object of government," American law has always tended to undermine its own moral foundations. Individual freedom is no friend to law.

In our times, moreover, we live increasingly specialized lives, in narrowing enclaves of work, knowledge, and residence. At the same time, mobility and social change make us more aware of diverse groups, modes, and morals. The experience and perception of diversity is an inescapable political fact, one which makes us doubt the justice of applying traditional rules and uniform standards to differing communities and individuals.

Public law and policy reflect this. Traditionally, legislators wrote laws excluding women from dangerous or arduous jobs, overlooking exceptions in favor of the general rule that women are less strong than men. Laws based on gender classification had the additional advantage of being clear and relatively easy to enforce. Recently, however, the courts have ruled that gender is a "semi-suspect" category in terms of due process of law because it is unfair to individuals, whatever its value as a general rule. The courts reason in this way: if the legislature aims to protect the weak, it should make *strength*, not gender, a qualification for heavy labor. In the same way, it can be argued that a mandatory retirement age is unfair to those old people who retain their powers; justice, in these terms, requires a test of *competence* rather than age. The Supreme Court will carry this argument only so far: it has held, for example, that the law may take account of the fact that widows have greater economic difficulties than widowers. Nevertheless, in relation to age and gender, the Court's direction indicates that general rules must yield in favor of observed diversities.

In rejecting any simple equation of physical characteristics with qualities of skill and spirit, the courts—and with them, public policy—have turned from measures which are relatively unambiguous to standards which are much more arguable. Administration and litigation—the discretionary judgment of cases—grows at the expense of statutes and general rules of law.

The Framers trusted that laws and institutions, designed on the basis of the "science of politics," could channel and direct both change and diversity, reducing the need for statesmanship and civic virtue. Today, the declining power of the laws implies that the Framers' faith must be moderated if not abandoned. Constitutional government, which is dependent on human virtues, requires more public attention to the education of statesmen and citizens. The Constitution can still be the shield of the republic, but only if we are strong enough to bear it.

The Ascendancy of the Executive

It is no secret that the balance of the American constitutional system has acquired a pronounced tilt: the executive is ascendant. Change and diversity demand quick action and flexibility, which in turn imply discretion. Power is routinely delegated to the President, limited only by relatively vague guidelines and standards; in practice, the President is often more restrained by the inertia of bureaucracy than by law. Woodrow Wilson saw it in 1908: "we have grown more and more inclined from generation to generation to look to the President as the unifying force in our complex system."

The President's role in war and foreign policy is an extreme but decisive example. The Framers assumed that the President must have discretionary power to defend the country in emergencies such as an attack on the citizens or territories of the republic. They also presumed, however, that Congress would have time to deliberate on and to evaluate the President's action. Accordingly, they gave Congress the power to "declare war"—to give war a legal status extending beyond the right to respond to armed attack. Similarly, the Framers trusted that public opinion and the courts would be able, after the fact, to pronounce on the President's actions, imposing political sanctions where necessary or at least denying the legitimacy of what had been done.

A Presidential decision to wage thermonuclear war, on the other hand, would not be subject to retrospective deliberation and judgment in any way that matters. The President's action would be wholly decisive. Thermonuclear war, in other words, is inevitably beyond the hindsighted reach of law.

Faced with the decline of retrospective limitations on Presidential power, Congress has demonstrated a growing desire to limit the President *before* the event, attempting to exert some kind of legislative supervision over decisions and processes which might lead to war. The War Powers Act of 1973, for example, requires the President to give Congress his reasons for committing troops to combat and to withdraw those troops after sixty days unless Congress specifically authorizes them to remain. Congress may also order the President to withdraw American troops from any undeclared war at any time by a majority vote of both houses. The War Powers Act, in short, attempts to limit the term and the extent of Presidential discretion. In a major crisis, however, the War Powers Act would not tie the hands of the President, and—facing a less pressing emergency—President Carter evaded the Act in 1980 when he dispatched the abortive mission to rescue American hostages in Iran. Moreover, the War Powers Act is based on a "legislative veto"—the ability of one house to block executive action—a technique which has been held unconstitutional in a case involving immigration and naturalization.

Nevertheless, it is hard to fault the intention behind the War Powers Act. The Constitution unquestionably allows Congress to limit the President through the "power of the purse," as Congress had done in refusing to grant funds for the Reagan administration's "covert" war in Nicaragua. Yet this negative policy can take away the President's power to respond to unforeseen circumstances. The War Powers Act reflects Congress's appreciation of the *need* for flexibility and Presidential discretion. In passing the War Powers Act, Congress was attempting to strengthen its specifically political controls over foreign policy, allowing the President to act but forcing him to persuade and to give reasons for his policies. The War Powers Act, in other words, is less concerned with laying down rules of *conduct* than in providing for the evaluation of *judgment*, and that emphasis marks its contemporaneity.

As we depend more on our leaders, we have a greater need to know who they *are*: qualities of judgment and character are at least as important as positions on the issues in assessing a candidate for President. We all know that what political leaders say is not necessarily what they will do: in Lebanon, President Reagan proclaimed his unwillingness to "surrender" just before he withdrew American forces. Change greatly increases the likelihood that unexpected events will shatter hopes, policies, and ideologies, throwing leaders—and the rest of us—back on the first principles of the soul. In the years following World War II, Henry A. Wallace opposed the Cold War and advocated accommodation with the Soviet Union, policies which were major themes of his third-party candidacy in 1948. But Wallace, like Woodrow Wilson, was at bottom a moralist: confronted with the invasion of South Korea, Wallace by 1951 was calling Stalin a "devil," proclaiming that communism "invades the sacredness of the human soul," and asserting that the Soviet Union sought world domination. Had Wallace been in office—and, after all, he was Vice President from 1941–1945—it is possible that he might have changed from a dove into an apocalyptic hawk. Voters, obviously, need to discern such possibilities before the event.

American democracy, in other words, relies more and more on those quasi-constitutional institutions which give citizens some ability to evaluate and to trust their leaders. The state of those institutions, however, does not inspire confidence. Television, dominating the media, is itself constrained by its dependence on pictures. Comment is possible only in the context of "photo opportunities"; the medium is defined by the visible, preoccupied with style and image, focused on the superficialities of human character. The medium is also limited by the need to attract a mass audience. Television executives, fixated on "ratings" and "market shares," tend to adapt programming to the habits and present tastes of viewers. Early in the 1984 campaign, Walter Mondale was warned that his sentences were too long: television audiences, the argument went, will watch only a few seconds of campaign news, and any thought that cannot be reduced to a slogan will not be covered at all. Such simplification does more than protect viewers' time: it makes it difficult for any candidate to challenge their current beliefs and perceptions. Regulation can improve television's treatment of politics. Nevertheless, television can never be well adapted to politics, since what matters politically is so often invisible, subtle, and substantive; television is even less suited to inquire into a candidate's soul.

Political parties can offer better guidance and protection. Party leaders are likely to know candidates on the basis of long-term familiarity and firsthand experience—or, at least, through well-informed hearsay. In fact, while voters are often dangerously attracted to outsiders with new faces, party leaders and professionals prefer known qualities to uncertain magic. In this respect, parties provide a "check and balance" vital to constitutional government. But parties can perform this function only to the extent that voters trust party leaders to act as "gatekeepers," mediating between citizens and candidates. The political loyalties and friendships which traditionally cemented American parties were rooted in memory and in relatively stable localities; both have been weakened, if not shattered, by change. Moreover, the political party has been subject to a persistent intellectual critique, part of the attack on institutions in the name of individual diversities. Influenced by that criticism, reform legislation since the Progressive era has been consistently hostile to party organizations. Federal campaign finance laws, for example, give public money to Presidential candidates rather than to political parties. That money, in turn, is spent almost entirely on the mass media. The law encourages an electoral politics defined in terms of individual candidates with mass followings, virtually legitimating mass society. It would be possible, by contrast, to give at least half of public campaign funds to state and local parties, strengthening rather than debilitating the structures of political mediation. The political trends, however, run in the opposite direction.

In fact, the contemporary public is increasingly without gatekeepers. Even when citizens belong to interest groups, they are apt to feel distant and disaffected, as so many members of trade unions do. The print media, so well suited to exploring the characters of candidates, have declined in favor of television, and various forms of direct access to the public are replacing contact through local organizations. Citizens, more and more, are on their own, so many faces in the crowd.

This ought to alarm us. The Framers neglected civic virtue, preferring to rely on political mechanics. Nevertheless, the Framers recognized that there is a sphere of great and fundamental political decisions—Locke had called it the "prerogative"—in which leaders and citizens must act without, or even in spite of, the rule of law. In our time, the prerogative pervades political life, and any constitutional republic rests, to a growing extent, on the virtue of its statesmen and citizens.

The Problem of Private Power

In the famous argument of *The Federalist* No. 10, Madison contended that republican government will best be protected against the "mischiefs of faction" by a large republic comprising a great number of competing interests. The "republican principle"—majority rule—guards against minority factions; a large and diverse regime reduces the risk of majority faction because majorities must be complex coalitions, which are unlikely to agree about very much or for very long. One side of the Framers' effort to limit private power, then, presumes a marketplace of interests in which groups and factions check and balance one another, teaching "circumspection"—a timid, cautious, and calculating awareness of the interests of others.

The contemporary United States, on the other hand, is characterized by private power organized on a scale which the Framers do not seem to have envisaged. The great corporations and mass associations are "private governments" on which citizens *depend*, but to which they can create no *alternative*. Citizens know that, in practice, they cannot create a new television network, a new automobile company, or a new industrial trade union; every student knows the inescapable, life-defining power of the Educational Testing Service. Ordinarily, we have some choice between such groups and associations—though, given mergers, the terms of choice may be narrowing—but, basically, the relationship between private governments is oligopolistic. Competition is imperfect, limited both by the implicit and explicit agreements between such firms and associations and by the restrictions which tend to rule out new entrants. Such private governments have an obvious impact on public policy through their command of money, communications, and organizational skill. In fact, a considerable sphere of public power is controlled, or even directly exercised, by private governments. (State bar, medical, and other professional examinations, for example, are normally designed and conducted by private professional organizations.)

Political scientists, fascinated by the pluralistic side of Madison's argument, have sometimes lost sight of the fact that the Framers placed *primary* reliance on the "republican principle" of majority rule as a check on private power. The Framers had no doubt that government must be strong enough to control and rule the private order. In fact, they recognized that such supremacy is essential to free government, since private life is the foundation of public freedom: "In the general course of human nature," Hamilton wrote, "a power over a man's subsistence amounts to a power over his will."

The government created by the Constitution is designedly a powerful one, armed with almost total power to command commerce, money, and credit. Intended to be ascendant over the states, the Federal government was also meant to school and guide the acquisitive passions— "sharpsighted" but also shortsighted—which the Framers regarded as the natural bases of civil life. The Constitution envisions a government able to create and protect the *kind* of marketplace and the *sorts* of private power suitable to free government.

In our time, the power of private government calls for a public government able to regulate private rule, holding it accountable to public standards in much of its internal life as well as in its external relationships. This has long been recognized in the case of private governments with a particularly crucial relation to public life. In the White Primary cases, for example, the Supreme Court ruled that political parties cannot exclude blacks—or, presumably, violate other public standards in defining membership. Even though parties are formally private associations, the Court observed, primaries are an "integral part" of the democratic process. In 1953, the Court held that a private political club which held straw votes whose winners habitually won the Democratic primary was also a "public" institution within the meaning of the Fourteenth Amendment.

In the same way, the privately owned mass media control *access* to the public. They act as chairpersons in our public debate, deciding whom to recognize and on what terms. For some time, public regulations have laid down standards for the media—fairness, equal time, public service broadcasting, family viewing, and the like. We need more regulation of the media; for example, cable television, now treated as wholly private, should be required to observe standards of fairness, and there are important questions to be raised about bias and quality in news programs.

It seems generally recognized, however, that the media, like the parties, have become an "integral part" of the democratic process.

Public government also intrudes into the internal government of unions and corporations. Federal laws regulate labor relations and set some of the terms for hiring and firing, supervise union elections and finance, and set a number of public standards for the conduct of business. Given the growing size of corporations and the burgeoning of corporate political action committees, it seems likely that more public intervention will be necessary in the interest of democratic life. To say this is only to recognize the most obvious aspect of private power.

One area, however, deserves special mention. Computer technology gives private organizations unique power to inquire into the private lives of citizens. Financial, medical, and psychological records are already less than secure. The growing technology of surveillance, creating ever-more-sophisticated modes of eavesdropping, only magnifies the problem. In many ways, the technology of *1984* has really arrived on schedule. Obviously, public agencies pose threats beyond the powers of private organizations. But the technology of electronic inquisition emphasizes that privacy has become more a legal and political idea than an economic or social fact.

Given existing technology, we cannot prevent the great corporations or the federal government from having access to information about our private lives. Nor would it always be desirable to do so: the new technologies, for example, give the IRS some hope of controlling the tax-evading "black economy." But we can hope to contain such intrusions, holding them accountable to public standards in order to limit the *misuse* of such information. We no longer have any real privacy unless it is protected *in* and *by* politics; public life is increasingly the source and support of private freedom.

The Contemporary Meaning of Political Freedom

The Framers phrased the Bill of Rights negatively, and, as a result, the first ten amendments seem to imply that a citizen is free if government leaves him or her alone. The language of the Bill of Rights, in other words, appears to presume individuals who, by nature or by rearing, have all the social and psychological requisites of liberty.

In theory, the Framers did believe that human beings are "by nature, free," meaning that we have no natural obligations and are bound legitimately only by our consent. In these terms, nature endows us with a *right* to be free, but does not make us free in *fact*. In practice, the Framers knew that government is necessary to free us from weakness and fear, parochialism and shortsightedness. They expected government under the Constitution to be liberative, enhancing our human powers. Nevertheless, the Framers' view of human nature did lead them to play down the positive side of freedom, the social and psychological conditions that make freedom real.

The essence of freedom—self-rule—is impossible without courage, and civil liberty demands its own sort of valor. This is obvious in the case of the citizen's military obligations, but the need for daring extends beyond the armed services. Courage is a civil as well as a military virtue. There is bravery in law-abidingness. Decent citizens know that the law is not perfect: they realize that some people will evade taxes, throwing the burden of supporting the common good on those who pay; they know that some people will break the law, injuring us in ways for which the political system offers no real remedy. Citizens, however, must be willing to suffer these hurts, abiding in the law for the sake of political society as a whole. Decency is a hard discipline, which demands risk and sacrifice; civil virtue is gentle, but not weak.

Even more courage is required of self-governing citizens who share in the making of laws. That role gives us the right to participate in civic deliberation. It also imposes the duty to dissent, the obligation to argue against the government or—much harder—against prevailing opinion, if either appears to be in the wrong. Confronted with a strong, consistent majority, individuals may doubt even the evidence of their own senses, and mass democracy makes matters worse. As individuals, contemporary Americans are relatively powerless and insignificant parts of the whole, all too subject to that psychological oppression that Tocqueville called the "tyranny of the majority." In a small group, a majority of six to four is reversible if I change the vote of one person; in the United States, the same majority is transformed from a close contest into an overwhelming landslide, as Reagan's victory in 1984 demonstrates. Individualism, by telling us to go alone, increases the likelihood that we will go along: civic courage is destroyed when we feel weak and isolated—and when we are convinced that what we do is unimportant. We can act heroically, but only if our suffering and sacrifice has a point.

Citizens need *dignity*, the conviction that their actions are noticed and remembered. The greatest heroes have friends whose love and good opinion is more important than life or comfort, those who can both shame and give honor. Similarly, civic virtue requires relationships which are strong enough to outweigh the numbers of even a considerable majority. Civic freedom, in other words, presumes civil friendship.

The contemporary Supreme Court implicitly recognized this princi-

ple in *Miranda* v. *Arizona*. In that now famous case, the Court held that
an individual is not "free" when questioned by the police even if he or she
is not abused physically. The Court recognized that loneliness—at least,
under conditions of stress—imposes a psychological coercion such that
we cannot be said to speak or act freely without the active support of
counsel. Negative rights against government are not enough to make us
free: we need a government which assumes the responsibility of *reminding* us of our rights to counsel and *providing* that counsel if necessary.

The *Miranda* doctrine points beyond the rights of the accused to a
basic principle of contemporary constitutionalism. In this age of routin-
ized crisis and social fragmentation, too many American citizens find
themselves, like the accused in *Miranda*, under stress and alone. More
and more Americans feel the lack of community. Family and locality are
embattled by change, and their instability weakens the bases of trust and
commitment, the capacity for friendship and the arts of civic association.
The Framers took such relationships more or less for granted; today, they
desperately need the encouragement and protection of public authority.

Civil speech, too, is no longer restrained by the old commonalities
and moral agreements. To some extent this is pure gain, the result of
overcoming old bigotries and drawing new groups into civic life. This
diversity, however, may mean that society lacks the coherence to enforce
standards of civility. "Fighting words" and group libels—racism and
sexism, for example—assault the core of a citizen's identity; if good
manners and social pressure cannot rule out such language, government
may have to do so. More positively, government can help to create
effective forums for civil argument and deliberation. Public authority, in
other words, has an increased responsibility for fostering public speech.

There are obvious dangers in this doctrine, but for the Constitution
these are dangerous times. To secure the future of constitutional government, it will be necessary to attend to the very foundations of civil
freedom.

List of Contributors

William M. Beaney is a professor of Constitutional Law at the University of Denver College of Law. He was the Cromwell Professor of Law at Princeton University. He is the author or co-author of numerous books on legal topics including *The Right to Counsel in American Courts.*

Jett B. Conner is the chairman of the Political Science Department at Metropolitan State College. He has taught at North Texas State University. He was a National Endowment for the Humanities Fellow in 1977 and is working on a book-length study of the political thought of Thomas Paine.

George Dennison is the Acting Academic Vice President of Colorado State University. He has taught at the University of Arkansas, University of Washington, and Colorado State University. He is the author of *The Dorr War: Republicanism on Trial* and a variety of articles on legal history.

Ira Glasser is the Executive Director of the American Civil Liberties Union. He was the Director of the New York affiliate of the ACLU. He has written and lectured extensively on civil rights and civil liberties in America.

Dennis Hale is an assistant professor of Political Science at Boston College. He has written numerous scholarly articles on American politics. Currently he is working on a biography of James Michael Curley.

Vincent Harding is a professor of Religion and Social Transformation at the Iliff School of Theology in Denver, Colorado. He was the chairman of the History and Sociology department at Spelman College and the director of the Martin Luther King Memorial Center. He is the author of *The Other American Revolution* and *There Is a River*, the first of a three-volume history of the black struggle for freedom in the United States.

David E. Kyvig is a professor of History at the University of Akron. He is the author of *Repealing National Prohibition*. Recently he edited *Law, Alcohol, and Order: Perspectives in National Prohibition.*

Wilson Carey McWilliams is a professor of Political Science at Rutgers University. He has taught at Oberlin College and Brooklyn College. He is the author of numerous articles and books including *The Idea of Fraternity in America*, which won the National Historical Society Prize in 1974.

Harvey C. Mansfield, Jr. is a professor of Government at Harvard University. He has been a Guggenheim and National Humanities Center Fellow. He is the author of many articles and books on political thought, including *The Spirit of Liberalism*. He is currently preparing a book on American constitutionalism.

Richard D. Miles is a professor of History at Wayne State University. He is the author of several articles and numerous reviews on eighteenth-century America. He is presently doing research on the original understanding of the American Revolution and new nation.

Michael Nelson is an associate professor of Political Science at Vanderbilt University. He has written, edited, and co-authored articles and book-length studies of the Presidency and bureaucracy. He is writing a book on the history of American bureaucracy.

Stephen Pepper is an associate professor of Law at the University of Denver College of Law. He has published a number of law review articles on the issue of the church and state. He is currently engaged in research extending his work on freedom of religion.

Edwin M. Yoder, Jr. is a syndicated columnist with The Washington Post Writers Group. He has written for the *Charlotte News*, the *Greensboro Daily News*, and the *Washington Star*, where he won a Pulitzer Prize for Editorial Writing in 1979. He is the author of numerous articles and is working on a study of the 1946 Supreme Court which will be published by Holt Rinehart.

ABOUT THE EDITOR

Adolph H. Grundman is a professor of History at Metropolitan State College, Denver, Colorado. He has been a visiting professor at Michigan State University and the University of Illinois. He has written several articles on American legal and social history.

Selected Additional Readings

The topics covered in this volume have generated a considerable bibliography. The titles below offer suggestions for readers desiring to explore one or more of these areas of study more deeply. In the first section of the book, Richard D. Miles presented a full discussion of the historical literature devoted to the study of the Constitution and its background. Excerpts from this literature and important articles are found in such convenient collections as Leonard W. Levy, ed., *Essays on the Making of the Constitution*(1969); Gordon Wood, ed., *The Confederation and the Constitution: The Critical Issues*(1979); and James Morton Smith, ed., *The Constitution*(1971). The documents of the Convention and constitutional ratification are collected in Max Farrand, *The Records of the Federal Convention of 1787*, 4 vols.(1911, 1937) and Jonathan Elliot, ed., *The Debates in the Several State Conventions on the Adoption of the Federal Constitution*, 5 vols.(1876). Anti-Federalist thought is documented and interpreted in Cecilia Kenyon, ed., *The Antifederalists*(1966) and Herbert J. Storing, ed., *The Complete Anti-Federalist* 7 vols.(1982). A good introduction into the life and work of Charles Beard is Richard Hofstadter's *The Progressive Historians: Turner, Beard, Parrington*(1968). Examinations of why Americans rallied so quickly behind the Constitution after its ratification include Frank I. Schecter, "The Early History of the Tradition of the Constitution," *American Political Science Review* 9(1915); Max Lerner, "Constitution and Court as Symbols," *The Yale Law Journal* 46(1937); Wesley Frank Craven, *The Legend of the Founding Fathers*(1956); and Michael Lienesch, "The Constitutional Tradition: History, Political Action, and Progress in American Political Thought," *The Journal of Politics* 42(1980). Two studies of the Bill of Rights are Robert A. Rutland, *The Birth of the Bill of Rights*(1955) and Irving Brant, *The Bill of Rights: Its Origin and Meaning*(1965). The life and thought of Thomas Paine are considered in David Freeman Hawke, *Paine*(1974) and Eric Foner, *Tom Paine and Revolutionary America*(1976). Conyers Read, ed., *The Constitution Reconsidered*(1938) is a collection of scholarly essays written for the sesquicentennial anniversary of the Constitution. Modern studies of slavery and the Constitution include David Brion Davis, *The Problem of Slavery in the Age of Revolution, 1770–1823*(1975) and William W. Freehling, "The Founding Fathers and Slavery," *American Historical Review* 77(1972). Scholars consider J.G.A. Pocock's *The Machiavellian Moment:*

Florentine Political Thought and the Atlantic Republican Tradition (1975) a pathbreaking reinterpretation of American culture, with its substitution of classical republicanism for Lockean individualism. John P. Diggins, *The Lost Soul of American Politics: Virtue, Self-Interest, and the Foundations of Liberalism*(1985) rejects this attempt to revise the basis of American culture.

In considering the themes discussed in the second section of this volume, one point of departure is to compare one of the editions of *The Federalist Papers* to Alexis de Tocqueville, *Democracy in America*, trans., George Lawrence, ed., J.P. Mayer(1966). James H. Kettner, *The Development of American Citizenship, 1608–1870*(1978) describes the problem of defining citizenship in the United States. Books which analyze the relationship between church and state are Elywyn A. Smith, *Religious Liberty in the United States: The Development of Church-State Thought Since the Revolutionary Era*(1972); Leo Pfeffer, *Church, State and Freedom*, rev. ed.(1967); and Mark De Wolfe Howe, *The Garden and the Wilderness: Religion and Government in American Constitutional History*(1965). Historical interpretations of bureaucracy in the United States are Stephen Skowronek, *Building a New American State: The Expansion of National Administrative Capacities, 1877–1920*(1982); Ellis Hawley, *The Great War and the Search for a Modern Order: A History of the American People and Their Institutions, 1917–1933*(1979); and Theodore Lowi, *The End of Liberalism: Ideology, Policy, and the Crisis of Public Authority*(1969). Alan P. Grimes, *Democracy and the Amendments to the Constitution*(1978) and Clement E. Vose, *Constitutional Change: Amendment Politics and Supreme Court Litigation since 1900*(1972) discuss the history of the amending process.

The final section of this volume covers such broad topics as the role of the judiciary in a constitutional democracy and the effects of rapid change and pluralism on American political institutions and the law. A good survey of the judiciary is found in G. Edward White, *The American Judicial Tradition: Profiles of Leading American Judges*(1976). Bernard Schwartz's *Super Chief: Earl Warren and His Supreme Court—A Judicial Biography*(1983) is an immense but readable biography of the Chief Justice whose name is closely identified with activism in civil rights and civil liberties. A good introduction to the debate over the nature of judicial review is John Hart Ely's *Theory of Judicial Review*(1980). J. R. Pole's *Pursuit of Equality in American History*(1978) is an excellent history of one of America's most fundamental values. Yehoshua Arieli, *Individualism and Nationalism in American Ideology*(1964) examines these values in America prior to the Civil War.

Seymour Martin Lipset, *The First New Nation*(1963) traces the relationship between individualism and equality in some of his chapters. A sympathetic and exhaustive history of the school desegregation case is Richard Kluger's *Simple Justice: The History of Brown v. Board of Education and Black America's Struggle for Equality*(1975). Two books that are critical of Brown's progeny are J. Harvie Wilkinson III, *From Brown to Bakke: The Supreme Court and School Integration, 1954–1979*(1979) and Lino Graglio, *Disaster by Decree: The Supreme Court's Decisions on Race and Schools*(1976). A careful examination of the issues raised by affirmative action is found in R. Kent Greenawalt's *Discrimination and Reverse Discrimination: Essay and Materials in Law and Philosophy*(1979). Harvard Sitkoff, *The Struggle For Black Equality, 1954–1980*(1981) surveys the various facets of the civil rights movement. Stephen B. Oates's *Let the Trumpet Sound: The Life of Martin Luther King, Jr.*(1982) is a detailed biography. David Garrow's *The FBI and Martin Luther King, Jr.: From "Solo" to Memphis*(1981) is an important supplement. Alan Reitman, ed., *The Pulse of Freedom, American Liberties: 1920–1970s* (1975) describes the role of the American Civil Liberties Union in the defense and advancement of rights in America. Richard E. Morgan's *Disabling America: The "Rights Industry" In Our Time*(1985) is critical of activist lawyers and groups. Alan Crawford, *Thunder on the Right: The "New Right" and the Politics of Resentment*(1980) and John S. Saloma III, *Ominous Politics: The New Conservative Labyrinth*(1984) discuss the activism of conservative organizations. George Nash, *The Conservative Intellectual Movement in America*(1979) provides a good survey of conservative thought in the United States since World War II. Louis Hartz, *The Liberal Tradition in America*(1955) remains a classic treatment of liberal thought in America. Austin Ranney, *The Doctrine of Responsible Party Government: Its Origins and Present State*(1962) sketches the scholarly critique of political parties between 1870 and 1915. Books which discuss contemporary American politics are: Walter Dean Burnham, *The Current Crisis in American Politics*(1982); Thomas Byrne Edsall, *The New Politics of Inequality*(1984); and Austin Ranney, *Channels of Power: The Impact of Television on American Politics*(1983). Arthur M. Schlesinger, Jr., *The Imperial Presidency*(1973) describes the expansion of Presidential power since 1787. Alan F. Westin, *Privacy and Freedom*(1967) and David Burnham, *The Rise of the Computer State*(1983) focus on the right of privacy and how it is threatened by modern technology. Lois Banner, *Women in Modern America*(1974); William Chafe, *Women and Equality*(1978); and Leo Kanowitz, *Women and the Law: The Unfin-*

ished Revolution(1969) provide a history of women and their treatment under the law. Robert L. Heilbroner, *An Inquiry Into The Human Prospect*(1974) considers how different the future of the nation and the world is likely to be and what these changes will mean for democratic institutions.